Presidents from Eisenhower through Johnson, 1953–1969

**Recent Titles
in The President's Position: Debating the Issues**

PRESIDENTS FROM EISENHOWER THROUGH JOHNSON, 1953–1969

Debating the Issues in Pro and Con Primary Documents

JOHN A. KING, JR. WITH JOHN R. VILE

The President's Position: Debating the Issues
Mark Byrnes, Series Editor

Greenwood Press
Westport, Connecticut • London

Library of Congress Cataloging-in-Publication Data

Presidents from Eisenhower through Johnson, 1953–1969 : debating the issues in pro
   and con primary documents / [compiled by] John A. King, Jr. with John R. Vile.
      p.cm. — (The President's position: debating the issues)
   Includes bibliographical references and index.
   ISBN 0-313-31582-5 (alk. paper)
   1. Presidents—United States—History—20th century—Sources. 2. United States—
Politics and government—1953–1961—Sources. 3. United States—Politics and
government—1961–1963—Sources. 4. United States—Politics and government—
1963–1969—Sources. 5. Eisenhower, Dwight D. (Dwight David), 1890–1969—Political
and social views—Sources. 6. Kennedy, John F. (John Fitzgerald), 1917–1963—Political
and social views—Sources. 7. Johnson, Lyndon B. (Lyndon Baines), 1908–1973—
Political and social views—Sources. I. King, John A. (John Allan), 1972– II. Vile, John
R. III. Series.
E176.1.P92135 2006
973.92'092'2—dc22   2005019207

British Library Cataloguing in Publication Data is available.

Library of Congress Catalog Card Number: 2005019207
ISBN: 0-313-31582-5

First published in 2006

Greenwood Press, 88 Post Road West, Westport, CT 06881
An imprint of Greenwood Publishing Group, Inc.
www.greenwood.com

Printed in the United States of America

The paper used in this book complies with the
Permanent Paper Standard issued by the National
Information Standards Organization (Z39.48-1984).

10 9 8 7 6 5 4 3 2 1

CONTENTS

SERIES FOREWORD

When he was running for president in 1932, Franklin D. Roosevelt declared that America needed "bold, persistent experimentation" in its public policy. "It is common sense to take a method and try it," FDR said. "If it fails, admit it frankly and try another. But above all, try something." At President Roosevelt's instigation, the nation did indeed take a number of steps to combat the Great Depression. In the process, the president emerged as the clear leader of American public policy. Most scholars see FDR's administration as the birth of the "modern presidency," in which the president dominates both domestic and foreign policy.

Even before FDR, however, presidents played a vital role in the making of public policy. Policy changes advocated by the presidents—often great changes—have always influenced the course of events, and have always sparked debate from the presidents' opponents. The outcomes of this process have had tremendous effects on the lives of Americans. The President's Position: Debating the Issues examines the stands the presidents have taken on the major political, social, and economic issues of their times as well as the stands taken by their opponents. The series combines description and analysis of those issues with excerpts from primary documents that illustrate the position of the presidents and their opponents. The result is an informative, accessible, and comprehensive look at the crucial connection between presidents and policy. These volumes will assist students doing historical research, preparing for debates, or fulfilling critical thinking assignments. The general reader interested in American history and politics will also find the series interesting and helpful.

Several important themes about the president's role in policy making emerge from the series. First, and perhaps most important, is how greatly the president's involvement in policy has expanded over the years. This has happened because the range of areas in which the national government acts has grown dramatically and because modern presidents—unlike most of their predecessors—see taking the lead in policy making as part of their job. Second, certain issues have confronted most presidents over history; tax and tariff policy, for example, was important for both George Washington and Bill Clinton, and for most of the presidents in between. Third, the emergence of the United States as a world power around the beginning of the twentieth century made foreign policy issues more numerous and more pressing. Finally, in the American system, presidents cannot form policy through decrees; they must persuade members of Congress, other politicians, and the general public to follow their lead. This key fact makes the policy debates between presidents and their opponents vitally important.

This series comprises nine volumes, organized chronologically, each of which covers the presidents who governed during that particular time period. Volume one looks at the presidents from George Washington through James Monroe; volume two, John Quincy Adams through James K. Polk; volume three, Zachary Taylor through Ulysses S. Grant; volume four, Rutherford B. Hayes through William McKinley; volume five, Theodore Roosevelt through Calvin Coolidge; volume six, Herbert Hoover through Harry Truman; volume seven, Dwight D. Eisenhower through Lyndon Johnson; volume eight, Richard Nixon through Jimmy Carter; and volume nine, Ronald Reagan through Bill Clinton. Each president from Washington through Clinton is covered, although the number of issues discussed under each president varies according to how long they served in office and how actively they pursued policy goals. Volumes six through nine —which cover the modern presidency—examine three presidencies each, while the earlier volumes include between five and seven presidencies each.

Every volume begins with a general introduction to the period it covers, providing an overview of the presidents who served and the issues they confronted. The section on each president opens with a detailed overview of the president's position on the relevant issues he confronted and the initiatives he took, and closes with a list of recommended readings. Up to fifteen issues are covered per presidency. The discussion of each issue features an introduction, the positions taken by the president and his opponents, how the issue was resolved, and the long-term effects of the issue. This is followed by excerpts from two primary documents, one representing the president's position and the other representing his opponents' position. Also included in each volume is a timeline of significant events of the era and a bibliography of sources for students and others interested in further research.

As the most prominent individual in American politics, the president received enormous attention from the media and the public. The statements, actions, travels, and even the personal lives of presidents are constantly scrutinized. Yet it is the presidents' work on public policy that most directly affects American citizens—a fact that is sometimes overlooked. This series is presented, in part, as a reminder of the importance of the president's position.

Mark Byrnes

PREFACE

This book highlights some of the most important issues in the history of the presidencies of Dwight D. Eisenhower, John F. Kennedy, and Lyndon B. Johnson and how those issues shaped and reflected America at the time and after. Because the literature on this period—and the Cold War of which it is a part—is so vast, we have utilized a number of criteria to limit the scope of this project. The book is primarily one of political history—it is the history of presidents and the issues that they considered to be the most important. We have further limited our choice of issues to those that exemplify the general views and philosophies that each president brought to his office. When further refinement was needed, we looked for issues that continue to have a legacy in American life today.

Consistent with companion volumes in this series, we have approached each issue from the standpoint of opposing viewpoints, presenting both the president's position on the issue and the resistance he encountered in his attempts to advance his policy or program. In the process, we have highlighted the role that the differences among presidents played in terms of personality, experience, style, and beliefs about the role of the federal government and the place of the United States in the world. Cold War conditions were such that despite these differences, the three presidents also shared a number of ideas and convictions about their duties, about the obligations of the federal government, and about American identity. We have highlighted such commonalities.

A chronological progression of events guides the organization of the issues within each section of this book. Where possible, we have accompanied the discussion of each issue by primary source documents that exemplify at least two sides of the topic, the president's position on the one hand, and that either of an opponent or critic, or that of an advisor who counseled a different direction, on the other. The inclusion of primary sources allows readers to identify the ways that historians use primary source documents, along with secondary literature, to draw conclusions about historical events, and to give readers a chance to reach some of their own conclusions about the issues. We have further included a selective bibliography and timeline to assist readers to organize their thoughts on this time period and to seek out further reading related to it.

Comments from the Authors:

JOHN KING

I am grateful to Kevin Ohe at Greenwood Press, Mark Byrnes at Middle Tennessee State University, the series editor, and Amy Sturgis, my friend and colleague, and the author of two other volumes in this series, for including me in this project. To Kevin and Mark, their patience has been appreciated more than they can imagine by someone who took on several new projects and activities at the same time, and did not complete any of them with the promptness with which he is accustomed. To Amy, her friendship and encouragement has meant more to my success than she realizes. I am especially grateful to J.F. Donnelly and Susan Socolow, outstanding teachers and historians themselves, and those who comprised the faculty of the History Department at Vanderbilt University during my time there, who inspired me and helped instill in me an enthusiasm for historical inquiry. Mike Ferguson and Michael Stokes—I am thankful for your friendship, your encouragement, and the models of professionalism and dedication that you have provided. I am indebted to my students at Ransom Everglades School, particularly the members of the Class of 2002, for the intellectual challenges they have provided, their encouragement, and their friendship. And lastly, neither this book, nor any of my accomplishments, academic or otherwise, would have come to fruition without my family: Mom, Dad, Kevin, Jamie, David, and Alexis, for whose love and support a line of gratitude here could never be sufficient, but for which I am eternally grateful.

JOHN R. VILE

In addition to adding my appreciation to the individuals mentioned above, I want to extend special thanks to John King, to Mark Byrnes, and to the editors at Greenwood for including me in this project. I would like to thank Sue Alexander, Sharon Parente, Al Camp, Ken Middleton, Mayo Taylor, Neil Scott, and others in the Middle Tennessee State University Library for helping me locate materials and to Pam Davis, Harry Veach, and Hilary

Stallings for assistance with computer formatting. More generally, I thank my students, administrators, and colleagues at MTSU for their continuing support. John King took the lead in writing this book and in compiling key documents, and I am glad to have been able to play a part in the final product.

TIMELINE

1953

January 20	Dwight D. Eisenhower inaugurated U.S. president
January 21	U.S. launches the *Nautilus*, first atomic-powered submarine
March 12	Department of Housing, Education, and Welfare created
April 16	President Eisenhower delivers "Chance for Peace" speech
June 19	Convicted spies Julius and Ethel Rosenberg executed at Sing-Sing prison
July 27	Armistice signed ending Korean War; partitions Korean peninsula at 38th parallel and establishes demilitarized zone around border
August 19–22	CIA sponsors coup in Iran to overthrow Mohammed Mossadegh and install U.S. ally Shah Reza Pahlavi
December 8	Eisenhower delivers "Atoms for Peace" speech at the United Nations

1954

April 22–June 17	Army-McCarthy hearings televised
May 7	French forces defeated in Vietnam at Dienbienphu; signals the end of the French effort to preserve their colony in Indochina
May 17	U.S. Supreme Court bans segregation in public schools in *Brown v. Board of Education*

June 16	Guatemala exiles backed by CIA and Nicaraguan government lead invasion of Guatemala; within two weeks oust Guatemalan President Jacabo Arbenz
August 20	Eisenhower signs Atomic Energy Act creating the Atomic Energy Commission
September 8	Southeast Asian Treaty Organization formed including the United States, Australia, New Zealand, Pakistan, Malaysia, Great Britain, France, Thailand, and the Philippines

1955

January 28	Congress authorizes use of force in Formosa against Chinese shelling of Taiwan
April 12	Polio vaccine approved safe for public use
May 14	Warsaw Pact created by Soviet Union and its communist satellite countries in Eastern Europe
July 18–23	Geneva Four Power Summit; Eisenhower proposes "Open Skies" plan
September 23	Eisenhower suffers a heart attack while vacationing in Denver, Colorado
December 1	Rosa Parks refuses to abandon bus seat; Martin Luther King, Jr. initiates 38 day Montgomery bus boycott

1956

February 24	Khrushchev gives "De-Stalinization Speech"
March 12	Southern Congressmen protest desegregation in the Southern Manifesto
April 10	Soviet troops invade Hungary to put down protests; apprehend and ultimately execute reformist President Imre Nagy
July 26	Egyptian government seizes control of Suez Canal from British and French; provokes attacks by Israel (October 29) and Britain and France (November 5)
June 29	Eisenhower signs National Defense Highways Act expanding federal funding for national highway system
Oct 13–Nov 7	British and French forces invade Egypt to reclaim control of the Suez Canal
November 6	Eisenhower reelected U.S. president

1957

| January 5 | Eisenhower promulgates Eisenhower Doctrine calling for aid to Middle Eastern countries resisting aggression from communist nations (Congressional bill |

	authorizing use of U.S. forces for Eisenhower Doctrine signed March 9)
January 10	Martin Luther King, Jr. helps form Southern Christian Leadership Conference
July 29	U.S. Senate ratifies treaty establishing International Atomic Energy Agency
September 9	Eisenhower signs Civil Rights Act of 1957; establishes Civil Rights Section in the Justice Department; gives federal government authority to obtain court injunctions to prevent discrimination in voting
September 24	Eisenhower sends federal troops to Little Rock, Arkansas after Gov. Orville Faubus refuses to allow nine black students to attend Little Rock public high school
Oct 4	Soviets launch *Sputnik,* first earth orbiting satellite

1958

January 31	Americans launch *Explorer I,* first American earth-orbiting satellite
March 27	Nikita Khrushchev becomes Premier of Soviet Union
May 26	Eisenhower opens first commercial nuclear power plant at Shippingsport, Pennsylvania
July 17	Eisenhower sends American troops to Lebanon to protect stability of Lebanese government
July 29	Eisenhower signs bill creating National Aeronautic and Space Administration (NASA)
August 28	Chinese forces threaten to invade Taiwanese islands of Matsu and Quemoy; U.S. Seventh Fleet responds to defend Taiwan
Sept 2	Eisenhower signs National Defense Education Act expanding federal funding for education
Sept 12	U.S. Supreme Court refuses to postpone desegregation at Little Rock High School in *Cooper v. Aaron*

1959

January 3	Alaska becomes forty-ninth U.S. state
January 5	Fidel Castro takes power in Havana, Cuba
August 21	Hawaii becomes fiftieth U.S. state

1960

January 2	John F. Kennedy announces candidacy for the U.S. presidency
February 1	Sit-ins begin at Woolworth's lunch counter in Greensboro, North Carolina
May 1	American U-2 spy plane shot down over Soviet Union

| November 8 | John F. Kennedy defeats Richard M. Nixon in U.S. Presidential election |

1961

January 3	U.S. breaks diplomatic relations with Cuba
January 17	Eisenhower warns of a military-industrial complex in his Farewell Address
March 1	Kennedy signs bill establishing the Peace Corps
March 13	Kennedy announces the "Alliance for Progress" between U.S. and Latin America
April 17–19	CIA backs Cuban exiles in invasion of Cuba at the Bay of Pigs
May 3	Freedom Rides to integrate the nation's interstates begin; Freedom Riders board buses in Washington, D.C.
May 5	Astronaut Alan B. Shepard becomes the first American in space
May 25	Kennedy signs Minimum Wage law raising minimum wage from $1 to $1.25
May 20	Federal troops deployed in Montgomery to ensure access of black students to schools
June 3–4	Kennedy meets with Soviet Premier Nikita Khrushchev at Vienna Conference
August 13	Berlin wall erected enclosing East Berlin

1962

February 20	American astronaut John Glenn becomes first human to orbit the earth
April 11	Kennedy attacks the $6 per ton increase in the price of steel implemented by six major U.S. steel companies
September 30	James Meredith first black student admitted to the University of Mississippi; 3,000 federal troops required to put down riots
October 11	Kennedy signs Trade Expansion Act to promote foreign trade
October 18	U-2 spy planes photograph medium-range ballistic missiles in Cuba
October 22	Kennedy appears on national television to announce missiles in Cuba and U.S. quarantine
October 27	Khrushchev announces that Soviet missiles will be withdrawn from Cuba

1963

| Mar 18 | U.S. Supreme Court extends the right to counsel to the indigent in *Gideon v. Wainwright* |

May 2–10	Children's march and violence in Birmingham, Alabama
May 28	Civil rights demonstrations in Jackson, Mississippi
June 10	Self-immolation of Buddhist monk Thich Quang Duc in Saigon; Vietnam protests authoritarian methods of South Vietnamese government
June 11	Gov. George Wallace blocks the entrance of two black students at the University of Alabama
June 11	Black civil rights leader Medgar Evers assassinated outside his home
June 20	U.S. and U.S.S.R. establish hot-line connection between White House and Kremlin to reduce possibility of accidental nuclear exchange
July 25	Limited Test Ban Treaty signed; bans testing of nuclear weapons in space, the atmosphere, or underwater
August 28	250,000–400,00 black civil rights activists gather at the March on Washington for Jobs and Freedom; Martin Luther King, Jr. delivers "I Have a Dream" speech
November 2	South Vietnamese President Ngo Dinh Diem assassinated
November 22	U.S. President John F. Kennedy assassinated

1964

March 23	Johnson announces "War on Poverty"
July 2	Johnson signs Civil Rights Act of 1964; bans discrimination in public accommodations based on race and religion; bans discrimination in employment based on race, religion, or sex
August 2	*USS Maddox* reportedly fired at by three North Vietnamese warships off the coast of Vietnam in the Gulf of Tonkin
August 4	Three civil rights workers found interred in unmarked grave in Mississippi
August 5	Congress passes Gulf of Tonkin Resolution giving the president authority to use "all necessary measures" to prevent attacks and repeal aggression on U.S. forces in Vietnam
September 3	Johnson signs Wilderness Act expanding acreage of federally protected lands
October	Students seize administration and classroom buildings in free speech protests at the University of California at Berkeley

December 14	U.S. Supreme Court affirms Constitutionality of Civil Rights Act of 1964 in *Heart of Atlanta Motel v United States*

1965

Feb. 1–March 9	Martin Luther King, Jr. and Student Nonviolent Coordinating Committee (SNCC) lead marches from Selma, Alabama to state capital in Montgomery to protest for voting rights
February 21	Malcolm X assassinated while speaking at a rally in Harlem in New York City
February 13	Johnson approves Operation Rolling Thunder bombing campaign in Vietnam
February 26	Johnson decides to commit fist U.S. ground troops to Vietnam
March 2	Operation Rolling Thunder begins in Vietnam
March 8	Two battalions of U.S. Marine Corps arrive in Vietnam
April 11	Johnson signs Elementary and Secondary Education Act expanding federal funding for public education
April 28	14,000 U.S. Marines invade Dominican Republic to prevent Communist takeover
June 7	U.S. Supreme Court rules that the right to privacy covers the right of married couples to use contraceptives in *Griswold v. Connecticut*
July 30	Johnson signs Medicare bill providing heath insurance for Americans over age 65
August 6	Johnson signs Voting Rights Act giving federal government authority to disqualify votes from polls using discriminatory registration policies
August 10	Johnson signs Housing and Urban Development Act; creates cabinet-level Department of Housing and Urban Development (HUD) to coordinate federal efforts to construct public housing and work toward urban renewal
August 11–16	Riots erupt in Watts in Los Angles, California leaving 34 dead and $200 million in losses
October 3	Johnson signs Immigration bill ending use of national origins quotas in immigration
October 22	Johnson signs Highway Beautification Act

1966

June 13	Supreme Court announces decision in *Miranda v. Arizona* leading to the requirement that those arrested

	by police be informed of their Fifth Amendment rights
June 30	National Organization for Women (NOW) founded

1967

January 27	American astronauts Grissom, White, and Chaffee killed on Apollo launch pad in fire that occurred during testing
October 2	Thurgood Marshall sworn in as first black U.S. Supreme Court Justice
October 22	March on Pentagon to protest American involvement in Vietnam
November 21	Johnson signs Air Quality Act

1968

January 23	North Korean ships seize American *USS Pueblo* off the coast of South Korea, holding 82 American seamen hostage for eleven months
January 31	Vietcong attack more than 20 cities in South Vietnam in Tet Offensive; U.S. and South Korean troops spend four weeks retaking cities in South Vietnam; turning point in Vietnam War
March 16	347 Vietnamese killed by American soldiers in Vietnam at My Lai Massacre
March 31	Johnson speaks to nation on national television; announces that he will not seek reelection
Aril 1	U.S. bombing campaign halted in Vietnam
April 4	Civil Rights leader Martin Luther King, Jr. assassinated outside hotel in Memphis, Tennessee
April 11	Johnson signs Fair Housing Act banning racial discrimination in public housing
April 23	Students for a Democratic Society takeover at Columbia University
June 5	Democratic presidential candidate Robert F. Kennedy assassinated in Los Angeles
July 1	U.S. and Soviet Union sign Nuclear Non-Proliferation Treaty to control dissemination of material for nuclear weapons

1969

January 20	Richard Nixon inaugurated president of United States
June 11	Homosexuals protest at Stonewall Bar in New York
July 20	American astronaut Neil Armstrong walks on moon
Aug 15–17	Woodstock Festival takes place in upstate New York

INTRODUCTION

Like the era of the French Revolution, about which novelist Charles Dickens wrote in *A Tale of Two Cities*, the years from 1953 to 1969 were at once, "the best of times and the worst of times." Not long before this period began, America had emerged from World War II as the dominant of the world's two superpowers. After a brief readjustment to a peacetime economy, America prospered consistently throughout the period, experiencing only minor recessions in the fifties and enjoying an unprecedented phase of sustained economic growth from 1961 to 1968. Cultural developments like the proliferation of McDonalds' fast-food restaurants, rock-and-roll music, the invention and use of the birth control pill, and the growth of the suburbs influenced American life in important ways that are still shaping the nation. American political, economic, and cultural leaders of the period also made profound contributions to the American state and to American society.

The presidents of the period were especially important players. The war hero Dwight D. Eisenhower renewed American's confidence in the presidency while building an infrastructure both at home and within American forces across the globe. A dashing John F. Kennedy brought youth and optimism to America, promising greatness for Americans as they embarked on a "New Frontier," while managing Cold War crises with a public confidence and grace. Finally, a former teacher from Texas, Lyndon B. Johnson, though beleaguered by the tragedy of a war abroad and chaos in cities and on college campuses at home, expanded the power and responsibility of the national government beyond what even President Franklin D. Roosevelt had imagined when he introduced his New Deal programs during the Great Depression. Eisenhower's interstate highway system still traverses the nation today; Kennedy's legend lives on with the "baby boom" generation; and national programs that Johnson initiated continue to serve millions of Americans.

THE CIVIL RIGHTS MOVEMENT

The struggle for civil rights, equality, and opportunity posed unique challenges to each of the presidencies highlighted in this book. Having made headway during World War II in the courts and in politics, civil rights activists intensified their push for equality, working not only for political and legal advances, but turning their attention to social venues as well. With a victory in the U.S. Supreme Court's landmark decision in *Brown v. Board of Education* (1954), which overturned the previous policy of "separate but equal" and banned racial segregation in schools, civil rights activists sought not only to ensure that the *Brown* decision was enforced in education, but also to expand political and economic opportunity into other areas.

The Cold War presidents faced difficult political decisions as they fleshed out their stances on civil rights. They confronted the proper role of the federal government, the desire to limit "bad press" for America across the globe, and the struggle to appease constituencies that included black voters, racist Southerners and civil rights supporters. Guided by a mix of political considerations and personal convictions about the use of the power of the federal government and often distracted or preoccupied by other interests, Eisenhower and Kennedy approached the issue of African American civil rights moderately and cautiously. By contrast, President Johnson made civil rights the centerpiece of his agenda for domestic policy, and by the end of the decade the nation had eliminated legal segregation and had protected due process rights for blacks in most aspects of society. Progress was sometimes costly. Racists lynched Emmett Till, an innocent African American teenager, for looking at a white woman and assassinated leaders of the civil rights movement like Harry T. Moore, Medgar Evers, Malcolm X, and Martin Luther King, Jr. Racial tension continued, and many African Americans still felt isolated, ignored, and oppressed. The wave of urban riots that overtook such U.S. cities as Watts, Detroit, Chicago, Cleveland, and Newark from the summers of 1965 through 1968, testified to such feelings.

OTHER PROTEST GROUPS

African Americans were not the only ones who voiced their frustrations with the American system and organized, mobilized, and took action during this period. Affluent students, frustrated by what they perceived as the staleness and uniformity of the fifties, and by the Vietnam War and military conscription during the sixties, engaged in political demonstrations that (like the incident May 4, 1970 at Kent State, where national guardsmen fired on student demonstrators) sometimes ended in violence. They also found diversions in rock and psychedelic music, eastern religions, alcohol, drugs, and sex. This culminated in the wild, three-day Woodstock festival in upstate New York in August 1969, which combined all these elements with musical performances by such popular musicians as Bob Dylan, Jimi Hendrix, and Jefferson Airplane.

The National Organization of Women took shape in the early 1960s to further the "rights revolution" and rekindle support for an Equal Rights Amendment. Inspired by the achievements of the black civil rights movement and energized by the publication of Betty Friedan's *The Feminine Mystique* in 1963, members expressed discontent with the limitations of their traditional roles as mothers and housewives and sought to expand their opportunities in America and gain greater control over their own lives. Not coincidentally, the women's movement also appeared in the wake of the introduction of "the pill" for birth control in 1961 and as pressure to legalize abortions began to mount. As women pressed for liberation from traditional restrictions on their roles in society and sought more control over their own place in the community, they became increasingly concerned with gaining greater control over their own bodies as well.

A variety of other groups participated in the quest for liberation in the 1960s. Led by Cesar Chavez, migrant farm workers protested low wages and substandard living and working conditions. Homosexuals staged a riot in New York City on June 11, 1969 at the Stonewall Bar that brought national attention to the discrimination that gays and lesbians faced. Students for a Democratic Society protested materialism and authoritarianism in America by staging rallies and occupying classrooms and administration buildings on college campuses across the nation.

CONDITIONS AT HOME AND ABROAD

America prospered economically in the 1950s and 1960s, but, clearly, not all Americans participated in this affluence. Moreover, as some prospered, their expectations, not only for prosperity but for opportunity and liberation from the trappings of mainstream America, increased: "All of these developments promoted grand expectations. . . .This optimistic spirit—the feeling that there were no limits to progress—defined a guiding spirit of the age and, over time, unleashed ever more powerful popular pressures for expanded rights and gratifications."[1]

Across the globe, developing nations were seeking more autonomy and greater equality on the world stage. As America was emerging as the world's most powerful nation and her citizens were becoming ever more confident about their role in the world, not all U.S. allies were reaping the benefits of American power and prosperity. Because all three presidents placed a high strategic and psychological value on winning the war on communism, the nation funneled a good deal of money to its allies. For example the United States supplied large sums of money in the early 1960s to make Chile a "showpiece" of one of President Kennedy's foreign policy initiatives, the Alliance for Progress. On the other hand other allies, less important strategically, or more stable politically, attracted less interest from the foreign policy establishment in the United States. In many cases, American assistance only fattened the coffers of corrupt political and economic elites in those countries, leaving the majority of the population living amid underdeveloped conditions, if not in squalor. The CIA supported President Mobutu Sese Seko of the Congo, even though he used the nation's rich natural resources largely for personal gain. Clearly, the United States was balancing strategic national security interests against less tangible foreign policy concerns. Attempting to counterbalance perceived Soviet expansionism, America further extended its military might to Korea, Vietnam, Laos, Germany, Guatemala, the Dominican Republic, and Cuba through both overt and covert military deployments. The allure of America's material culture, which then Vice President Richard Nixon highlighted in his informal July 25, 1959 "kitchen debate" with Nikita Khrushchev at the American National Exposition in Moscow, reinforced the nation's military and diplomatic power.

THE THREAT OF COMMUNISM AND THE U.S. RESPONSE

Americans in the 1950s and 1960s based their foreign policy on their overwhelming fear of communism, the political ideology based on the idea of class warfare and a dictatorial political structure that first came to power in the Soviet Union, and spread to Eastern Europe, China, and Cuba. Americans viewed the tenets of communism, and its corresponding political system, as diametrically opposed, and therefore threatening, to the American way of life. Americans saw communism as an ideology that valued a large bureaucratic state organization vesting power in the government at the expense of individual freedom. Americans were convinced that communism was inherently expansionist, threatening not only those who lived within the system, but those on the outside as well.

The idea of "containment" thus dominated most foreign policy decisions made in the United States during the years of the Cold War. Developed in 1947 by sovietologist George Kennan, containment prescribed a two-fold approach to the menace of communism, predicated on American vigilance and diligence. First, Americans should check the expansion of communism wherever it occurred. Kennan argued that if the United States contained communism within its existing boundaries, it would eventually collapse. Bolstered by this belief, Eisenhower backed the overthrow of a government in Guatemala, Kennedy deployed money and troops to Southeast Asia, and

Johnson sent Marines to the Dominican Republic and expanded American involvement in Vietnam. The second, less well-remembered aspect of containment, which Kennan also promulgated, called on Americans to project a unified and coherent image of domestic happiness and tranquility. Because communism could expand both by force and by psychological and ideological appeal, Kennan reasoned that military power alone could not contain communism. Americans thus needed to counter the communist promise of an equitable distribution of wealth, which was popular in newly independent nations, with its own positive example of expanding economic prosperity and opportunity. America's domestic responses to its own economic downturns and social tensions were thus tied to its ability to win friends and allies abroad. Some historians have argued that this concern motivated presidential support for civil rights, especially during the Eisenhower and Kennedy years. Promote a favorable image of capitalism and democracy, keep communism from gaining strength, and wait it out—in the end, Kennan, and soon most Americans, believed, communism was doomed.

The quest for nuclear superiority added to the ideological contest with global communism. The "arms race" between the United States and the Soviet Union was another playing field for the Cold War. Each of the two superpowers tried to outgun the other by creating thousands of nuclear warheads, along with missiles, jets, submarines, tanks, and other instruments of war. This race to build more weapons generated new philosophies of war and diplomacy. Perhaps the two most notorious doctrines were those of brinksmanship and mutual assured destruction (MAD). Brinksmanship, in essence, applied the old car game of "chicken" to the standoff between the world's two nuclear superpowers, urging the United States not to back off from its threats to use nuclear weapons to defend itself. MAD, based on the premise of deterrence, described the military strategy of building such a stockpile of weapons that the adversary was assured of its own destruction, even if it achieved its objective of ruining its enemy. However risky they may have been, these ideas drove the thinking and policymaking of both Americans and Soviets during the Cold War. Moreover, the United States and the Soviet Union each maneuvered to gain strategic positions around the globe. At the height of the Cold War, the Soviets had stationed missiles in Cuba, ninety miles off the coast of the United States, while American missiles targeted Moscow from just across the Soviet-Turkish border.

Just as the bulwarks of democracy and communism sought ideological allies, they worked feverishly to secure military alliances as well. These efforts were largely responsible for the proliferation of regional organizations after World War II. The North Atlantic Treaty Organization (NATO), the Rio Treaty of Reciprocal Assistance, the Southeast Asian Treaty Organization (SEATO), the Warsaw Pact, and other such regional alliances were designed to trigger the automatic military response of member states in the event of foreign attack. While providing for stability, such alliances also highlighted the danger that just a fraction of the world's arsenal could destroy all of civilization. Although the Cold War never erupted into nuclear conflict, it generated fear and terror throughout the world.

AN AGE OF ANXIETY AND CONSENSUS

The threat and fear of communism penetrated deep into American life in the 1950s. The anxiety of the age helped shape domestic politics, economics, and culture. In the first year of the decade, the government accused Alger Hiss, the president of the Carnegie Foundation for International Peace, of being a secret communist who engaged in espionage by passing State Department documents to the Soviets. Hiss was convicted of perjury when he denied giving State Department information to his accuser, the communist agent, Whitaker Chambers. Within two weeks of Hiss's conviction, the Federal Bureau of Investigation (FBI) arrested scientist Klaus Fuchs, who confessed to providing the Soviets with information about U.S. efforts to develop an atomic bomb. Fuchs led authorities to Julius Rosenberg and his wife Ethel, who were convicted in 1951 of being part of a spy ring providing information to Russian spies about the Los Alamos laboratory and the efforts there to develop atomic weapons. Convicted of conspiracy to commit espionage, both Rosenbergs received death sentences, which were carried out in June 1953.

All this led to the now shameful episode know as McCarthyism, during which a maverick Wisconsin senator, Joseph McCarthy, bandied about accusations of communist sympathizing against everyone from State Department officials, to Hollywood film stars, to high-ranking military officials. Thus, the fear posed by the Cold War extended from the contest to develop nuclear weapons to science and cinema in American life. The now infamous bomb shelters that dotted the suburban underground, the air-raid drills that interrupted school days throughout America, and the double meanings of the B-movies of the 1950s and 1960s, reflected and enhanced the frightened and confused atmosphere of the Cold War era.

Historians have dubbed the 1950s the "Age of Anxiety" because Americans so feared the expansion of communism and the unprecedented power of nuclear weapons. To cope with that anxiety, Americans joined together to form a sense of cultural conformity that has led other historians to dub the decade the "Age of Consensus." Although some scholars are challenging that characterization of the 1950s, a look, literally, at the landscape of America in the 1950s verifies the consensus of Americans during those years. Undoubtedly, rock and roll divided America's youth and older Americans; Alfred Kinsey's books on the thoughts and sexual practices of men and women, published in 1948 and 1953 respectively, caused a rift between the more socially conservative minded and those of a more liberal bent; and racial tensions, though showing some signs of easing, fractured some American communities in the 1950s and led, in part, to "white flight" to the suburbs. However, expanding suburbs, fast-food franchises, and the growth of church memberships in America also evidenced significant cultural uniformity and consensus.

President Eisenhower's Highway Act connected America from coast to coast and border to border. Highways allowed, if not encouraged, Americans to reside in suburbs that were located outside the city limits, further away from work and markets, and such urban maladies as poverty, racial tension, crime, and pollution. President Johnson's Great Society programs would aim at eradicating such problems and extending the prosperity and consensus of the suburbs to all Americans.

Religion remained an important component of American life during the 1950s. Religion provided a sanctuary for Americans seeking solace from the frightening world of communist ideological threats and the prospects of nuclear devastation, and, in addition to satisfying spiritual needs, it arguably played into the American desire for consensus. Both church attendance and membership increased during this period. In 1954, Congress added the phrase "under God" to the flag salute, reinforcing the words "in God we trust" on American coins and the Protestant tradition that so many Americans shared.

This consensus of the 1950s had a dark side as well. Assimilationists opposed accommodations for special groups, such as educational programs in foreign languages for those who were not fluent in English, and argued against tolerance. Suspicion of ethnic origin, as well as unconventional political affiliation, was commonplace. The McCarran-Walter Act of 1952 affirmed the national origins quotas that had been a part of immigration policy since the 1920s, and retained the bias against immigrants from nations outside Western Europe and the Western Hemisphere. The nation did not remove these quotas and their ethnic preferences until the adoption of the Hart-Cellar Immigration Act of 1965 during the administration of President Lyndon Johnson.

INTELLECTUAL CURRENTS

Despite the affluence and the sense of consensus of the early postwar period, not all Americans benefited from the economic upswing, and not all agreed on how to make postwar prosperity more inclusive. John Kenneth Galbraith's *The Affluent Society*, Michael Harrington's *The Other America*, and Gunnar Myrdal's *Challenge to Affluence* criticized the American postwar obsession with productivity and economic growth at all costs. They argued that socioeconomic structures were preventing some Americans, notably the poor, immigrants, and minorities, from accessing the affluence in which so many white suburbanites flourished. As Americans moved into the 1960s, many groups expressed their frustrations with these structures and the status quo of the 1950s. Recognizing that the nation had made little progress on the desegregation front in the years since the *Brown* decision, civil rights protestors resorted to more confrontational protests, marches, and boycotts. Paradoxically, law enforcement officials resisting desegregation in the South, furthered the cause by effectively forcing Eisenhower and Kennedy to mobilize troops in support of desegregation.

Intellectuals also encouraged black civil rights and expanded the discussion from legal equality to equal economic opportunity. In 1965 Daniel Patrick Moynihan published *The Negro Family: The Case For National Action*, a study linking culture and economic well-being. Moynihan observed that the traditional correlation between unemployment and the rate of growth of the welfare rolls was aberrant in black communities in the early 1960s. He found that even though the unemployment rate was declining, welfare participation was growing. He observed that the number of black children growing up in single-parent homes was rising dramatically in the 1950s and 1960s. Moynihan concluded that the deterioration of the black family in America was linked to the "dependency rate," that is, the percentage of people on welfare. Critics argued that Moynihan was blaming victimized poor black families for their own economic woes and the deterioration of the communities in which they lived. President Johnson, however, responded more favorably to Moynihan's report, and took it into account in shaping his proposed Great Society. Welfare, community action programs, housing, immigration, education, and the model cities efforts, with their emphasis on families and the importance of local communities, all reflected the influence of Moynihan's study.

Other intellectuals also contributed to the increased momentum for reforms that emphasized a focus on families in poor communities. Required by the 1964 Civil Rights Act, the Coleman Report, formally entitled "Equality of Educational Opportunity," concluded in 1966 that a child's family was a better predictor of how a child would perform in school than the school the child attended or the resources the child used. Similarly, the report of the Kerner Commission, which President Johnson commissioned in 1967, focused on the progress of civil rights legislation, integration, and equal opportunity. The Kerner Commission warned that by 1967 the legislation of the Great Society was not achieving its stated objectives, which included integration and economic development, but that two separate white and black societies were emerging in America.

SUMMARY

All of these forces influenced politics during the Cold War era. Dwight Eisenhower was president during most of the 1950s when politics reflected the consensus of the age. The fear of communism and the quest to defeat it drove both foreign and domestic policy, affecting projects as diverse as the space race and the construction of a national system of highways. Early in the 1960s, a new president exuded optimism and idealism, confidence and bravado. John Kennedy announced a "New Frontier" in America and the world. He promised to bring a new energy to attack racism, poverty, and recession at home, while fighting communism in new and innovative ways abroad. Because an assassin's bullet tragically cut Kennedy's life short, we will never know how well he would have fared as he pursued the challenges of the "New Frontier," and his three years as president left a larger legacy of hope than of accomplishment. Kennedy's successor, Lyndon Johnson, was even more ambitious. Johnson pledged to pacify the frontier of an increasingly restless America with the blueprints for a "Great Society." Johnson announced broad plans to protect the environment and consumers and to guard minorities from discrimination and the poor from lack of opportunity. Johnson's "Great Society" held the promise to fulfill the call of George Kennan's containment policy for a tranquil and prosperous society in America. The war in Vietnam, the frustration of those not participating in the affluence of America, and the youthful spirit and energy of the baby boomers, just then coming of age, sidetracked Johnson's dreams; facing war, riots, and protests, midway through his five years in office, Johnson was frustrated and exhausted, and his plans for a "Great Society" were threatened, if not derailed.

The Cold War embodied both fear and progress. Until the 1990s, Americans had never enjoyed the sustained economic growth they did in the 1960s. Innovative time-saving devices, the birth control pill, computers, advances in medicine, television, and the electric guitar made the Cold War era exciting. Many Americans were getting rich in the 1950s and 1960s, buying dream houses in the suburbs, raising families patterned after the Cleavers (of *Leave It To Beaver*) and other television families. Although some Americans disapproved, all three of the Cold War presidents covered in this volume backed initiatives that dramatically expanded the role of the federal government in American life. During this period the government began providing new services and benefits to all Americans, from federal funding for education, to federal protections of wilderness areas, to protections against discrimination. During the same time, Americans had to deal with the ever-present threat of nuclear war, which loomed over their idyllic suburban lives, and endure the traumas of major wars in Korea and Vietnam, which combined to claim the lives of more than 110,000 American soldiers and contributed to domestic divisions. Americans also suffered from the psychological effects of several crises that nearly led to nuclear exchange between the world's two superpowers, and the endless upheaval caused by American intervention in the affairs of other nations. By the 1960s, Americans confronted constant news of conflicts not only between the United States and foreign powers but also among Americans themselves. While many Americans lived prosperous lives during the Cold War, others struggled for economic opportunity, equality, and acceptance. At the end of the 1960s, American society was more affluent, more integrated, and more connected than it had ever been, but it also had more destructive power in its arsenal, and a greater responsibility and commitment to its own people and to the world than it had ever previously assumed.

NOTE

1. James T. Patterson, *Grand Expectations: The United States, 1945–1975* (New York: Oxford University Press, 1996), 317.

DWIGHT DAVID EISENHOWER

(1953–1961)

INTRODUCTION

Although Republicans dominated the presidency through much of the late nineteenth and early twentieth centuries, Democrats captured the Oval Office with the election of Franklin D. Roosevelt in 1932 and held it through the administration of Harry S. Truman, who was elected in 1948. Things changed with the election of 1952. Both parties had courted World War II hero, Dwight D. Eisenhower, but he ran as a Republican presidential candidate against Illinois Democrat Governor Adlai Stevenson and won 55 percent of the popular vote in a landslide.

Republicans used the slogan K_1C_2—Korea, Communism, Corruption—to characterize the putative failures of the outgoing Truman Administration. Democrats found themselves defending a situation where American troops were bogged down in a military stalemate in Korea. They were further undercut by the paranoia generated by Republican Senator Joseph McCarthy of Wisconsin, which was sweeping across America from Washington to Hollywood. Not wanting to alienate voters who were attracted to McCarthy or provoke him into a dirty war of words, Eisenhower refused to attack the senator during this campaign, but Eisenhower made Korea central to his critique of the incumbent party. Eisenhower pledged not only to resolve that crisis in which American troops had been stalemated for more than two years, but also to strengthen America's resolve against communism more generally. According to Eisenhower and the Republicans, the Truman administration had "lost" China, failed to employ containment in Korea, and been unable to protect the national security secrets of the United States, as evidenced by the spy trials of Alger

Hiss and the convictions of Julius and Ethel Rosenberg for passing atomic secrets to the Soviets.

Eisenhower argued that Truman's domestic policy also needed fixing and threatened national security. Eisenhower contended that the New Deal and Fair Deal programs of Presidents Franklin Roosevelt and Harry Truman had enlarged the federal government too much and had inappropriately involved the federal government in the economy of the United States, particularly through federal regulations and controls on business. Eisenhower charged that big budgets and a shaky economy affected not only the quality of life in America, but also made America vulnerable to international communism, failing to provide the right example of capitalism and democracy and making the maintenance of the American military more difficult. Viewed both as a moderate Republican on domestic affairs, and an able statesman, Eisenhower easily won the favor of Americans.

SENATOR MCCARTHY POSES PROBLEMS
FOR THE NEW ADMINISTRATION

Senator McCarthy soon became a thorn in the new president's side. The senator held up Eisenhower's first nomination in the Senate, that of Walter Bedell Smith for Undersecretary of State. McCarthy did not like Smith's praise for another State Department official, John Paton Davies, who McCarthy had placed on his infamous list of State officers who were "known communists." McCarthy suggested that Smith's support for Davies could evidence Smith's own sympathies with the Soviet Union and urged careful scrutiny of his appointment and even his role in government. Smith, however, had been Eisenhower's trusted aide since World War II, serving as the general's top assistant in Europe. Furious with McCarthy, Eisenhower was determined to ruin him.

Eisenhower's strategy, though, was consistent with the management style he used throughout his presidency, what historian Fred I. Greenstein has dubbed "The Hidden Hand Presidency." Despite a fairly intimate involvement in most issues, and a tight control over members of his administration, Eisenhower projected the public image of a rather hands-off, behind-the-scenes president who allowed his appointees to do most of his work for him. More than one historian has characterized Eisenhower's notion of the presidency as "Whiggish" (a political designation, partly derived from English precedents, characteristic of some early nineteenth-century American politicians) for his aloofness, avoidance of partisanship, and his conception of limited federal government. Moreover, Eisenhower considered his presidential image to be crucial. The president should exemplify dignity and prestige and remain above the fray of down and dirty politicking. Accordingly, he planned to destroy McCarthy by ignoring, rather than by publicly rebuking, him.

After the election, McCarthy continued his antics, even traveling overseas to investigate the broadcasts of the Voice of America and American libraries in Europe. McCarthy's investigations created fear. After McCarthy alleged that State Department libraries in Europe contained over 30,000 books authored by communists, Secretary of State John Foster Dulles banned the works of communist authors in State Department libraries. Some librarians, afraid of being caught with suspect volumes, even burned some books. In public Eisenhower remained detached from the fray, consistently refusing requests from friends and aides to rebuke McCarthy.

Significantly, Eisenhower, those in his administration, and Republicans in general did not object to the intent of McCarthy's investigations. As cold warriors and staunch anticommunists, they too feared subversion, and acknowledged that the threat of the communist menace internally was significant. Dulles at times even called it more serious than the expansion of communism abroad. Eisenhower thus developed his own apparatus for investigating the loyalty of government employees and dismissing those who threatened national security.

The paranoia of the fifties placed the president in a tough spot. While weighing whether to pardon convicted spies Julius and Ethel Rosenberg from a death sentence and what responses he should make to communist advances in Korea, Indochina, Guatemala, and China, Eisenhower had to take account of public fears. Although he disliked the tactics and drama of McCarthyism, Eisenhower feared that criticizing the McCarthy investigations or pardoning the Rosenbergs might falsely convey a softening in the White House on communism and specifically on internal subversion.

In the end, Eisenhower's strategy succeeded. He managed to work through the entire McCarthy episode without even mentioning the senator's name in public or commenting specifically on any of his activities. As McCarthy became more brazen in his allegations throughout 1953 and 1954, his support among the public soon began to diminish. He went too far when he turned his attacks against the Protestant clergy, the CIA (headed by Secretary of State John Foster Dulles's brother, Allen), General George Marshall, and the United States Army. Although polls gave McCarthy between a 50 and 60 percent popularity rating in January 1954 after he made his initial accusations against the army, by the time he conducted nationally televised hearings questioning the loyalty of high-ranking army men in the summer of 1954, he had lost his credibility. Censured by an overwhelming vote in the Senate in August 1954, McCarthy lost his influence in government and became a tragic political figure. Eisenhower's patience paid off, and McCarthy proved to be his own undoing.

BIG GOVERNMENT AND THE ECONOMY

In addition to resolving the scare of McCarthyism and negotiating a truce to end the stalemate in Korea, Eisenhower had other items on his agenda. Despite some campaign rhetoric critical of Democratic programs and the evolution of big government, Eisenhower did not set out to roll back the New Deal. Although Eisenhower believed that excessive government intervention threatened individual freedom, and he attempted to reduce federal controls in business and generally shrink the size of the federal government, overall Eisenhower's domestic program continued to expand the federal government.

Because he recognized the important role the government played in the life of Americans, Eisenhower did not enact reforms radically. Even more dedicated to balanced budgets than to downsizing the role of the federal government, he resisted congressional pressure to include tax cuts in his first budget, which many fellow Republicans favored. However, his pragmatic view of the relationship between the government and the economy and the priorities of the Cold War led to only three balanced budgets in eight years. Although the president initially resisted any government intervention in the economy, a recession that started early in Eisenhower's presidency generated pressure that persuaded him to sanction the use of interest rates and the management of the national debt to encourage economic recovery. Even if it meant running a budget deficit, government spending was justified to provide an economic stimulus.

As opposed to the self-regulating laissez-faire view of the "Invisible Hand" that had characterized Republican economics of the 1920s, one historian has characterized Eisenhower's own policies as the "Barely Visible Hand." These policies allowed the federal government to play a role in the American economy, even while maintaining an aloof attitude toward economic developments. Eisenhower's domestic agenda was consistent with what his supporters of the day called "Modern Republicanism." This view of government was more sympathetic and activist than the staunch conservatism of many Republicans in the 1950s, that of Senate Leader Robert Taft (R-OH) and Senator William Knowland (R-CA), for example, but it was a far cry from the liberalism of the New Deal era. This is evidenced by the criticism directed against Eisenhower. Liberals at times referred to him as "Eisen-hoover," while conservative Senator Barry Goldwater (R-AZ) complained that the president ran a

"Dime Store New Deal." In fact, the president's domestic policy, like his foreign policy, was cautious, guarded, and, most importantly, pragmatic.

THE SIZE OF THE NATIONAL GOVERNMENT

Just as Eisenhower adapted his position on balanced budgets and the role of the federal government in the economy to prevailing economic circumstances, he also eased his stance on the size and purpose of the national government. He tweaked some liberal programs to reduce dependency on the federal government. Thus, Public Law 480 overhauled farm policy, and, in particular, subsidies for agricultural products. Although the program did not eliminate federal subsidies for farmers, it subjected agricultural goods to increased market forces, and put food surpluses to better use than they had been in the past. Acknowledging the political, psychological, and economic importance of some New Deal programs, Eisenhower expanded Social Security, the minimum wage, and unemployment insurance. Eisenhower supported the Atomic Energy Act of 1954, which allowed for government funding of atomic research; the Interstate and Defense Highways Act in 1956, which was the largest federal public works program in American history; and the National Defense Education Act in 1958, which represented an increased federal commitment to the funding of public education.

President Eisenhower also proved less conservative, and more pragmatic, on civil rights than some might have expected in 1952. He did not endorse the 1954 Supreme Court decision in *Brown v. Board of Education*, which banned racially segregated schools and set the precedent for the civil rights movements of the 1950s and 1960s. However, in his second term, Eisenhower used federal power to enforce desegregation. He also proposed and signed a civil rights bill in 1957, the impact of which Congress minimized with amendments.

MILITARY POLICIES: STRATEGIC THEORY

Certain Cold War factors influenced Eisenhower's domestic policy. He realized that a strong economy and a contented and compensated workforce were essential to effective containment policy. Yet some of Eisenhower's philosophical convictions about government policy did not sit so well with those on his foreign policy team, and the president's ideas about domestic and foreign policy were not always easy to reconcile. Eisenhower's commitment to a balanced budget clashed with the military concerns of the Cold War. The defense budget had increased 300 percent during the Korean War, and the effort to keep pace with the Soviets in the race for bigger and more destructive atomic weapons suggested no end to escalating defense costs. Furthermore, Eisenhower believed strongly that foreign aid to allies for military and economic development should be a key component of American foreign policy. Truman's foreign spending had been substantial, especially during the years of the Marshall Plan, which provided massive aid to West European allies. Ironically, while Eisenhower struggled to wring more money out of Congress for foreign aid throughout his two terms, he also squared off, primarily with members of his own party, to bring defense spending, like overall spending, under control. He argued that security was not only a function of the superiority of the arsenal but that a strong economy and domestic policy were also important. The president contended that unlimited spending on defense would force cuts in domestic programs such as Social Security, and he therefore called for a "new look" in defense strategy, based on more powerful weapons, strengthened alliances, and reduced costs.

When after the death of Soviet Premier Joseph Stalin in 1953, the Soviet government signaled that cooperation—or at least détente, a relaxation of tensions—with the Soviet Union was possible, Eisenhower called on both Americans and Soviets to embrace what he called, in the title of a speech to the American Society of Newspaper Editors, "The Chance for Peace." The speech included a list of specific, practical invitations to the Soviets to compromise on global issues like Korea and self-determination, but the real impact came toward the end of the speech when the president highlighted disarmament, equating the costs of the arms race with the lack of spending on schools, hospitals, power plants, and social services. Guns, warships, and rockets, Eisenhower implored, signified "a theft from those who hunger and are not fed, those who are cold and are not clothed." Eisenhower suggested that if the Soviets were also ready to conclude the Cold War and commence a war on poverty and underdevelopment, both nations could redirect the resources used to build arms to the development of infrastructure, health care, and economic development across the globe. The media hailed Eisenhower's speech for its logic, moderation, and sincerity, and it provided hope for an easing of Cold War tensions. Americans were pleased to see Eisenhower take the "propaganda initiative" away from the Russians. The speech also outlined a general philosophy for the Eisenhower presidency—a definition of national security that included the defense of the American way of life with a strong military, as well as with social spending and the management of consistent economic development.

The Cold War did not come screeching to a halt as a result of the president's "Chance for Peace" address. Many "hot" spots continued to require the attention of American foreign policy, and despite a new Soviet leadership apparatus, the United States could not abandon containment. Both Eisenhower and Secretary of State John Foster Dulles exemplified the attitudes of "Cold Warriors" of the age. Staunchly anticommunist, they believed, like most Americans, that the Soviets were bent on expansion, and they crafted U.S. policy to contain this threat. Some historians have argued that Eisenhower and Dulles dramatically expanded, even transformed, the idea of containment by deploying the American military, overtly and covertly, in Latin America, Asia, and the Middle East. Much of this critique is due to the rhetoric of the Secretary of State, who had harshly criticized the Truman administration's approach to containment and frequently talked of U.S. foreign policy designed for "liberating captive peoples." Although some expected Eisenhower to apply this doctrine to Soviet satellite nations, in practice, Eisenhower and his foreign policy team did not so much alter the containment policy as he strengthened and applied it more aggressively than had Truman.

Dulles believed that Truman's approach to containment and the guidance of NSC-68 (the National Security Council policy document, promulgated in 1950, which called for a more aggressive containment policy and dramatically increased military spending to project an image of strength and vigilance) led to costly and futile policies like America's response to the North Korean invasion of South Korea. Dulles argued that focusing merely on "resistance to aggression," as NSC-68 advocated, created "treadmill policies" that were inefficient and ineffective. In its place, Dulles wanted a defense policy predicated on deterring aggression and regional wars (thus, obviating the need to "resist"), and only if a war did break out, striking with the full force of the American arsenal such that American action was corrective rather than simply resistant. The crises in Taiwan, which pitted the United States as the protector of the Nationalist Chinese government in exile, exemplified this new defense strategy by threatening dire consequences if the Chinese pursued an aggressive policy.

Eisenhower and Dulles, then, did not change the prevailing view of the objectives and tactics of foreign policy. They simply further defined the containment policy, which had only been formulated in 1947, as they responded to the myriad of incidents across the globe during the 1950s. In fact, the role that the United States played in the Middle East under Eisenhower in the mid-1950s looked remarkably similar to the policy of the United States in Greece and Turkey under Truman in 1947. Containment during the Eisenhower years meant support of all noncommunist regions, whether they were particularly friendly to the United States or not. The United States aggressively extended containment tactics beyond the Soviet border, expanding Truman's earlier focus on Turkey, Greece, and Korea to Central America, Africa, and the Middle East. Thus, although Eisenhower had criticized Truman in the election of 1952 for the stalemate in Korea, and for other weaknesses in foreign affairs, once Eisenhower took office, "republican command merely gave the old product new sponsorship,"[1] even if this new "sponsorship" reflected a more aggressive and strong-willed posture.

FOREIGN POLICY: FORGING ALLIANCES

Eisenhower's conception of American defense included America's allies. The idea of mutual security was important to the President. It helps to account for his insistence on spending for foreign aid, his interest in various forms of European unification, and the formation of other regional alliances. A strong believer in economic diplomacy and the importance of economic development among America's allies, Eisenhower devoted his attention almost immediately to strengthening American relations with countries in Western Europe. He encountered stiff opposition from Senate Republicans, and even to some extent from Dulles, when he requested foreign aid spending each year. Eisenhower's most difficult foreign aid fight was probably his first when he surprised Congressional Republicans by requesting $5.8 billion for foreign aid in the 1954 budget. This was almost $2 billion less than Truman had asked for in his last budget but far more than those who were seeking to reduce federal spending believed necessary. Many conservatives viewed expenditures for foreign aid, like liberal social spending at home, as handouts. They ultimately reduced Eisenhower's budget request for foreign aid by 22.3 percent.

The forging of alliances was central to the foreign policy of Eisenhower and Dulles, even if, at least in the first term, this activity took a back seat to the emphasis on the "new look" and massive retaliation. Eisenhower viewed the European allies as essential to help contain the Soviets in Europe and protect the integrity of the postwar arrangements in Germany and Berlin. Eisenhower viewed collective security and economic assistance as central components of American foreign policy. Given his general fiscal conservatism, the President clearly sought foreign aid for allies not because he valued handouts but because he thought that strong allies, capable of manufacturing and maintaining their own military, and sustaining their own economic development, benefited not only American national security in the immediate term, but also could serve to reduce American spending on foreign aid in the long term. Thus, Eisenhower worked hard to convince Europeans of the importance of establishing the European Defense Community (EDC)—they had signed a treaty creating this union, which would sponsor an all European army, but the French were holding up ratification of the treaty. Eisenhower thought the EDC would strengthen America's security in Europe vis-à-vis its allies and direct some of the costs for defending Europe from the United States to the Europeans themselves.

WORLD HOT SPOTS

Korea

The most immediate foreign policy crisis confronting Eisenhower after becoming president was the war in Korea. U.S. troops, under the auspices of the United Nations, had been bogged down in this "police action" in Korea since 1950, and in early 1953 little progress was evident in the war against the North Koreans and their Chinese and Soviet backers. Defying the advice of most of his foreign policy advisors, including his Secretary of State, Eisenhower resisted pressure to escalate the war and push the communists out of the Korean peninsula entirely. Instead, the president brought enough pressure to bear on the parties involved to bring the war to a close. Although neither side "gained" anything after three years of fighting and hundreds of thousands of casualties, Eisenhower rightly claimed that the United States had advanced its foreign policy objective of containing communism by preventing its expansion from North Korea.

China

Republicans had criticized the Democrats for "losing" China at the end of World War II. As a result of the Communist victory on the mainland, the leaders of the old Nationalist Chinese government fled to the island of Taiwan off the coast. During the Eisenhower administration, the United States continued to recognize the Nationalist Government as the "true" China and committed itself toward defending this Nationalist regime against Communist aggression. This resulted in a series of confrontations with the Communist Chinese who flexed their muscles in this area.

Vietnam

Korea and China were not the only Asian crises facing Eisenhower. In Indochina, the French were fighting to preserve one of the last vestiges of their colonial empire. By the early 1950s, they seemed destined to lose that struggle. Although they had been holding out for nearly ten years in Vietnam against the nationalist forces of Ho Chi Minh, by 1953 the situation was desperate, and the French called on the United States for increased support. They sought continuing finances for the struggle (by 1953 the American government was providing the majority of the financing for the French effort), military hardware, especially planes, and even personnel. Both Eisenhower and the French used the aforementioned EDC as a bargaining chip. While the French tried to trade ratification of the EDC for more U.S. assistance in Vietnam, the United States did the opposite, but for American policymakers the equation was not that simple. American concerns in Vietnam did not end with the question of whether and to what degree to support an ally.

The nationalist forces working to liberate Vietnam from the French were not innocuous rebels who posed no difficulty for the United States. Instead, the Vietnamese nationalists, backed by the Chinese and to a lesser degree by the Soviet Union, planned to install a communist regime in Vietnam. American policymakers were naturally inclined to help the French fend off the Vietnamese nationalists. After all, containment formed the basis of American foreign policy, and the "new look" was based on the use of definitive forces, not a replication of the stalemate of Korea. However, after just having concluded their major involvement in Korea, Americans were tired of war, and deploying forces to fight a guerilla war in Vietnam was hardly consistent with the "new look" defense policy which sought to reduce defense spending and avoid intervention in small regional conflicts. In addition, America's image in the world was at stake.

While alliances in Europe were important for the military advantage they provided, alliances in other areas of the world were crucial as well, and thus the behavior of America in those regions shaped the nature of American relations with potential allies. Eisenhower feared that involving American forces in Vietnam to fight alongside the French colonialists would ruin America's reputation as a champion of freedom. Dulles expressed concern about alienating smaller allies with thunderous talk of massive retaliation and nuclear warfare; taking the side of French imperialists could only serve to further frighten America's friends in the Third World, leading them to question the intentions of the United States and the value of their friendship. Ultimately, Eisenhower resigned himself to accept the French withdrawal from Vietnam and, as in Korea, a negotiated peace that partitioned a country. But this did not put American concerns in Southeast Asia to rest.

THE DOMINO THEORY

Eisenhower's most influential legacy in American foreign policy may have been his promulgation of the "domino theory," which shaped American foreign policy in the Third World until the end of the Cold War. In a news conference on April 7, 1954, he emphasized the importance of Southeast Asia to the United States for the resources like rubber, metals, and oil that it provided. More importantly, he warned that the United States could not abandon Southeast Asia because the region resembled a row of dominos. By this analogy, if one fell, the rest were sure to follow very quickly. As a result, Eisenhower argued that the United States needed to contain communism in North Vietnam in order to save all of Southeast Asia, and eventually areas beyond, from communist expansion. Consequently, the United States supported the most anticommunist leader they could find in South Vietnam, Ngo Dinh Diem, in order to preserve the "freedom" of the former

French colony. Through a dictatorial political apparatus and ruthless treatment of any who opposed him, Diem maintained some sense of stability in South Vietnamese politics at least until the early 1960s.

Eisenhower also turned to the formation of a defensive alliance in the region to prevent the collapse of more "dominos." The Southeast Asia Treaty Organization (SEATO), based on the North Atlantic Treaty Organization (NATO) in Europe, bound the United States and the non-communist countries of the region like Australia, New Zealand, Indonesia, Malaysia, and others in a reciprocal defensive alliance, which called on all the members of the organization to respond if any other were to be attacked by a foreign power. Although obligating the United States to future commitments, SEATO helped contain communism and avoid immediate conflict.

Avoiding direct involvement in Vietnam also helped Eisenhower avoid division at home. Eisenhower saw the maintenance of domestic tranquility as a critical concern. He remembered the divisiveness that the Korean War, McCarthyism, and recession had created in the immediate postwar period. Deploying troops in Vietnam would have provoked criticism at best and, at worst, vigorous dissent.

TIES BETWEEN FOREIGN AND DOMESTIC POLICIES

Eisenhower's concern to avoid internal infighting also explains his hesitancy on civil rights. Although his loyalty to and respect for the law and the Constitution ultimately led him to involve the federal government in the cause of civil rights in the South, until 1957 Eisenhower's lack of support for the civil rights movement was not based on racism or disinterest, but on his fear that federal support for civil rights, specifically forced integration, would result in turmoil if not violence and revolt. Similarly, this attitude accounts for the minimalist domestic agenda of the Eisenhower presidency until he thought that Cold War pressures made a more ambitious domestic policy imperative.

Americans had just emerged from the worst economic catastrophe in American history and the most destructive war that the world has known. Eisenhower believed that Americans preferred consistency over change, consensus over risks, and tranquility over turmoil. Consequently, he did his best to ensure the security of Americans' territory, their way of life, and most importantly, their quality of life. Significantly, the nation remained prosperous throughout most of his term in office.

NOTE

1. Herbert S. Parmet, *Eisenhower and the American Crusades* (New Brunswick, NJ: Transaction Publishers, 1999), 269.

ENDING THE KOREAN WAR

The war in Korea was probably the most important issue in the election of 1952. American troops were bogged down in Korea after having been deployed as part of a United Nations peacekeeping action in 1950. Consistent with America's containment policy, American troops had responded to the June 1950 invasion of South Korea, a noncommunist but dictatorial regime, by the communist government of North Korea. North Korea's stated purpose in the war was to reunite a nation that had been cut in two by a treaty following World War II. By contrast, many Americans viewed the North Korean communist government as bent on expanding its territory and influence. Instead of simply repulsing the North Koreans, U.S. and South Korean troops initially had attempted to reunite the Korean peninsula under one government, provoking China to enter the conflict. By 1951 the war had become a gory fight along the pre-1950 boundary between North and South Korea. Few Americans questioned the necessity of America's immediate response to preserve the status quo in Korea, but many criticized Truman's handling of the war, which resulted in over 50,000 U.S. casualties, and war weariness was growing. During the 1952 presidential campaign, Eisenhower attacked Truman's foreign policy for allowing the war to get started in the first place. Eisenhower promised that as president he would make ending the war his top priority, even if he had to travel to Korea to do it.

Shortly after being elected, even before his inauguration, Eisenhower visited the front lines of the conflict. He surveyed these circumstances and appraised the troops. He met with almost every military leader in South Korea, as well as South Korean President Syngman Rhee and Mark Clark, the commander of UN forces in Korea. These two leaders and others close to Eisenhower had designs for another push to reunite Korea. Eisenhower realized that these aggressive plans would only further provoke the Chinese, escalate the war, and make the use of atomic weapons more likely. Besides, the United States had succeeded in "containing" communism by driving the communist aggressors back out of South Korea. Once Eisenhower took the option of pushing the communists out of North Korea off the table, the only remaining options were a negotiated settlement to the war or continued stalemate on the battlefield. Eisenhower deemed the latter "intolerable." How to achieve a settlement with terms favorable to all parties involved was less obvious.

In February 1953, Clark, Dulles, and others pressured Eisenhower to take a more aggressive stance in Korea, as they feared that the Chinese were preparing to launch an offensive push back into the South. Some even argued in favor of using atomic weapons in Korea, a dicey proposition given the possibility that the Soviets would respond in kind. Eisenhower did not favor this tactic, but he pressured the Chinese into a settlement by keeping the threat of the use of atomic weapons an active possibility. Eisenhower also pulled back the Seventh Fleet of the U.S. Navy from the coast of China, placing another subtle pressure on the Chinese. The United States had deployed this fleet as a buffer between mainland China and the nationalist Chinese government exiled on the island of Formosa since 1949. By removing the fleet, the United States removed a physical barrier to nationalist attacks on the mainland, even as the United States maintained political pressure on the nationalists to refrain from such attacks. According to historian Stephen Ambrose, "the greatest pressure, by far, was his [Eisenhower's] own reputation." Ambrose argues that Eisenhower's use of "every weapon at his disposal" against Germany in World War II, combined with the presence of American atomic weapons in Asia and Eisenhower's use of language, which referred to a stalemate in Korea as "intolerable," ultimately accounted for the Chinese and North Korean willingness to negotiate an end to the war.[1]

By April 1953, all signs pointed to this willingness. The Indian government set forth a proposal that appealed to both the United States and the Chinese. Spurred in part by Indian fears that a new administration in the United States might otherwise be inclined to pull out of Asia completely, leaving a power vacuum and clearing the way for a war of "Asians and Asians," a phrase that Eisenhower had employed during his presidential campaign, the Indian plan included the continuation of the partition of Korea. Less than pleased with the terms of the Indian proposal, South Korean President Rhee insisted that the people of the peninsula did not want an armistice that preserved the division of Korea. Instead of the Indian proposal for peace, he wanted the removal of UN and Chinese troops from the Korean Peninsula, a mutual defense agreement between the United States and South Korea, and military assistance. Rhee threatened to continue fighting even if UN troops left him. Realizing that the opportunity for peace was at hand in the Indian proposal, Eisenhower threatened to abandon South Korea, pulling out American troops, ceasing military aid, and reneging on the promised funds for reconstruction of South Korea at the conclusion of the war if Rhee failed to recognize and yield to the authority of the UN to broker peace in Korea. While American and UN diplomats were trying to convince Rhee to go along with the peace, Chinese and North Korean forces unleashed an offensive that resulted in the death of 14,000 UN troops, mostly South Korean, and a gain of seven miles along the border of North and South Korea. Rhee ultimately realized that South Korea could not conduct the war on its own or survive without U.S. support, and he agreed to cooperate with the terms of a peace conducted by the UN.

The truce was signed on July 16 without much fanfare in the United States Eisenhower and others warned that the United States could not take solace in the ending of hostilities in Korea. Global communism would only look elsewhere to turn its aggression, and therefore the United States must remain vigilant and on guard. American foreign policymakers would spend the next forty years attempting to thwart the expansion of communism across the globe.

Some in the United States, from both parties, criticized the Korean armistice because Eisenhower did not press for an unqualified victory. After all, the war ended basically as it began, with a divided Korea, with a communist government in the North, an anticommunist government in the South, and foreign troops keeping guard on the border. As excerpts from an article in *Barron's* magazine cited by Representative Lawrence Smith (R-WI) indicates, however, criticism was muted in part because those who had sought total victory had previously felt abandoned by Truman, and thought that, without such an aim, it was best to conclude a peace than to continue the carnage. The peninsula remains divided still, more than fifty years after the conclusion of the Korean War. North Korea continues to be governed by a communist dictator, and hostilities between the two countries continue to preoccupy neighboring nations as well as the United States, particularly as the specter of North Korean acquisition of nuclear weapons looms over the peninsula.

NOTE

1. Stephen Ambrose, *Eisenhower: Soldier and President* (New York: Touchstone, 1990), 302–303.

PRESIDENT EISENHOWER TO THE PRESIDENT OF THE REPUBLIC OF KOREA (RHEE), (APRIL 23, 1953)

DEAR MR. PRESIDENT: Since my return to Washington 2 I have had an opportunity carefully to study your letter of April 9.

As I said in my message 4 delivered to you April 17 by Ambassador Briggs, because of their sufferings and sacrifices in the common cause the Korean people may be sure that the United States will never forget Korea or cease to be concerned for its welfare and security.

Also, as you well know, I am deeply sympathetic with the aspirations of yourself and the Korean people to bring an end to the artificial and unnatural division of your country, and to expel the Chinese aggressors from all of Korea.

However, I would be lacking in candor if I did not state that I was deeply disturbed at the implication of your letter of April 9, not only for Korea but for the efforts being made to deal with the problem of Communist aggression by the collective action of free peoples.

I think it important that we reiterate certain fundamental facts inherent in the situation.

First, the action taken by the United Nations in Korea was to assist your valiant country in repelling the armed attack directed against it initially by the North Korean regime and subsequently by the Chinese Communists. This has successfully been accomplished.

Second, the task of repelling the armed attack having been accomplished it would not be defensible to refuse to stop the fighting on an honorable basis as a prerequisite to working out the remaining issues by peaceful means.

Third, the United States and the United Nations have consistently supported the unification of Korea under conditions which would assure its freedom and independence. Neither the United States nor the United Nations has ever committed itself to resort to war to achieve this objective. To do so would be a complete negation of the basic tenets of this country and the United Nations.

Fourth, any agreement to stop the fighting on an honorable basis presupposes a willingness on the part of both sides to discuss the remaining issues and to make every reasonable effort to reach agreement thereon. As I said in my address of April 16 an honorable armistice "means the immediate cessation of hostilities and the prompt initiation of political discussions leading to the holding of free elections in a United Korea." If an honorable agreement is reached to stop the fighting, the United States intends to proceed promptly, vigorously and in good faith to seek by all appropriate means, in full consultation with your Government, to achieve a settlement of the problems confronting your country with the objective of achieving a true peace. These efforts would, of course, be entirely nullified if your Government should take actions which could not be supported by this or other governments supporting the defense of your country. I am also certain that you recognize that any such action by your Government could only result in disaster for your country, obliterating all that has been gained at such sacrifice by our peoples.

I am confident that if a spirit of mutual respect, trust and confidence so essential to the accomplishment of the high task upon which our countries are engaged can be maintained, we shall be successful. However, if unhappily the objective of a true peace proves to be unattainable, sober consideration will then have to be given as to what should be done under those circumstances.

Ambassador Briggs will shortly be communicating further with you concerning the questions which you raised with him in your conversation of April 14.5

Sincerely, DWIGHT D. EISENHOWER

Source: *Foreign Relations Series of the United States, 1952–1954*, Vol. XV, *Korea* (Washington, DC: Government Printing Office), 929–930.

PRESIDENT OF THE REPUBLIC OF KOREA, SYNGMAN RHEE
TO PRESIDENT EISENHOWER (APRIL 9, 1953)

DEAR PRESIDENT EISENHOWER: I have often thought of writing you, but refrained from doing so for fear of encroaching upon your valuable time. The moment has come, however, when I have to inform you of what steps we must take regarding the Korean war situation. I know without doubt the sincerity of your determination to settle the Korean war with honor as soon as possible. I know also that the opposition to your policy on the part of foreign powers, as well as of the peace-at-any-cost circles, is so strong that any Administration might feel hampered and handicapped. Under this circumstance, the Korean people again suffer disappointment, although they are not disappointed with you but in the whole situation.

If this situation is allowed to continue, Korea cannot survive as an independent nation and it will be made another China. Perhaps that is what some United Nations members would wish. If Korea were given to the Soviets, nonetheless, all the so-called free nations will be in grave danger of being the next victims, one by one.

At all events, either as a result of the Indian resolution or of the Communists' recent offer of peace negotiations, if they arrange a peace agreement allowing the Chinese to remain in Korea, we have to ask all the friendly nations whose armed forces are now fighting in Korea and who do not desire to join with us in our determination to defeat aggressive communism and drive up to the Yalu River, to withdraw from Korea. Any nation which will join with us in our efforts to drive the Chinese Communists out of Korean territory will be welcomed to work with us. In this we must reiterate our original announcement that we will not move one step beyond our age-old national boundary line without your request. . . .

With prayers for your health and success,
Sincerely yours, SYNGMAN RHEE

Source: *Foreign Relations Series of the United States, 1952–1954*, Vol. XV, *Korea* (Washington, DC: Government Printing Office), 902–903.

THE PRESIDENT OF THE REPUBLIC OF KOREA (RHEE)
TO PRESIDENT EISENHOWER (MAY 30, 1953)

DEAR MR. PRESIDENT: . . . I earnestly wish I could see my way clear to make a public statement, as requested, pledging to accept any armistice you may deem necessary. But we are fearfully aware, on the other hand, that to accept any armistice arrangement which would allow the Chinese Communists to remain in Korea would mean to the Korean nation, in terms of eventualities, an acceptance of a death sentence without protest. It is a hard thing for a nation to do. Furthermore, even if I personally agree to such an arrangement, it will not help the matter very much, as subsequent developments, I fear, will show.

... None of these proposals from other sides has proved to be acceptable to all and consequently there has come about a stalemate in negotiation, in addition to this stalemated war. Whatever academic arguments there may be against it, we cannot but feel that rough and rudimental justice calls for Korea making one first and last proposal on its own part. From our own point of view, the Korean problem which the United Nations started to settle by military means when they sent their armed forces to fight Communism and kept on fighting for three years should be settled by punishing the aggressors, unifying Korea and thus firmly establishing the collective security of all free nations. This would be honorable and just for all concerned .... I submit the following as a rough outline of what we propose as something to be preferred to any arrangement leaving Korea divided and letting the Chinese Communists stay on in Korea.

We propose a simultaneous withdrawal of both the Communist and United Nations forces from Korea....

The United States will agree to come to military aid and assistance immediately without and consultation or conference with any nation or nations, if and when an enemy nation or nations resume aggressive activities against the Korea Peninsula....

Adequate supplies of arms, ammunition and general logistic materials will be given Korea with a view to making it strong enough to defend itself without needing American soldiers to fight in Korea again....

In case the idea of simultaneous withdrawal is found unacceptable to either or both of the negotiating parties, I beg you to allow the Koreans to continue the fighting, for this is the universal preference of the Korean people to any divisive armistice or peace.... it is beyond question that we cannot any longer survive a stalemate of division....

Due to the lack of a firm and steady policy on the part of the free world, we have lost already too many nations to the Soviets. The longer this policy continues, the more free nations will be forced to join with the enemy of Democracy. To disappoint the Koreans is to disappoint most of the anti-Communist elements everywhere. The United States will in the end find itself a democratic oasis in a Communist desert. I trust that the people of America will never sell out their freedom and democratic institutions at the price of peace.

Most sincerely yours,

Syngman Rhee

Source: *Foreign Relations of the United States, 1952–1954*, Vol. XV, *Korea* (Washington, DC: Government Printing Office), 1124–26.

"BITTER TRUCE—IT'S BETTER TO BE HONEST ABOUT KOREA." ARTICLE IN *BARRON'S* MAGAZINE (JUNE 15, 1953)

This truce, if it comes, will be a very bad one—that is what Syngman Rhee is saying. Surely a good many Americans already know this in their hearts. The justification for making peace now is that many months ago this country and its allies abandoned the search for decisive victory; that to go on fighting a war of attrition means a needless sacrifice of American life; and the possibility we may yet get back those American prisoners (General Dean among them) who the Communists have not already butchered. These are compelling reasons for ending the bloodshed and for hoping that in the end Mr. Rhee will bow to the inevitable. But to accept the inevitable is something different from applauding it. When a man faces a Hobson's choice, he might as well admit it. It is time, we think to put away deception and face the hard, unpalatable facts.

Source: Cited by Lawrence H. Smith (R-WI) in Vol. 99, *Congressional Record*, Appendix, A3434, June 10, 1953.

THE "NEW LOOK" OF MASSIVE RETALIATION

Eisenhower's vision for American foreign policy extended well beyond an end to the military standoff he had inherited in Korea. A balanced budget and reforms in U.S. defense policy were two of Eisenhower's biggest issues in his 1952 campaign. These two ideas came together when Eisenhower proposed his 1954 budget with its "New Look" for American armed forces. Eisenhower predicated the "New Look" on getting what Secretary of Defense Charles Wilson called, "more bang for the buck," that is, a more powerful military for less cost. Eisenhower reasoned both that America's defense policy was inefficient, outdated, and ineffective, and drew resources away from better causes, such as social spending and research on the use of atomic energy for peaceful rather than destructive purposes. Defense spending had increased threefold during the era of the Korean War. With the war over, Eisenhower wanted to cut the number of men in the army and its budget by almost a third and slash the budget for the navy by more than 20 percent. Funding for the air force could be increased, Eisenhower agreed, though only slightly, because that branch of the armed service would become more important in the "New Look" of the American military.

The Truman Administration had set target dates for increased in spending. One such date had been 1954, when the Pentagon had expected the Soviet Union to have the ability to deliver a working hydrogen bomb. By contrast, Eisenhower proposed to tailor any military buildup to its afford-ability and in relationship to overall spending.

With advances in technology, both with respect to warheads and delivery systems, and increases in the numbers of nuclear weapons, by the early 1950s most agreed that a nuclear exchange would result in mutual destruction of the two superpowers. A nuclear attack by one on the other was a no-win proposition. Thus, deterrence was perhaps the nuclear arsenal's most important function. Moreover, Americans increasingly believed in the inevitability of Soviet attempts at expansion, which meant the need for a tougher American defense policy. Therefore, the National Security Council replaced NSC-68, which emphasized resisting aggression wherever it arose, with NSC-162/2, which called for a reduction of spending on ground forces in favor of a nuclear-based military strategy. Accordingly, the "New Look" defense policy, which Secretary of State John Foster Dulles announced and described on behalf of the Eisenhower Administration in a famous speech of January 12, 1954, placed the highest value on a military capable of conducting a general war based on what Dulles called "massive retaliation." Dulles reasoned that the veiled threats of the use of nuclear weapons had forced the Chinese to the negotiation table in Korea, and therefore the deterrent of nuclear weapons should form the basis of U.S. defense policy. Massive retaliation suggested an outlook based almost solely on nuclear weapons as opposed to conventional arsenals. Eisenhower and Dulles believed the threat of massive retaliation could prevent small-time conflicts. Accordingly, Dulles contended that American defense policy should rely on "a great capacity to retaliate, instantly, by means and places of our choosing." America would respond to future conflicts with "massive force," that is, the delivery of nuclear warheads by air, not the deployment of a 100,000 man army. Against this position, neither the Soviets nor the Chinese would be able to sponsor regional events like the Korean War without fearing the wrath of the American nuclear arsenal. Dulles and Eisenhower were convinced that this deterrent would prevent Russian military activities outside of Eastern Europe.

Not everyone concurred with the "new look" that Eisenhower and Dulles brought to defense spending. Not surprisingly, some leaders of the military establishment balked at the projected reduction for military spending. General Matthew Ridgeway, for example, expressed confusion about why military spending would be cut when the threat against which the military was designed to counter was increasing. Policymakers too voiced concern about the "new look." Senator John F. Kennedy (D-MA), looking particu-larly to deteriorating events in Asia, continuing tensions in Korea, and heightening instability in Indochina, questioned whether reductions in military spending and a revamping of military strategy were timely. Similarly, in an exchange with Senator Homer Ferguson (R-MI), Senator Albert Gore, Sr. (D-TN) maintained that despite the concept of the "new look," the climate simply did not warrant a military philosophy based on less money and future technologies. Despite these objections, Congress could do little but vote to appropriate the reduced monies requested by Eisenhower for defense, even if congressmen would have liked to see larger military budgets. Thus Eisenhower and Dulles embarked on their course to give the U.S. military a "new look."

This new defense philosophy rendered armed services designed for miniscule, or even many conventional, episodes of warfare inefficient and unnecessary. Maintaining and deploying a large standing army was costly and put the lives of great numbers at risk. Military spending and planning was redirected to the development of delivery systems for nuclear weapons, and to more powerful nuclear devices, such as the hydrogen bomb, and placed increased emphasis on air power. In addition, the "New Look" emphasized cutting-edge military technology, and the research and development of new hardware suited for the nuclear era. Led by Eisenhower's appointment as Chairman of the Joint Chiefs of Staff, Admiral Arthur Radford, an ardent advocate of the development of atomic weapons, the navy put into high gear its program for the Polaris missile, a nuclear missile launched from a submarine, and took on a greater air-sea orientation, expanding the use of aircraft carriers and nuclear submarines. The army also began to implement the "new look," refining tactical nuclear weapons to be used on the battlefield. It developed the first antiaircraft missiles, the Nike Ajax, which eventually became operational with nuclear warheads, and the Hawk missile to defend against low-flying aircraft. Most important though was air power, which became central to U.S. military policy. The creation of the Air Force Academy in 1954 exemplifies the elevated status and importance of the flyers. The air force also improved its hardware, adding planes and replacing propeller-driven bombers with B-47 jets so that by 1955 the American armed services included 1,750 aircraft capable of carrying nuclear warheads into Russia. Not only did the "new look" call for expanded offensive capabilities by air, but it also enhanced air defenses, with the army's antiaircraft missiles and the installations of new radar warning systems in northern Canada and Alaska.

Between 1953 and 1959 the number of nuclear weapons in the American arsenal increased from 1,500 to 6,000. Despite public pronouncements to the contrary during the 1960 presidential campaign, this provided the United States with a huge advantage over the Soviet Union in missile development. More negatively, the rapid escalation in the building of new and more destructive weapons fueled an arms race that continued into the following decades. This escalation of the production of weapons of mass destruction, combined with a series of crises that nearly resulted in a nuclear exchange, led to discussions about the control and limitation of the production of these armaments by the late 1950s. Fifty years later, the United States and Russia are still working to control the development and distribution of nuclear weapons, and the United States is once again exploring defensive weapons.

JOHN FOSTER DULLES ON MASSIVE RETALIATION (1954)

The Need for Long-Range Policies

This "long time" factor is of critical importance.

The Soviet Communists are planning for what they call "an entire historical era," and we should do the same. They seek, through many types of maneuvers, gradually to divide and weaken the free nations by overextending them in efforts which, as Lenin put it, are "beyond their strength, so that they come to practical bankruptcy." Then, said Lenin, "our victory is assured." Then, said Stalin, will be "the moment for the decisive blow."

In the face of this strategy, measures cannot be judged adequate merely because they ward off an immediate danger. It is essential to do this, but it is also essential to do so without exhausting ourselves.

When the Eisenhower administration applied this test, we felt that some transformations were needed.

It is not sound military strategy permanently to commit U.S. land forces to Asia to a degree that leaves us no strategic reserves.

It is not sound economics, or good foreign policy, to support permanently other countries; for in the long run, that creates as much ill will as good will.

Also, it is not sound to become permanently committed to military expenditures so vast that they lead to "practical bankruptcy."

Change was imperative to assure the stamina needed for permanent security. But it was equally imperative that change should be accompanied by understanding of our true purposes. Sudden and spectacular change had to be avoided. Otherwise, there might have been a panic among our friends and miscalculated aggression by our enemies. We can, I believe, make a good report in these respects.

We need allies and collective security. Our purpose is to make these relations more effective, less costly. This can be done by placing more reliance on deterrent power and less dependence on local defensive power.

This is accepted practice so far as local communities are concerned. We keep locks on our doors, but we do not have an armed guard in every home. We rely principally on a community security system so well equipped to punish any who break in and steal that, in fact, would be aggressors are generally deterred. That is the modern way of getting maximum protection at a bearable cost.

What the Eisenhower administration seeks is a similar international security system. We want, for ourselves and the other free nations, a maximum deterrent at a bearable cost.

Local defense will always be important. But there is no local defense which alone will contain the mighty landpower of the Communist world. Local defenses must be reinforced by the further deterrent of massive retaliatory power. A potential aggressor must know that he cannot always prescribe battle conditions that suit him. Otherwise, for example, a potential aggressor, who is glutted with manpower, might be tempted to attack in confidence that resistance would be confined to manpower. He might be tempted to attack in places where his superiority was decisive.

The way to deter aggression is for the free community to be willing and able to respond vigorously at places and with means of its own choosing.

Source: John Foster Dulles, "The Evolution of Foreign Policy," *Department of State Bulletin*, 30 (January 25, 1962): 107–110.

SENATOR ALBERT GORE, SR. (D-TN) (JUNE 16, 1954)

[on the reduction of military spending]
Mr. Gore: In this troubled and distraught world, when we face dangers which are clearly recognizable, what is the justification for the feeling... that the Congress should reduce expenditures for national defense?...

Mr. Ferguson (R-MI): ... we do not have any use for the other divisions at the present time, and the men involved might better be employed in civilian industry, helping to increase the national wealth and to produce materials for the military, instead of being in positions where they are not needed....
Mr. Gore: Does the Senator entirely write off the value of having a strategic reserve, ready for use in case of immanent danger? Is the Senator saying that, because we are not involved in a specific conflict at the moment, we do not have need for a national defense reserve ready for instant and quick employment?...
Mr. Gore: Is this the New Look budget?... Does the Senator still believe in the so-called New Look program... which I understand to be nonworkable in this day of world peril?...
Mr. Ferguson: Yes.... It represents a different conception. We expect some criticism of it, naturally.... But I believe... that the budget represented in the figures contained in this bill is a proper budget for the defense of America.

Mr. Gore: I should like to say, as one Member of the Senate, that I believe it is a desperate gamble with the national defense, a desperate gamble with national security and the freedom of the world, a desperate gamble with the chance of having peace, instead of war. The New Look program has already proved its failure in Indochina, and yet we are still considering a program which was prepared on the assumption that it would work....

[on future military hardware]

Mr. Gore: The able Senator...has raised the question...whether it is more in the interest of national defense to have blueprints or planes. I do not mean that in the extreme sense.... There is always the problem of obsolescence.... I know it is said that every place becomes obsolescent the day it is turned out by the factory. Obsolescent by what standard? By the standard of future plans. But we cannot hide behind the plans for the future and permit our defense for the present to be cut drastically....

Mr. Gore: ...our strength and the adequacy of our strength must be judged comparatively with what a possible enemy may have. The Senator has stated that he wants the United States Air Force and the military strength of the United States to be superior to any possible enemy.... The situation is not static...it is not changing to our advantage...it is changing to our disadvantage.

Source: *Congressional Record*, Vol. 100, Pt. 16, 8321–8330.

ATOMS FOR PEACE

In spite of Eisenhower's "New Look" policy for American defense, based on an increased nuclear deterrent, the President did not eschew efforts to promote the use of atomic energy for peaceful measures. In fact, Eisenhower devoted a great deal of attention to "atoms for peace" and disarmament during his administration. Eisenhower's two primary goals as president, domestic tranquility and world peace, formed the basis of all of his more specific initiatives, and his views on atomic energy were no different. While Eisenhower appreciated the importance of a formidable nuclear arsenal for American defense, he also realized the potential of atomic energy for more productive means. As early as his "Chance for Peace" speech in April 1953, the President suggested that resources then being devoted to the development of weapons of mass destruction could and should be redirected to other causes. But he delivered his most important commentary on atomic energy in an address to the United Nations General Assembly in December 1953, when he announced his

"Atoms for Peace" policy. The next year, Congress passed the Atomic Energy Act, creating the Atomic Energy Commission (AEC) "to encourage widespread participation in the development and utilization of atomic energy for peaceful purposes." This was the first time that the U.S. government permitted the general use of atomic energy for peaceful purposes, and the first time that the government gave private industry access to classified government information and involved it in the production and application of atomic energy. Thus, while the military forged ahead with the development of increasingly powerful atomic weapons of destruction during the 1950s, other branches of the government and private industry focused on employing the power of the atom for more productive purposes.

In his speech to the United Nations, Eisenhower contended that although only a few of the world's countries possessed the know-how to build and deliver atomic weapons, the consequences of that fact threatened the existence of the entire world.[1] He conceded that although the principle of deterrence guided U.S. nuclear policy, the "capability of devastating retaliation, is no preventive, of itself, against the fearful material damage and toll of human lives that would be inflicted by surprise aggression." Amid this backdrop of "dread" and "doom," however, Eisenhower lamented wasteful spending on the development of weapons capable of "hideous damage," and proposed creating an International Atomic Energy Agency under the authority of the United Nations to supervise a global effort to transform the power of atomic energy into "universal, efficient, and economic usage." The President outlined a plan for the International Atomic Energy Agency in which governments involved in atomic research, including the Soviet Union, would contribute from their stockpiles of uranium and fissional material. The Agency would direct and supervise efforts to develop peaceful uses for atomic energy, particularly in medicine, agriculture, and electric power. In this way, Eisenhower argued, "contributing powers would be dedicating some of their strength to serve the needs rather than the fears of mankind." With this proposal, Eisenhower sought not only to accomplish the objectives for atomic energy he outlined, but also to assuage some of the fears of allies and potential allies, and their sense of alienation, regarding the intent of the United States and its nuclear arsenal to which the "New Look" and its accompanying rhetoric had contributed. Eisenhower hoped that this cooperative effort would facilitate improved communication between the United States and the Soviet Union on myriad topics and thereby reduce the tension between the two countries and the likelihood of aggression.

Negotiations began immediately, and an international conference on the peaceful use of atomic energy met in 1955, but it took three years to create the International Atomic Energy Agency. Americans were not prepared to wait for the rest of the world to embark on their own projects to develop uses for atomic energy beyond weapons. With the creation of the United States Atomic Energy Commission (AEC) in 1954, the United States government committed itself to the use of atomic energy for "peaceful purposes." The Atomic Energy Act of 1954 created essentially three functions for the AEC: first, to continue research and development of nuclear weapons; second, to encourage and facilitate private use of atomic energy for peaceful means; and third, to establish a set of safeguards to protect the public from the dangers of commercial uses of atomic energy. In accordance with Eisenhower's "Atoms for Peace" initiative, the Act supported U.S. assistance not only to domestic power producers, but also to other nations for building power-producing nuclear reactors. The AEC also represented an attempt to bring private industry into the atomic energy business, an area which the Atomic Energy Act of 1946 had previously restricted to government agencies. The AEC is illustrative, or at least consistent with, the general philosophy of the Eisenhower Administration, which valued private initiative and disliked government monopoly and government interference. Although the Atomic Energy Act easily passed Congress, indicating general agreement both in political circles and among the public about the need to apply nuclear power to nonmilitary uses, the implementation of the efforts of the AEC followed less smoothly.

The emphasis on private initiative was one of the primary sticking points. The AEC put into development five prototype nuclear power plants, each experimenting with a different method of power production based on atomic energy. AEC chairman Lewis E. Strauss argued that the "use of atomic energy in the framework of the American free enterprise system" was inherent in the mission of the AEC and that the quickest and most efficient way to commercial use of nuclear power was through private industry. Accordingly, the AEC provided information, demonstrations, testing, loans, and other economic incentives for the private construction of nuclear power plants. The financial outlay required for the construction of these plants, however, and the dangers of working with nuclear power prevented an all-out building boom of nuclear power plants by private industry, much to the dismay of many in the AEC and in Congress, who had hoped that with the Atomic Energy Act, intensified efforts would be directed at civilian uses for atomic energy.[2] Disputes also arose over safety issues, as members of Congress became concerned that the AEC was not balancing its eagerness to stimulate private initiative in atomic energy with its obligation to ensure public safety.

In addition to domestic programs aimed at peaceful uses of atomic energy, the United States supported similar efforts across the globe. Naturally, European programs attracted a substantial amount of attention. Just as the United States had supported European integration efforts with respect to defense (the European Defense Community) and industry (the European Coal and Steel Community [ECSC]), the United States strongly endorsed Euratom, a consortium of European countries dedicated to building an atomic energy industry in Europe similar to ECSC. The United States also concluded numerous agreements with foreign nations to provide material, information, and training. Perhaps the most important result of these efforts, an agreement of cooperation between the United States and the Soviet Union, established a framework for the exchange of unclassified information on peaceful uses of nuclear energy between the two nations.[3] Even though these agreements did not represent any formal agreements regarding the use of atomic energy, or arms control, they laid the groundwork for future such treaties. Eisenhower relentlessly called for the suspension of nuclear testing and disarmament, especially during his second term, and pronounced the willingness of the United States to enter into binding test ban agreements. These pleas produced no results during Eisenhower's term in office, but they set the stage for the Limited Test Ban Treaty, which the United States and the Soviet Union signed in August 1963 prohibiting nuclear explosions in the atmosphere, underwater, or in space, and restricting underground explosions.

The most far-reaching result of Eisenhower's call for the use of "Atoms for Peace" was the creation of the International Atomic Energy Agency (IAEA). While many advocates of atomic energy in the United States viewed this agency with great sympathy, some opposed U.S. membership in the international organization. Raising questions about radiation, fallout, the potential for an international trade in atomic materials, and regulation, similar to those raised about domestic power programs, opponents of the international treaty, like Republican Senator John Bricker of Ohio (who, since his start in the Senate, had consistently opposed American membership in treaties and organizations, which, he contended, required the United States to surrender sovereignty), also feared that the treaty would have many adverse and perhaps even unpredictable consequences. Despite such concerns, the Charter for the IAEA was created in 1956, and by 1957 the ratification of the Charter by 29 states, including the United States, made the provisions of the charter binding on its members.

With the proliferation of domestic atomic energy production and the creation of new knowledge and technologies, the administration of the domestic program became more difficult and unwieldy, but also more rewarding. In 1957 the Shippensberg (Pennsylvania) prototype plant became the first full-scale nuclear power plant in operation. In 1963, the Jersey Central Power and Light Company announced that it would build a nuclear power plant on the Toms River. Predicting that the nuclear plant would be competitive with fossil fuel plants, this represented the first time a company elected to produce nuclear power without government incentives. By 1974, the United States had 233 nuclear power stations either under construction or in the planning stages. This dramatic growth in the productive capacity of U.S. industry became more than the AEC could handle effectively. Ultimately, in 1974 the Nixon administration disbanded and reorganized the AEC and created the Nuclear Regulatory Commission (NRC) and the Energy Research and Development Administration (ERDA). This reorganization finally addressed the concerns of many who criticized the structure of the AEC at the outset. The NRC could now focus primarily on public safety and regulation, while the ERDA worked on facilitating development of better uses and more efficient production for atomic energy. Thus, the conflict of interest within one agency was removed.

NOTES

1. This truth became graphically evident only three months after the "Atoms for Peace" address, when the United States began tests on a new series of nuclear weapons over the Pacific. A Japanese fishing vessel, 82 miles "nearby," returned to shore with much of its crew requiring hospitalization from the effects of radioactive fallout from the explosion of the American device.

2. J. Samuel Walker, *A Short History of Nuclear Regulation, 1946–1999*, Nuclear Regulatory Commission, <http://www.nrc.gov/SECY/smj/shorthis. htm#AEC>.

3. *Institutional Origins of the U.S. Department of Energy*, <http://www.dpi.anl. gov/dpid/instorig/instorig.html>, 8–9.

ATOMS FOR PEACE ADDRESS GIVEN BY DWIGHT D. EISENHOWER BEFORE THE GENERAL ASSEMBLY OF THE UNITED NATIONS ON PEACEFUL USES OF ATOMIC ENERGY, NEW YORK CITY (DECEMBER 8, 1953)

Madame President, Members of the General Assembly:

... I know that the American people share my deep belief that if a danger exists in the world, it is a danger shared by all—and equally, that if hope exists in the mind of one nation, that hope should be shared by all....

I feel impelled to speak today in a language that in a sense is new—one which I, who has spent so much of my life in the military profession, would have preferred never to use.

That new language is the language of atomic warfare.

The atomic age has moved forward at such a pace that every citizen of the world should have some comprehension, at least in comparative terms, of the extent of this development of the utmost significance to every one of us. Clearly, if the people of the world are to conduct an intelligent search for peace, they must be armed with the significant facts of today's existence....

Today, the United States' stockpile of atomic weapons, which, of course, increases daily, exceeds by many times the explosive equivalent of the total of all bombs and all shells that came from every plane and every gun in every theatre of war in all of the years of World War II.

A single air group, whether afloat or land-based, can now deliver to any reachable target a destructive cargo exceeding in power all the bombs that fell on Britain in all of World War II.

In size and variety, the development of atomic weapons has been no less remarkable. The development has been such that atomic weapons have virtually achieved conventional status within our armed services. In the United States, the Army, the Navy, the Air Force, and the Marine Corps are all capable of putting this weapon to military use.

But the dread secret, and the fearful engines of atomic might, are not ours alone.

. . . the secret is possessed by our friends and allies, Great Britain and Canada . . . . The secret is also known by the Soviet Union. . . .

If at one time the United States possessed what might have been called a monopoly of atomic power, that monopoly ceased to exist several years ago. . . .

. . . let no one think that the expenditure of vast sums for weapons and systems of defense can guarantee absolute safety for the cities and citizens of any nation. The awful arithmetic of the atomic bomb does not permit any such easy solution. Even against the most powerful defense, an aggressor in possession of the effective minimum number of atomic bombs for a surprise attack could probably place a sufficient number of his bombs on the chosen targets to cause hideous damage.

Should such an atomic attack be launched against the United States, our reactions would be swift and resolute. But for me to say that the defense capabilities of the United States are such that they could inflict terrible losses upon an aggressor—for me to say that the retaliation capabilities of the United States are so great that such an aggressor's land would be laid waste—all this, while fact, is not the true expression of the purpose and the hope of the United States . . . .

. . . my country's purpose is to help us move out of the dark chamber of horrors into the light, to find a way by which the minds of men, the hopes of men, the souls of men every where, can move forward toward peace and happiness and well being.

In this quest, I know that we must not lack patience.

I know that in a world divided, such as ours today, salvation cannot be attained by one dramatic act.

I know that many steps will have to be taken over many months before the world can look at itself one day and truly realize that a new climate of mutually peaceful confidence is abroad in the world.

But I know, above all else, that we must start to take these steps—now. . . .

The United States would seek more than the mere reduction or elimination of atomic materials for military purposes.

It is not enough to take this weapon out of the hands of the soldiers. It must be put into the hands of those who will know how to strip its military casing and adapt it to the arts of peace.

The United States knows that if the fearful trend of atomic military buildup can be reversed, this greatest of destructive forces can be developed into a great boon, for the benefit of all mankind.

The United States knows that peaceful power from atomic energy is no dream of the future. That capability, already proved, is here—now—today. Who can doubt, if the entire body of the world's scientists and engineers had adequate amounts of fissionable material with which to test and develop their ideas, that this capability would rapidly be transformed into universal, efficient, and economic usage.

To hasten the day when fear of the atom will begin to disappear from the minds of people, and the governments of the East and West, there are certain steps that can be taken now.

I therefore make the following proposals:

The Governments principally involved, to the extent permitted by elementary prudence, to begin now and continue to make joint contributions from their stockpiles of normal uranium and fissionable materials to an international Atomic Energy Agency. . . .

The more important responsibility of this Atomic Energy Agency would be to devise methods whereby this fissionable material would be allocated to serve the peaceful pursuits of mankind. Experts would be mobilized to apply atomic energy to the needs of agriculture, medicine, and other peaceful activities. A special purpose would be to provide abundant electrical energy in the power-starved areas of the world. Thus the contributing powers would be dedicating some of their strength to serve the needs rather than the fears of mankind.

The United States would be more than willing—it would be proud to take up with others "principally involved": the development of plans whereby such peaceful use of atomic energy would be expedited.

Of those "principally involved" the Soviet Union must, of course, be one. . . .

Against the dark background of the atomic bomb, the United States does not wish merely to present strength, but also the desire and the hope for peace.

. . . the United States pledges before you—and therefore before the world—its determination to help solve the fearful atomic dilemma—to devote its entire heart and mind to find the way by which the miraculous inventiveness of man shall not be dedicated to his death, but consecrated to his life.

I again thank the delegates for the great honor they have done me, in inviting me to appear before them, and in listening to me so courteously. Thank you.

Source: Dwight D. Eisenhower Library, <http://www.eisenhower.utexas.edu/atoms.htm>

SENATOR JOHN BRICKER (R-OH), "ATOMS FOR PEACE, ATOMS FOR POWER, ATOMS FOR WAR" (JUNE 18, 1958)

We are dealing with a subject matter which promises good or evil to the world; and this whole program is fraught with grave dangers which the Senate should consider before it votes to ratify the statue.... I oppose ratification of the statue of the International Atomic Energy Agency in its present form. The activities of this global atomic energy agency will, more probably than not, produce the following undesirable consequences:

First, a universal, enforceable plan of disarmament will become far more difficult . . . to achieve.
Second, the danger of worldwide atomic warfare will be increased.
Third, radiation hazards to world health may exceed limits which are biologically and morally tolerable.
Fourth, the military potential of Communist countries will be enhanced to some extent.

For these reasons, approval of the treaty as written would be, in my judgment, an act of suicidal folly.

The phrase "atoms for peace" which has been repeated time and time again on the floor of the Senate during the past few days, when applied to the pending treaty, is a misnomer. The treaty is not limited to international cooperation in the benign uses of the atom. If the treaty concerned only peaceful applications of atomic energy, I would favor ratification without amendment or reservation. . . .

However, the treaty does concern something more than "atoms for peace." It is not limited to safe atomic science. It also involves "atoms for power," and the very real danger that "atoms for power" will become "atoms for war." . . .

It is a pity that atoms for peace has been so often equated with the production of electric power. Industrial atomic power development involves grave health hazards, extreme military dangers, and benefits considerable less than those which are now being derived from safe atomic science.

What the treaty involves primarily is an international nuclear power program. The legislative history of the treaty and its specific provisions indicate that the International Atomic Energy Agency will be concerned principally with atoms for power, and only secondarily with atoms for peace....

There is nothing in the statue that controls the end use of nuclear power. To promote such a program under an atoms-for-peace trademark is deceptive, to say the least.... Does anyone deny that a nation's powerplants are vital to the successful prosecution of war. It would indeed be anomalous for the United States to prohibit the export of conventional fuels and other strategic material to its potential enemies, while at the same time providing them by treaty with enriched uranium, the most strategic material of all....

I might say that in my judgment not only would the pending treaty not lead to an enforceable inspection system and arms control, but it might enhance the war potential and the arms potential of many countries which are not now in the bomb field....

Until there are adequate safeguards ... I think the Senate would be very foolish to go ahead with a treaty which would turn over the safeguards not to ourselves or to our allies, but to 80 countries represented by 23 countries, of which we will have one vote.

Source: *Congressional Record*, Vol. 103, Pt. 7, 9472–9489.

THE TAIWAN STRAITS CRISIS

Despite all the talk of "Atoms for Peace," nuclear weapons were at the core of American foreign policy, and the threat of their deployment was persistent and real during the Cold War. In foreign policy, words alone were rarely a sufficient deterrent. Dulles's "massive retaliation" policy and his strategy of brinksmanship were quickly put to the test in Asia. Since the 1950s, American diplomats have been challenged by the dilemma over China policy, and more specifically, over the American position on Taiwan. In 1949, when the Communist regime of Mao Zedong ousted the Nationalist government of Chiang Kai-shek, the latter fled to Taiwan (Formosa) and the small group of islands surrounding Taiwan, known as Matsu, Quemoy, and the Tachens. Since 1949, the Nationalist government has existed in exile on Taiwan, claiming, like the mainland regime, to be the legitimate government of all of China. Although President Truman initially stated that American foreign policy would be neutral on Taiwan, when the Korean War commenced in 1950, American policymakers pledged American protection for Taiwan and deployed troops to the region.

As a strategy to pressure Communist China during the Korean War, President Eisenhower dismantled the American military blockade of

Taiwan. Nationalists on Quemoy and Matsu, the two islands closest to the Chinese mainland in the Formosan group (only about two miles off the coast), took advantage of the absence of American intermediaries to conduct raids against the Communist government on the mainland. Fed up with the agitation of these Nationalist actions, the Communist Chinese forces began shelling Quemoy and Matsu in September 1954, hoping to destabilize and quash the Taiwanese government and bring the islands under the control of the mainland government. At the time, Secretary of State Dulles was concluding a treaty for the defense of Taiwan, the U.S.-Nationalist Chinese Mutual Security Pact, which was signed on December 2, 1954. There was a catch. The treaty called only for American defense of Taiwan, it did not require the United States to guard all of the islands surrounding Taiwan. Nonetheless, if the Communists took Quemoy and Matsu, Americans faced a potential war with Communist China in order to defend the fledgling Nationalist government on Taiwan.

Having just promulgated the "New Look" defense strategy, predicated on "massive retaliation," the Eisenhower foreign policy team jumped into action, with few apparent concerns over a hard-line response. The Joint Chiefs of Staff began planning a nuclear strategy for dealing with the crisis in Taiwan. Joint Chiefs Chairman Admiral Arthur Radford said he wanted to give China "a bloody nose." Dulles told the Senate in January that if the United States wished to remain a power in Asia, atomic war with China could be the cost. Acting on this advice, both houses of Congress passed the Formosa Resolution on January 29, 1955, giving the President nearly unlimited authority to deploy American forces to defend Taiwan and "related positions."[1] Meanwhile, both the president and Secretary of State issued public warnings to the Communist Chinese to back down. In early March Eisenhower insisted that the United States would not be part of an "aggressive war" in the Taiwan Straits. However, when asked at a press conference on March 16, 1955 about the possibility of the use of American nuclear weapons against China, the President stated, in a now famous quotation, "in any combat where these things can be used on strictly military targets and for strictly military purposes, I see no reason why they shouldn't be used just exactly as you would use a bullet." At the same time, Dulles promulgated a firm American allegiance to Taiwan. On April 23, 1955 the Communist Chinese began negotiations to end the crisis and ceased the shelling of the islands around Taiwan on May 1. The first crisis of the Taiwan Strait thus ended without the use of any American firepower. In the aftermath of these events, Eisenhower tried to convince Chiang Kai-shek to relinquish control of Quemoy and Matsu, so as to reduce the possibility of future conflicts over those islands. Fatefully, Chiang refused.

An arms race ensued in the Taiwan Strait as the United States fortified the Taiwanese regime. In August of 1958, the Communist Chinese government launched a new effort to take Quemoy. Some historians argue that Mao acted in 1958 to demonstrate Chinese independence from the Soviet Union. Sino-Soviet relations were fracturing at the time, and Mao and Khrushchev were neither seeing eye-to-eye on the goals or methods of international communism nor on their military obligations to one another. Although the Soviets warned the United States against aggressive intervention in the Taiwan crisis, Eisenhower again deployed forces to the region, including the U.S. Seventh Fleet. Yet again, Dulles threatened the use of overwhelming force, and the Joint Chiefs of Staff developed plans to use nuclear weapons against cities on the Chinese mainland. With public approval, American statesmen defined the crisis in terms of the Cold War. "We are not concerned about two little bits of real estate [Quemoy and Matsu] in the world," Eisenhower told the press. The issue was rather one of "communist territorial expansion by force" that could not be allowed to succeed. If the United States allowed the Communist Chinese to gain ground in the Taiwan Strait, he argued, the Chinese would act like an appeased Hitler at Munich.

Critics portrayed Eisenhower's resort to brinkmanship as extreme. European allies were appalled at the suggestion of the use of nuclear weapons and called emergency meetings of NATO to discuss the American attitude. One critic at home, the esteemed historian of Chinese history John King Fairbank (no relation to the primary author of this book), lambasted the administration, and Americans in general, for their lack of knowledge and understanding of the Chinese worldview. Fairbank contended that Americans, not the Chinese, were at fault for the uneasy relationship over Taiwan. Critics, like those in the Eisenhower administration itself, may have overreacted, for just as in the first Taiwan crisis, the second flare-up in the Taiwan Strait suddenly ended. After Eisenhower insisted that the United States would not ease its position in the region "in the face of armed aggression," in September 1958 the Communist Chinese government again proposed to resolve the crisis through negotiations. The Communists stopped shelling on October 6, and all sides met at the negotiating table.

The world certainly was not as close to nuclear war in these episodes as it would be in the early 1960s in Berlin and in Cuba, but the Quemoy and Matsu incidents marked important moments in the development of American foreign policy in the Cold War. Documents from the Chinese Communist government now indicate that it was never prepared to call the Administration's bluff in regard to the use of nuclear weapons. The American position on Taiwan thus lends credibility to Eisenhower's commitment to a "New Look" policy of "massive retaliation." The incidents continue to be important for beginning a half-century of tense relations between the United States and mainland China over the sovereignty of Taiwan. Although the United States had removed all of its military installations from Taiwan by the 1970s, the independence and legitimacy of Taiwan still depends greatly on the support of the United States, and the Taiwan Strait remains one of the tensest areas of global conflict. Routinely, the Communist Chinese government and the Nationalist government on Taiwan conduct war games, which inflame tensions in the region. In June 2001, for example, while the mainland Chinese government mobilized its army across the strait to conduct one of its largest war games in years, the Taiwanese government test-fired three Patriot missiles it had just received from the United States, as part of an arms deal that included 200 Patriot missiles, eight submarines, and a complement of destroyers.

NOTE

1. The precedent of the Formosa Resolution should not be lost. In 1964, Lyndon Johnson would ask for, and receive, in the Gulf of Tonkin Resolution, a similar authority from Congress to defend American interests in South Vietnam.

PRESIDENT DWIGHT EISENHOWER, "RADIO AND TELEVISION REPORT TO THE AMERICAN PEOPLE REGARDING THE SITUATION IN THE FORMOSA STRAITS" (SEPTEMBER 11, 1958)

...So the world is again faced with the problem of armed aggression. Powerful dictatorships are attacking an exposed, but free, areas. What should we do?...

I know something about war, and I never want to see that history repeated. But, my fellow Americans, it certainly can be repeated if the peace-loving democratic nations again fearfully practice a policy of standing idly by while big aggressors use armed force to conquer the small and weak.

Also we have more to guide us than history. We have the statements, the boastings, of the Chinese Communists themselves. They frankly say that their present military effort is part of a program to conquer Formosa.

It is as certain as can be that the shooting which the Chinese Communists started on August 23 had as its purpose not just the taking of the island of Quemoy. It is part of what is indeed an ambitious plan of armed conquest.

This plan would liquidate all of the free world positions in the Western Pacific area and bring them under captive governments which would be hostile to the United States and the free world. Thus the Chinese and the Russian Communists would come to dominate at least the Western half of the now friendly Pacific Ocean.

So, aggression by ruthless despots again imposes a clear danger to the United States and to the free world. . . .

I must say to you very frankly and very soberly, my friends, the United States cannot accept the result that the Communists seek. Neither can we show, now, a weakness of purpose—a timidity—which would surely lead them to move more aggressively against us and our friends in the Western Pacific area.

If the Chinese Communists have decided to risk a war, it is not because Quemoy itself is so valuable to them. They have been getting along without Quemoy even since they seized the China mainland nine years ago.

If they have now decided to risk a war, it can only be because they, and their Soviet allies, have decided to find out whether threatening war is a policy from which they can make big gains.

If that is their decision, then a Western Pacific Munich would not buy us peace or security. It would encourage the aggressors. It would dismay our friends and allies there. If history teaches anything, appeasement would make it more likely that we would have to fight a major war. . . .

I am striving to the best of my abilities to avoid hostilities; to achieve a cease-fire, and a reasonable adjustment of the situation. You, I think, know my deep dedication to peace. It is second only to my dedication to the safety of the United States and its honorable discharge of obligations to its allies and to world order. . . . We must not forget that the whole Formosa Straits situation is intimately connected with the security of the United States and the free world.

Source: *Public Papers of the Presidents of the United States, Dwight D. Eisenhower*, 1958 (Washington, DC: Government Printing Office), 694–699.

JOHN KING FAIRBANK, "CHINA: TIME FOR A POLICY" (APRIL 1957)

. . . [Taiwan's] independence is preserved only by our Seventh Fleet, Taiwan is . . . a concrete example of American 'imperialism.' . . . For us, the organized wrath of 600 million people in China is not something to go out and seek, yet by our principles we have little alternative. It takes an effort of imagination for us to recognize what we are really defending and confronting in the Formosa Straits. . . .

. . . our position in Taiwan . . . , is seriously isolated and may become steadily more vulnerable, so long as it stand on the one leg of American power and lacks diplomatic support . . . . Indeed we cannot overlook the possibility that, as the mainland builds up, its power of attraction by promise and threat may undermine Taiwan's capacity for independence, which is an American conception, ... more than a traditional Chinese conception....

The extremist positions, that we can solve our Chinese problem with the toughness of a nucleated MacArthurism, or on the other hand merely by being friendly and admiring like the fellow travelers, are both bankrupt....

... it remains a fact that Taiwan's independence has been the chief fruit of our China policy for seven years past and there is nothing on the horizon, except disaster, to alter it....

To negotiate or not to negotiate is a question not of principle but of expediency. Our diehard anti-Communists must accept the idea that when an evil becomes serious enough, it must be dealt with.... This need to negotiate gives us a positive reason to see Red China in the US, which exists as a forum where diplomatic dealings may avert the common danger of nuclear war....

Source: The Atlantic Online, <http://www.theatlantic.com/unbound/flashbks/china/fairbank.htm>

CIVIL RIGHTS

While foreign policy consumed much of Eisenhower's attention in the early years of his administration, domestic developments challenged the president's resolve early on as well. Although initial gains were minimal, African American civil rights had begun to make advances during World War II. Small pieces of legislation and several important Supreme Court decisions placed restrictions on discrimination as the contradiction between fighting for democracy and freedom abroad while preserving a system of segregation and discrimination at home confronted Americans. President Truman's important initiatives establishing an Office for Civil Rights and integrating the U.S. Army provided the movement with more momentum as President Eisenhower took office.

Eisenhower was cool to the issue of African American civil rights. Although Eisenhower was not a segregationist, his beliefs that the role of the federal government should be limited and that integration could not be forced deterred him from taking an aggressive stand on the issue early in his presidency. He thought that race relations would improve thanks to local initiatives. He feared that federal orders would only antagonize opponents of black civil rights and inflame the situation. However, the decision of the Supreme Court in the landmark *Brown v. Board of Education* (1954) case gave the reluctant President no choice but to deal with the issue. Ironically, the former Republican Governor of California, Earl Warren, the Chief Justice who delivered the *Brown* decision, had been Eisenhower's first appointment to the Supreme Court. Eisenhower later called Warren's appointment "the biggest damn fool mistake" he had ever made. Despite the rulings of the Court in 1954 and in a follow-up case in 1955 (*Brown II*), Eisenhower did not involve the federal government in the efforts of integration until events several years later left him no alternative but to employ federal power to enforce the Court's rulings.

Although little in the way of integration immediately followed the *Brown* decision, violence and confrontation did. Public defiance of the Court manifested itself in the South. Some Southern school districts chose to close schools rather than integrate. White Citizens Councils sprung up across the South, Southern white resisters beat and lynched African Americans, and white juries acquitted their "peers" of crimes, including murder, against African Americans. In a document known as the "Southern Manifesto," many Southern lawmakers publicly declared their intent to go against the *Brown* decision and prevent the integration of schools. In the meantime, the *Brown* decision emboldened African American civil rights advocates. In 1955 a refusal by Rosa Parks, a black seamstress, to give up her seat on a Montgomery city bus led to the Montgomery bus boycott, and Dr. Martin Luther King, Jr. rose to national prominence as the leader of a nonviolent movement for African American civil rights.

All the while Eisenhower kept the federal government aloof from the civil rights struggle. He refused to endorse the *Brown* decision and offered no federal assistance to integration efforts. Neither Eisenhower, nor Adlai Stevenson (who was once again his Democratic opponent for the presidency), made civil rights an issue in the election of 1956. By mid-1957 though, violence in the South had become intolerable for those in the Eisenhower Administration and many in Congress. Eisenhower gave moderate support to a civil rights bill promoted by his Attorney General and maneuvered through the Congress by the Senate majority leader, Lyndon Johnson (D-TX). The Civil Rights Bill of 1957 was the first federal civil rights legislation since Reconstruction. The bill created a Civil Rights Commission and authorized the Attorney General to step in when those registering to vote or integrate schools were precluded from doing so. Although Eisenhower endorsed the legislation, he pledged his faith in the respect of the American people for the law by ruling out the use of federal troops to enforce the *Brown* decision.

Eisenhower was forced to alter his stance in September of 1957 when Arkansas Governor Orval Faubus, who once declared that he would never be "outniggered," ordered the Arkansas National Guard to keep nine African American students from entering Little Rock's Central High School. Over a period of three weeks, circumstances in Little Rock escalated. A mob of whites threatening black students attempting to enter the school replaced the National Guard, which Faubus strategically withdrew. Unable to motivate either the Governor or the unruly crowd with words, Eisenhower federalized the National Guard and sent in 1,000 members of the 101st Airborne. Now the Guard, which only weeks earlier had surrounded the school to prevent the entry of African American students, was at Central High to ensure their safety.

Reactions to Eisenhower's handling of the crisis in Little Rock were mixed. Many white Southerners, such as Democratic Senator Richard Russell of Georgia, chastised him while civil rights advocates expressed concern over his hesitancy on the issue. Progress followed at a snail's pace. In 1960 only 1 percent of black children in the South attended school with white children. President Kennedy used federal troops to integrate the University of Mississippi in 1962 and again in 1963 to overcome Governor George Wallace's attempts to prevent blacks from attending the University of Alabama. Yet it is clear that the Civil Rights Act of 1957, along with the *Brown* decision and the commitment, however reluctant, of the federal government to enforce that opinion, gave proponents of African American civil rights hope and inspiration to persevere. President Kennedy capitalized on this momentum with his rhetoric both on the road to, and in, the White House. However, the nation did not make substantial progress on African American civil rights until the real force behind the Civil Rights Act of 1957, Lyndon Johnson, became president.

PRESIDENT DWIGHT D. EISENHOWER, NATIONAL ADDRESS ON LITTLE ROCK (SEPTEMBER 24, 1957)

Good Evening, My Fellow Citizens: —For a few minutes this evening I want to speak to you about the serious situation that has arisen in Little Rock. To make this talk I have come to the President's office in the White House. I could have spoken from Rhode Island, where I have been staying recently, but I felt that, in speaking from the house of Lincoln, of Jackson and of Wilson, my words would better convey both the sadness I feel in the action I was compelled today to take and the firmness with which I intend to pursue this course until the orders of the Federal Court at Little Rock can be executed without unlawful interference.

In that city, under the leadership of demagogic extremists, disorderly mobs have deliberately prevented the carrying out of proper orders from a Federal Court. Local authorities have not eliminated that violent opposition and, under the law, I yesterday issued a Proclamation calling upon the mob to disperse.

This morning the mob again gathered in front of the Central High School of Little Rock, obviously for the purpose of again preventing the carrying out of the Court's order relating to the admission of Negro children to that school.

Whenever normal agencies prove inadequate to the task and it becomes necessary for the Executive Branch of the Federal Government to use its powers and authority to uphold Federal Courts, the President's responsibility is inescapable. In accordance with that responsibility, I have today issued an Executive Order directing the use of troops under Federal authority to aid in the execution of Federal law at Little Rock, Arkansas. This became necessary when my Proclamation of yesterday was not observed, and the obstruction of justice still continues....

Our personal opinions about the decision have no bearing on the matter of enforcement; the responsibility and authority of the Supreme Court to interpret the Constitution are very clear. Local Federal Courts were instructed by the Supreme Court to issue such orders and decrees as might be necessary to achieve admission to public schools without regard to race—and with all deliberate speed.

During the past several years, many communities in our Southern States have instituted public school plans for gradual progress in the enrollment and attendance of school children of all races in order to bring themselves into compliance with the law of the land.

They thus demonstrated to the world that we are a nation in which laws, not men, are supreme.

I regret to say that this truth—the cornerstone of our liberties—was not observed in this instance.

It was my hope that this localized situation would be brought under control by city and State authorities. If the use of local police powers had been sufficient, our traditional method of leaving the problems in those hands would have been pursued. But when large gatherings of obstructionists made it impossible for the decrees of the Court to be carried out, both the law and the national interest demanded that the President take action....

The very basis of our individual rights and freedoms rests upon the certainty that the President and the Executive Branch of Government will support and insure the carrying out of the decisions of the Federal Courts, even, when necessary with all the means at the President's command.

Unless the President did so, anarchy would result....

Mob rule cannot be allowed to override the decisions of our courts....

The proper use of the powers of the Executive Branch to enforce the orders of a Federal Court is limited to extraordinary and compelling circumstances. Manifestly, such an extreme situation has been created in Little Rock. This challenge must be met and with such measures as will preserve to the people as a whole their lawfully-protected rights in a climate permitting their free and fair exercise. The overwhelming majority of our people in every section of the country are united in their respect for observance of the law—even in those cases where they may disagree with that law.

They deplore the call of extremists to violence....

At a time when we face grave situations abroad because of the hatred that Communism bears toward a system of government based on human rights, it would be difficult to exaggerate the harm that is being done to the prestige and influence, and indeed to the safety, of our nation and the world.

Our enemies are gloating over this incident and using it everywhere to misrepresent our whole nation. We are portrayed as a violator of those standards of conduct which the peoples of the world united to proclaim in the Charter of the United Nations. There they affirmed "faith in fundamental human rights" and "in dignity and worth of the human person" and they did so "without distinction as to race, sex, language or religion."

And so, with deep confidence, I call upon the citizens of the State of Arkansas to assist in bringing to an immediate end all interference with the law and its processes. If resistance to the Federal Court orders ceases at once, the further presence of Federal troops will be unnecessary and the City of Little Rock will return to its normal habits of peace and order and a blot upon the fair name and high honor of our nation in the world will be removed.

Thus will be restored the image of America and of all its parts as one nation, indivisible, with liberty and justice for all.

Good night, and thank you very much.

Source: *Public Papers of the Presidents of the United States, Dwight D. Eisenhower,* 1957 (Washington, DC: Government Printing Office), 689–694.

THE SOUTHERN MANIFESTO
(MARCH 12, 1956)

We regard the decision of the Supreme Court in the school cases as clear abuse of judicial power. It climaxes a trend in the Federal judiciary undertaking to legislate, in derogation of the authority of Congress, and to encroach upon the reserved rights of the states and the people.

The original Constitution does not mention education. Neither does the Fourteenth Amendment nor any other amendment. The debates preceding the submission of the Fourteenth Amendment clearly show that there was no intent that it should affect the systems of education maintained by the states.

The very Congress which proposed the amendment subsequently provided for segregated schools in the District of Columbia....

In the case of *Plessy v. Ferguson* in 1896 the Supreme Court expressly declared that under the Fourteenth Amendment no person was denied any of his rights if the states provided separate but equal public facilities. This decision has been followed in many other cases....

This interpretation, restated time and again, became a part of the life of the people of many of the states and confirmed their habits, customs, traditions and way of life.

It is founded on elemental humanity and common sense, for parents should not be deprived by Government of the right to direct the lives and education of their own children.

Though there has been no constitutional amendment or act of Congress changing this established legal principle almost a century old, the Supreme Court of the United States, with no legal basis for such action, undertook to exercise their naked judicial power and substituted their personal political and social ideas for the established law of the land.

This unwarranted exercise of power by the court, contrary to the Constitution, is creating chaos and confusion in the states principally affected. It is destroying the amicable relations between the white and Negro races that have been created through ninety years of patient effort by the good people of both races. It has planted hatred and suspicion where there has been heretofore friendship and understanding. . . .

Even though we constitute a minority in the present Congress, we have full faith that a majority of the American people believe in the dual system of government which has enabled us to achieve our greatness and will in time demand that the reserved rights of the states and of the people be made secure against judicial usurpation.

We pledge ourselves to use all lawful means to bring about a reversal of this decision which is contrary to the Constitution and to prevent the use of force in its implementation.

In this trying period, as we all seek to right this wrong, we appeal to our people not to be provoked by the agitators and troublemakers invading our states and to scrupulously refrain from disorder and lawless acts.

Source: 102 *Congressional Record* 4515–16 (1956).

GUATEMALA

While the *Brown* decision highlighted the paradox in America's Cold War rhetoric on "free societies," juxtaposing idealist visions of equality and segregation policy, Guatemala challenged that same rhetoric and the resolve of the Eisenhower foreign policy team abroad. American foreign policy in the 1950s was fairly straightforward. Consistent with Sovietologist George Kennan's ideas of containment, American foreign policy aimed to prevent the expansion of communism into places where it did not exist. This meant responding to Soviet military maneuvers, or those of its communist allies, such as in Korea. But containment also meant a vigilant watch on the "free world" for any evidence of communist meddling and an appropriate response to squelch any attempts at communist expansion, even in those cases where the military was not involved. The United States tested containment in response to communist military expansion in Korea in

1950; it tested the containment of more subtle communist incursions in Guatemala in 1954.

In the nation's first democratic election, held in 1954, Guatemalans elected Juan Jose Arevalo. Arevalo, a reform-minded president, embarked immediately on efforts to address the rampant inequality that had developed in Guatemala as a result of its colonial legacy, its history of dictatorial governments, and its agricultural-based economy. Arevalo's Secretary of Defense, Jacobo Arbenz Guzman won the election of 1950 to succeed Arevalo. Arbenz planned to carry the reforms of the previous decade even further. He invited reformers, including labor leaders and members of the Guatemalan Communist Party, into his government and set out to improve the quality of life for workers and peasants. In these efforts, Arbenz improved social welfare programs, launched a campaign to build roads and ports across the country, and, most importantly, announced Decree 900, an ambitious plan to redistribute uncultivated land from the hands of large landholders to peasants. Arbenz planned to expropriate fallow portions of major latifundias (plantations), compensating owners with government bonds. By 1954 Arbenz had redistributed 1.5 million acres of land to over 100,000 peasant families. One major obstacle stood in the way of an even more profound agrarian reform, an obstacle Arbenz later labeled "the octopus." The octopus was the United Fruit Company (UFCO), an American company that, with over 15,000 employees, was Guatemala's largest employer. The company owned more than 550,000 acres of land, and a 43 percent stake in the IRCA, a company that controlled most of Guatemala's railroads and was the country's second largest employer with a workforce of 5,000. More than 80 percent of the UFCO land was uncultivated, and therefore subject by law to expropriation. The Guatemalan government valued 200,000 acres of UFCO land at $627,572 for the purposes of expropriation and redistribution, based on the tax returns filed by UFCO. The company though disputed this figure, demanding $15,854,849 for the land. The company appealed to the U.S. State Department for help in dealing with the seemingly intransigent Guatemalans.

Fortunately for UFCO, State Department officials and Eisenhower advisors already had their eye on the Arbenz regime. Most on the Eisenhower foreign policy team, including Secretary of State John Foster Dulles, CIA Director Allen Dulles, and the President himself, believed that Arbenz, if he were not a communist himself, was at least "playing ball" with communists both within Guatemala and perhaps communist agitators sponsored by the Soviet Union. U.S. Ambassador to Guatemala, John Peurifoy, pointedly surmised that if Arbenz "is not a communist, he will certainly do until one comes along."[1] Arbenz had appointed no members of the Communist party to his cabinet and counted only three communist members of the Congress in his ruling coalition; nonetheless, although they differed on the methods that the United States should employ to deal with the perceived menace, the majority of those in the foreign policy-making circles of the State Department, CIA, and White House were convinced that Arbenz's reform efforts indicated his sympathy with communist ideology. A few in the State Department cautioned that Arbenz only viewed the Communists in Guatemala as useful allies, and that his sympathy toward them was pragmatic politics rather than evidence of an allegiance to international Communism. Some, like policy advisor Louis Halle, Jr., warned that aggressive U.S. actions could have detrimental results for the United States in the region that would outweigh the threat posed by affairs in Guatemala. However, Peurifoy sent frequent memos to the State Department warning of the imminent dangers of the Arbenz regime, and Eisenhower and his close advisors continued to regard Arbenz as a communist who had to go. The United States could not tolerate sympathy for communism in the Western Hemisphere, which it regarded as its "own backyard."

Eisenhower officials worked feverishly in the Organization of American States (OAS) to align nations in the Western Hemisphere against Guatemala. Beginning in March 1954, Secretary of State Dulles and the U.S. Ambassador to the OAS argued that communism, whether backed by a foreign power or not, represented an infiltration of a foreign power into the hemisphere, violating not only the Monroe Doctrine, a traditional benchmark for U.S. foreign policy, but also the Rio Treaty of Reciprocal Assistance. The Rio Treaty, signed in 1947, arranged for the collective response of all Western Hemisphere nations if any one was threatened by the "aggression" of a foreign power. Dulles argued that communist sympathy in the Arbenz regime, along with the land expropriations, clearly indicated that the communist ideology, if not Soviet agents themselves, had gained access to Guatemala, representing a threat to the sovereignty of Guatemala and to the entire hemisphere. Despite the arrival of two shiploads of Czechoslovakian armaments in Guatemala in May 1954, U.S. diplomats never convinced the majority of those in Latin American nations to view events in Guatemala as dangerous. Eisenhower decided that if the nations of the hemisphere collectively would not rid the region of the threat posed by the situation in Guatemala, the United States would handle the situation itself.

The United States certainly could not go around overthrowing democratically elected governments like the one in Guatemala, but covert United States operations had successfully replaced the Iranian regime with a U.S. favorite in 1953. Why not try again, this time closer to home? Eisenhower, the Dulles brothers, and a few other top aides began working on a plan to topple the Arbenz administration with disenchanted Guatemalans who had fled the country when the Arbenz reforms began. Their plan was not to build an army to overthrow Arbenz, but to create a situation in which Arbenz's own army turned against him. The CIA armed and trained a mere

200 rebels in Honduras, hoping that this ragtag group of exiles, along with the bombing of Guatemala City by CIA pilots, and the broadcasting of the sounds of war into Guatemala by the CIA, would convince the Guatemalan army, the largest in Central America, to give up its support for Arbenz. On June 18 the rebels, led by former Colonel Carlos Castillo Armas, who had served as a ruthless official in the dictatorship that ruled Guatemala from 1930 to 1944, moved into Guatemala. Arbenz resigned in seven days, convinced by his military that the United States was committed to destroying his government.

In the aftermath of the invasion, U.S. officials decided to support Castillo Armas's bid to run the military government, beginning one of the most unfortunate relationships of the Cold War. Castillo Armas dealt with opposition harshly, banning labor unions and all political parties but his own and imprisoning and killing those who opposed him. He returned land given to peasants during the Arbenz period to the original owners. He presided over a government that was fraught with corruption and plagued by his own inept mismanagement. In 1957, an assassin's bullet killed the Colonel, but a series of dishonest, repressive dictators followed. In 1961, Guatemala served as the staging ground for another American covert operation, the Bay of Pigs fiasco, which sought to overthrow the subsequent communist threat in the region, Fidel Castro in Cuba. Only in the 1990s have Guatemalans managed to restore stability and democracy to their nation. Scholars estimate that in the intervening years the political chaos resulted in the deaths of over 100,000 people in Guatemala and the displacement of hundreds of thousands more.

NOTE

1. Cited in Stephen G. Rabe, *Eisenhower in Latin America: The Foreign Policy of Anticommunism* (Chapel Hill: University of North Carolina Press, 1988), 47.

JOHN PEURIFOY, U.S. AMBASSADOR TO GUATEMALA TO THE DEPARTMENT OF STATE (DECEMBER 23, 1953)

As a result of my interview with President Arbenz, I am convinced Communists will continue to gain strength here as long as he remains in office. My staff agrees fully on this. Therefore, in view of inadequacy of normal diplomatic procedures in dealing with situation, there appears to be no alternative to our taking steps which would tend to make more difficult continuation of his regime in Guatemala....

I propose that...we carefully work out program designed to create situation in which non-Communists whether now supporting or opposing government would feel forced to coordinate their organizations and take action against government....

Department and Embassy should be able to work out program which while flexible enough to allow for adjustments to developments . . . , should be concrete enough to permit its implementation promptly . . . .Program should be applied in progressive steps which would build up increasing sense of urgency among non-Communist Guatemala.

Program should be undertaken with full realization it could provoke Guatemalan Government to swing sharply to left, to assume dictatorial power, to seek to win mass support through strongly nationalistic stand, and to expropriate or take other extreme reprisals against American companies in Guatemala. Guatemalan Government could be expected to make international issue of intervention, might ask my recall or even break off diplomatic relations with United States. It is quite conceivable it would lead to considerable bloodshed.

Nevertheless, implementation some such plan should not be deterred by these possible unpleasant consequences since continuance of present regime would also lead to most of them though at a slower pace and at the convenience of the Communists.

Source: *Foreign Relations Series of the United States, 1953–1954*, Vol. IV, *American Republics*, 1093–1094.

LOUIS J. HALLE, JR., POLICY PLANNING STAFF, MEMORANDUM TO THE DIRECTOR OF THE POLICY PLANNING STAFF (MAY 28, 1954)

Today the Fruit Company is, as it was becoming then, an agent of social betterment; but its past is not forgotten and what really counts is that, whether beneficent or maleficent in its practices, it remains the expression of Guatemala's economic colonialism.

The international Communist movement is certainly not the cause of the social revolution in Guatemala, but it has made the same effort there that it has made everywhere else to harness the revolutionary impulses— nationalism and social reform alike—and exploit them for its sown purposes. In Guatemala this effort has been less successful than in Vietnam and perhaps no more successful than it was in Mexico twenty years ago under the regime of Lazaro Cardenas. It has, however, been impressive in its success, all the circumstances considered. It has achieved a high degree of covert control over the reformist regime of President Arbenz and is dominant in the national labor movement.

The revolution in Guatemala is nationalist and anti-Yanqui in its own right. It is, in its own right, a movement for "social justice" and reform. If the international Communist movement had gained no foothold at all in Guatemala one might expect that the United Fruit Company, the Railways, and the Electric Power Company of Guatemala City would still be the victims of persecution in Guatemala.... All this is merely aggravated by the participation of Communism, which supplies a leadership and a body of tactical doctrine beyond the capacity of native resources alone....

The key to a wise choice [of action in Guatemala] lies in the answer to two questions: (1) What is the magnitude and immanence of any danger that the present situation hold for us? and (2) how much support for collective action can we expect from the rest of the inter-America community?... The real threat that Guatemala poses for her neighbors is that of political subversion through the kind of across-the-borders intrigues that is a normal feature of the Central American scene.... Finally, and above all, it might spread through the disposition the Latin Americans would have to identify themselves with little Guatemala if the issue should be drawn for them not as that of their own security but as a contest between David Guatemala and Uncle Sam Goliath.... The nationalistic and reformist elements in the Guatemalan situation have hitherto loomed larger for the Latin Americans than the element of international communism. They believe that we exaggerate the latter for our own purposes, and this belief is not weakened when we meet it with redoubled protestations....

If the above analyses are sound the conclusion must be that the time is not ripe for collective inter-American action.... This conclusion raises the question however, of what policy we should follow to expedite the ripening of time.

In this connection it seems to me that the two events which have so aroused us are as if calculated for our advantage. In the absence of undue excitement on our part they are bound to arouse alarm among Guatemala's neighbors, which alarm would tend to communicate itself throughout Latin America. If other like events ensued, that alarm would increase—but we would not ourselves be directly endangered....

If we should adopt, instead, the second alternative of intervening unilaterally with whatever force was necessary we would, in effect, be making a colony of Guatemala that we could maintain only by continued force, and by so doing we would turn all of Latin American against us to the advantage of the international Communist movement. If our intervention was less than decisive... we would have strengthened Communism in Guatemala while antagonizing Latin America generally. It would seem to me wise for us... to take a more relaxed attitude generally. In this connection we ought also avoid needlessly alarming and arousing our own public, for that would end by making the pursuit of a considered policy impossible.

Source: *Foreign Relations Series of the United States, 1952–1954*, Vol. 4, *American Republics*, 1139–1149.

THE HIGHWAY ACT

President Eisenhower initiated the largest and most ambitious public works program in American history. That program, the construction and consolidation of a system of interstate highways, is symbolic not only of Eisenhower's interests as president, but of the mentality of Americans in the 1950s as well. In the Age of Consensus and the Age of Anxiety, when Americans were looking to shared cultural traditions, beliefs, and practices to help them cope with the fears associated with the Cold War, an organized network of roadways criss-crossing the nation brought Americans closer together, culturally[1] and physically. It also provided a sense of economic and physical security by creating jobs and serving as a vast transportation network, not only for tourists and business travelers, but for the American military as well. The national government had studied the lack of national highways early in the twentieth century and had built some national highways before President Eisenhower signed the Federal Aid Highway Act in July 1956, also referred to as the National Defense Highway Act, but Eisenhower and other contemporary leaders made the issue of an interstate highway system a national concern. Whereas earlier proposals called for a joint effort by the states and the federal government, the Federal Aid Highway Act put into action a highway building program that received 90 percent of its funding from the federal government. Recognizing Eisenhower's important role in the building of the network of roads, President George H.W. Bush signed legislation in 1990 renaming the interstate highway system the "Dwight D. Eisenhower System of Interstate and Defense Highways."

During his time in Europe during World War II, the German national highway system, called the autobahn, impressed the then-Commander of the Allied Forces. Eisenhower marveled at the speed and efficiency with which German troops, and later Allied troops, were able to move across the country. He returned to the United States convinced of the need for a similar system of four-lane, national roadways. Despite the passage of a weak highway bill in 1954 that made little change in the way that highways were constructed and funded, Eisenhower was determined to reform fundamentally both the nation's highway system and the federal government's role in the design, construction, and maintenance of highways. In a speech later that year, which Vice President Nixon gave on the President's behalf, Eisenhower called America's highway system "inadequate locally, and obsolete as a national system." He listed five "penalties" of the highway system as it stood in 1954. These included the annual death and injury rate, traffic jams, the number of lawsuits related to highways, inefficiency, and "the appalling inadequacies to meet the demands of catastrophe or defense, should an atomic war come."[2] Eisenhower wanted a national highway system not only to enhance travel but to improve the economy by connecting America's major market areas, benefit defense by the movement of troops across the country, and provide for the evacuation of the civilian population in the face of a conventional or nuclear attack on an American city.

Few objected to the premise of an interstate highway system. Not all agreed, however, on how to fund the massive project. Eisenhower appointed a commission, headed by General Lucius Clay, to study the creation of a national highway system and the relationship between the federal government and the states in the building of the roadways. The Clay Commission's original proposal called for the federal government to pay the lion's share of the cost for a national highway system, and a bond issue to pay for the federal share of the cost, the bonds being retired over thirty years by revenue from gas taxes and highway user taxes that the national government collected. State governors initially resisted this plan, as they had hoped they would be able to eliminate the federal gas tax. More serious opposition came from those opposed to deficit spending, led by Senator Harry Byrd (D-VA). Representative Brady Gentry (D-TX) warned that funding the highways in this way was problematic for several reasons, including avoiding congressional regulation of government spending, the setting of a precedent for the funding of other projects in this way, and the inadequacy of the funds that would be raised. In addition, the trucking, tire, and petroleum industries all lobbied hard against the highway bills of 1955 because of the additional taxes proposed in the bills, not only on fuel, but on truck tires, the sale of trucks and trailers, and heavy vehicle usage. Although several different versions of the highway bill appeared in Congress in 1955, none included methods of financing without deficit spending and tax increases, making passage impossible.

Eisenhower remained dedicated to the national system of highways, however, and he reiterated his interest in the program in his 1956 State of the Union address. Accordingly, new highway bills surfaced in the House, this time with more creative financing plans, known as pay-as-you-go methods. In these kinds of financing plans, funds are raised as the project is implemented, rather than through bond issues, which raise all the necessary funds for a project at the outset. In April the House passed a highway bill that included an increase in the federal gas tax, from two to three cents, and the creation of a Highway Trust Fund, where revenue from taxes collected specifically to fund the construction of the interstate highway system would be placed. The Senate debated the bill next. Senator Byrd added a provision to the bill to prevent deficit spending within the Highway Trust Fund by requiring the Secretary of Commerce to reduce allocations to states if spending threatened to exceed the value of the Fund. Despite wrangling in conference committee, the bill was reported out, and it successfully passed both houses of Congress. Eisenhower signed it into law on June 29, 1956.

Although the national highway system was originally projected at 42,000 miles of roadway, by 2001, after several expansions, the system included over 45,000 miles of paved highways, designed for high-speed travel. A systematic numbering scheme names the highways. East-west highways end in 0 (I-10, I20, etc.), south-north highways in 5 (I-95, I-85, etc.), and highways that bypass cities are three digits and incorporate the major route's name (I-285 allows travelers to exit I-85, travel around the city of Atlanta, and then reenter I-85). The Federal Highway Administration within the U.S. Department of Transportation manages the interstate highway system and the Highway Trust Fund. In recent years, most notably the 1970s and 1980s, the federal government has used its role in the funding of interstate highways in order to bring states in line with policies the federal government favors. For example, amidst the oil crises of the 1970s, the federal government withheld highway funding from states that refused to bring speed limits down to 55 miles per hour. More recently, the national government has reduced funds for states that failed to raise their drinking age to 21.

NOTE

1. Some historians have argued that the highway system promoted cultural consensus, in fact, by keeping mainstream American culture insulated from the diversity of regional cultures. This argument suggests that transnational travelers avoided exposure to local cultures by remaining on the interstate highways, whereas prior to the highway system, these travelers passed through the core areas of regional cultures on local and state roads.

2. Cited in "Federal Highway Act of 1956: Creating the Interstate System," *Public Roads On-Line* (Summer 1996), <http://www.tfhre.gov/pubrds/summer96/p96su10.htm>

PRESIDENT DWIGHT D. EISENHOWER, MESSAGE TO CONGRESS (FEBRUARY 22, 1955)

Our unity as a nation is sustained by free communication of thought and by easy transportation of people and goods. The ceaseless flow of information throughout the Republic is matched by individual and commercial movement over a vast system of inter-connected highways criss-crossing the Country and joining at out national borders with friendly neighbors to the north and south.

Together, the uniting forces of our communication and transportation systems are dynamic elements in the very name we bear—United States. Without them, we would be a mere alliance of many separate parts.

The nation's highway system is a gigantic enterprise, one of the our largest items of capital investment. Generations have gone into its building.

Three million, three hundred and sixty-six thousand miles of road, traveled by 58 million motor vehicles, comprise it.... But, in large part, the network is inadequate for the nation's growing needs....

First: Each year more than 36 thousand people are killed and more than a million injured on the highways.... Reliable estimates place the measurable economic cost of the highway accident toll to the Nation at more than $4.3 billion a year.

Second: The physical condition of the present road net increases the cost of vehicle operation, according to many estimates, by as much as one cent per mile of vehicle travel. At the present rate of travel, this totals more than $5 billion a year. The cost is not borne by the individual vehicle operator alone. It pyramids into higher expense of doing the nation's business. Increased highway transportation costs, passed on through each step in the distribution of goods, are paid ultimately by the individual consumer.

Third: In the case of atomic attack on our key cities, the road net must permit quick evacuation of target areas, mobilization of defense forces and maintenance of every essential economic function. But the present system in critical areas would be the breeder of a deadly congestion within hours of an attack.

Fourth: ... Unless the present rate of highway improvement and development is increased, existing traffic jams only faintly foreshadow those of ten years hence.

To correct these deficiencies is an obligation of Government at every level. The highway system is a public enterprise. As the owner and operator, the various levels of Government have a responsibility for management that provides the economy of the nation and properly serves the individual user. In the case of the Federal Government, moreover, expenditures on a highway program are a return to the highway user of the taxes which he pays in connection with his use of the highways....

The Interstate Highway System must be given top priority in construction planning. But at the current rate of development, the Interstate network would not reach even a reasonable level of extent and efficiency in half a century. State highway departments cannot effectively meet the need. Adequate right-of-way to assure control of access; grade separation structures; relocation and realignment of present highways; all these, done on the necessary scale within an integrated system, exceed their collective capacity....

The obvious responsibility to be accepted by the Federal Government, in addition to the existing Federal interest in our 3,366,000-mile network of highways, is the development of the Interstate System with its most essential urban arterial connections....

A sound Federal highway program, I believe, can and should stand on its own feet, with highway users providing the total dollars necessary for improvement and new construction. Financing of interstate and

Federal-aid systems should be based on the planned use of increasing revenues from present gas and diesel oil taxes, augmented in limited instances with tolls.

I am inclined to the view that it is sounder to finance this program by special bond issues, to be paid off by the above-mentioned revenues which will be collected during the useful life of the roads and pledged to this purpose, rather than by an increase in general revenue obligations....

Source: Dwight D. Eisenhower Library, <http://www.eisenhower.utexas.edu/DI/InterstateHighways/InterstateHighwaysdocuments.html>

REP. BRADY GENTRY (D-TX), SPEECH TO THE ANNUAL CONVENTION OF THE AMERICAN AUTOMOBILE ASSOCIATION (SEPTEMBER 21, 1955)

... It is unfortunate that the highways needed by today's traffic will cost so much money. It can hardly be denied that most of our main highways are grossly inadequate and are causing our motorists great losses in time, deaths, injuries, and destruction to property. While we are told by eminent authorities that it will cost motorists more in actual dollars and cents to continue using our present roads than to pay the taxes necessary to modernize and then enjoy good thoroughfares, recent happenings in the Congress are proof that modern highways are no early certainty.

Several points of difference on this problem seem to divide us.... There is little question that the problem or financing caused the major opposition to this legislation or served as an excuse for such opposition....

The President, speaking through Vice President Nixon at a Governors' Conference in July 1954, called public notice to the need for a modernized system of highways. Subsequently the President appointed an advisory committee and named General Clay as chairman. The advisory committee forthwith appointed a staff, comprised of highway and financial experts. Characteristic or the committee approach to this problem was the instruction to the staff that it evolve a plan that would spend $25 billion on highways without increasing taxes or debt. Just think for a moment! Spend $25 billion without increasing taxes or debt! Your reaction must be that that simply could not be done. It would seem to be an utter impossibility.... In addition, regular Federal aid now $700 million, would be set at $600 million and frozen at that yearly figure for the next 32 years.

Up to the present, every dollar expended by the Government on roads has been subject to authorizing legislation by Congress, full budgetary control, complete appropriation procedure, has been paid out or general revenue, and accounted for within the statutory debt limit. Such is the pattern of present Federal financing. The advisory plan would discard each and every one of these safeguards of responsible financing. It would effectuate a complete and revolutionary departure from fiscal fundamentals and long recognized principles in Government practices. . . .

What was the testimony of Government witnesses concerning this? In effect, here is what they said: "These bonds are not debts or obligations of the Government, but they are moral obligations, and the Government will, of course, have to pay them. It will have to do that to protect Its credit." Doesn't it seem unusual that anyone would question classifying as debt something which they say the Government must pay? . . .

What was the result of all this mumbo jumbo of the committee plan? Everybody got what they wanted. The Treasury could rely on the recital in the bonds that they were not Government debts and thus say that neither the debt nor debt limit would be increased. The bond buyers, regardless of the bond recital, could rely not only on the further provisions of the legislation which did obligate the Government but also on the assurances of the Secretary of the Treasury that the Government would pay them. Who was losing by all this financial word-juggling? You taxpayers were losing and so was responsible fiscal policy.

If the Government is to do further major deficit spending, there should be no question of its true character and it should mean the same thing to all people . . . it is deficit financing, pure and simple. . . .

The idea of the Federal Highway Corporation is represented as the easy way. It is the painless solution. It would have us believe we are getting something for nothing—billions in highways, without debt and without taxes. What could be more vicious in its evil potentiality for a Government's fiscal soundness? It could be the beginning of a chain of Federal corporations, each nibbling away a portion of the Government's general revenues which, even during the boom time of the last few years, still have been insufficient for us to live within our income. . . . Just what will happen to the present manifold obligations of the Government if a great portion of its revenues are assigned to newly organized Federal corporations in order to secure new or greatly enlarged services? If this precedent is established, there is no earthly reason to doubt that other Congresses might utilize it to effect possible demoralization in Government financing. . . .

What do these facts mean? They mean that we have never had enough available tax revenue to build the highways we needed; that we don't have enough available tax revenue today; and, that we delude ourselves if we think we will solve this problem by deficit spending through bond issues. If we do this, we simply compound our problem by using a part of insufficient and greatly needed revenue in paying interest. . . .

Surely we will not at this late date take the easy road by yielding to fear and political expediency. That will never get us the highways our motorists need and should have. Certainly we ought to do that which will neither involve us in deadly precedent nor lead us into fiscal irresponsibility. Neither should we accept a plan that is wholly insufficient and can only result in growing highway inadequacies and greater financial losses. We need legislation that is not only fiscally responsible, but also equitable as between various road user groups. It should not be sufficient for a season only, but that which will give us the highway system required today and permit expansion as it is needed on tomorrow. Then and only then can we say that we are on the high road to solving out highway problem.

Source: *Congressional Record*, Vol. 102, Pt. 1, 501–504.

NATIONAL DEFENSE EDUCATION ACT

Eisenhower claimed throughout his presidency that education was as important as defense, but he did little to address the issue at a national level until the two issues became intertwined in the last years of his administration. In the mid-1950s, with baby boomers entering schools and the GI Bill boosting college enrollments, classroom space and teachers were both in short supply relative to the student population. Nonetheless, the federal government hardly addressed the issue. Sputnik, the satellite that the Soviets launched in 1957, finally got the attention of the federal government. Just as Sputnik kick-started the space program and led to stepped-up work on missile development, it also led the federal government to an unprecedented level of involvement in public education. In the words of Admiral Hyman Rickover, Americans were right to fear "world scientific and engineering supremacy" by the Russians: "We have let our educational problem grow much too big for comfort and safety," he argued. America must produce scientists and engineers at the same rate or better than the Russians in order to avoid losing "American technical supremacy."[1]

Rickover's sentiments represented those of many Americans in the late 1950s. The President responded with the National Defense Education Act (NDEA), targeting federal funds toward the teaching of mathematics, science, and foreign languages in secondary schools in reaction to a perceived disparity in education in these important Cold War disciplines between the education systems in the United States and the Soviet Union. If the National Defense Highway Act was the granddaddy of Eisenhower's domestic record in the first term, the NDEA, motivated by similar Cold War fears, was the centerpiece of Eisenhower's domestic program in the second.

The importance of the NDEA extends beyond just its place among the other pieces of domestic legislation responding to pressures of the Cold War. The NDEA is significant in two other respects: first, it represents the federal government's first serious involvement in public education. Although most states had fairly well-established systems of public education by the Civil War, the federal government only had dabbled in the funding of education by the 1950s; most federal education legislation, such as the Morrill Acts of 1862 and 1890, the Smith-Hughes Act of 1917, and the Serviceman's Readjustment Act of 1944 (the G.I. Bill), had aimed at collegiate and vocational education. In 1946 and 1954 federal legislation provided funds for school lunches and later for milk for those lunches. Not until the NDEA, however, did the federal government allocate funds specifically for the educational programs of secondary schools, thus setting the precedent for massive education legislation of the following years, most notably the Elementary and Secondary Education Act, part of President Johnson's "Great Society," in 1965. It is unlikely that Johnson would have been able to make such a substantial and broad commitment to public education without the initial federal foray into funding secondary education that the NDEA provided.

Second, the NDEA, like the National Defense Highway Act of 1956, profoundly illumines the philosophy of the Eisenhower presidency. Despite Eisenhower's cost-cutting rhetoric and his abhorrence of excessive federal interference in private and local matters, the NDEA, like the highway act, signified his pragmatism and flexibility amid the pressures of the Cold War. Just as Eisenhower defied his political convictions by allowing unbalanced budgets for a majority of the years of his presidency, in the case of education he expanded the federal government in nearly unprecedented ways.[2]

With the NDEA, state and local school systems received federal funding to improve curriculum and instruction in science, math, foreign languages, and "other critical subjects," to improve statistical services, and to reform guidance and counseling programs. But, postsecondary educational institutions were not left out of the NDEA either. Eisenhower's initial plans for education legislation after Sputnik consisted primarily of college scholarship programs, but pressure from Congress and others led Eisenhower to sign into law a much more comprehensive and far-reaching piece of education legislation. This revised legislation included a new program of scholarships and loans, as well as funds for colleges and universities to enhance foreign language study and training. In addition, the act provided funding for the study and promotion of increased use of multimedia, television, and motion pictures in education. Finally, in response to manpower shortages in certain areas of the defense industry, the legislation earmarked funds to spur vocational and technical study necessary to the national defense. With a projected cost of more than one billion federal dollars, the NDEA placed the government at the center of the daily life of Americans in a way that even much of the New Deal legislation had not.

Despite the atmosphere of the Cold War, the symbolic threat posed by the launching of Sputnik I and Sputnik II, and the anxiety that most Americans felt in the 1950s, not everyone endorsed the NDEA. Just as Americans feared communism, many feared the expansion of their own federal government, as they demonstrated in part by electing and reelecting Eisenhower. Prior to the 1950s, education had largely been the province of states and localities and some Congressmen saw the NDEA simply as a way to increase federal control over education, a place where some, like Senator Barry Goldwater (R-AZ), believed the federal government did not belong. Thus, part of the debate over the NDEA focused on the degree to which the act vested the federal government with control over local school systems. Some also worried that the pretense of "national defense" would give the federal government a blank check to determine what was taught (i.e., science and math) and how (i.e., multimedia).

Certain provisions of the act clearly reflect the Cold War context in which the legislation was passed. For example, Senator John F. Kennedy (D-MA) objected to the loyalty oaths required of scholarship recipients, arguing that they would dissuade potential students from applying and frighten universities and faculty from participating in the program. This resulted in a provision in the NDEA legislation strictly prohibiting "federal control" of education. As its defenders saw it, the NDEA merely established guidelines, the details of which states and localities would develop and implement. Others still argued that the program did not go far enough. Senator J. William Fulbright (D-AR) spoke at length in the Senate criticizing the Eisenhower education program, and took great pains to point out the differences from what he perceived as a complacent American attitude toward education and the strides made by the Soviet education system since the end of World War II. The issue of the optimal federal role remains central even in the twenty-first century, with the issues of funding for education and national educational standards dominating the current debate.

NOTES

1. Hyman G. Rickover, *Education and Freedom* (New York: E.P. Dutton, 1959), 59.

2. One could make the same argument in regard to the highway act, although that legislation could be called more "Whiggish," both because of its actual similarities to the national improvements programs of the Whig presidents of the nineteenth century, and because, unlike the education act, private industry played an important, if not central, role in the construction of the highways.

PRESIDENT DWIGHT EISENHOWER, SPECIAL MESSAGE TO THE CONGRESS ON EDUCATION (JANUARY 27, 1958)

To the Congress of the United States:
   Education best fulfills its high purpose when responsibility for education is kept close to the people it serves—when it is rooted in the home, nurtured

in the community, and sustained by a rich variety of public, private, and individual resources. The bond linking home and school and community—the responsiveness of each to the needs of the others—is a precious asset of American education.

This bond must be strengthened, not weakened, as American education faces new responsibilities in the cause of freedom. For the increased support our educational system now requires, we must look primarily to citizens and parents acting in their own communities, school boards and city councils, teachers, principals, school superintendents, State boards of education and State legislatures, trustees and faculties of private institutions.

Because of the national security interest in the quality and scope of our educational system in the years immediately ahead, however, the Federal government must also undertake to play an emergency role....

High quality professional personnel in science, engineering, teaching, languages, and other critical fields are necessary to our national security efforts. Each year, nevertheless, many young people drop out of high school before graduation. Many able high school graduates do not go on to college. This represents a waste of needed talent. Much of this waste could be avoided if the aptitudes of these young people were identified and they were encouraged toward the fullest development of their abilities....

National security requires that prompt action be taken to improve and expand the teaching of science and mathematics. Federal matching funds can help to stimulate the organization of programs to advance the teaching of these subjects in the public schools.

The Administration therefore recommends that the Congress authorize Federal grants to the States, on a matching basis, for this purpose. These funds would be used, in the discretion of the States and the local school systems, either to help employ additional qualified science and mathematics teachers, to help purchase laboratory equipment and other materials, to supplement salaries of qualified science and mathematics teachers, of for other related programs.

To help assure a more adequate supply of trained college teachers, so crucial in the development of tomorrow's leaders, the Administration recommend that the Congress authorize...

a. graduate fellowships to encourage more students to prepare for college teaching careers,
b. federal grants, on a matching basis, to institutions of higher education to assist in expanding their graduate school capacity.

Knowledge of languages is particularly important today in the light of America's responsibilities of leadership in the free world. And yet the American people generally are deficient in foreign languages....It is important to our national security that such deficiencies be promptly overcome. The administration therefore recommends . . .

   a. support for special centers in colleges and universities to provide instruction in foreign languages which are important today but which are not now commonly taught in the United States,
   b. support of institutes for those who are already teaching foreign languages in our schools and colleges. These institutes would given training to improve the quality and effectiveness of foreign language teaching . . . .

This emergency program stems form national need, and its fruits will bear directly on national security. The method of accomplishment is sound: the keystone is State, local, and private effort; the Federal role is to assist— not to control or supplant—those efforts.

The administration urges prompt enactment of these recommendations in the essential interest of national security.

Source: *Public Papers of the Presidents of the United States, Dwight D. Eisenhower*, 1958, 127–123.

JOHN F. KENNEDY ON THE LOYALTY OATH OF
THE NATIONAL DEFENSE EDUCATION ACT

Our most important natural resource is found in the Universities of the nation. It is here that we must begin our search for the scientific talent that this nation will need in peace or war. It is here that we find the reservoir of creative ideas and imaginative solutions for the infinite variety of problems we face as a nation. It is here that the leaders of our country are trained. Not the least important, it is here that the delicate flower of cultural achievement is nourished. . . .

[The National Defense Education Act] provides generally for Federal loans to students at institutions of higher learning. It announces that the security of the Nation depends upon the fullest development of the mental resources and technical skills of our young men and women, and encourages this development by the loan program.

When the bill passed Congress last year very little attention was paid to a section of the bill inserted on the Senate Floor which required any student who applied for a loan under it to sign an oath of loyalty and to make out an affidavit declaring that he did not believe in or support any organization which believed in or supported the overthrow of the United States Government by illegal methods. . . .

...nor was there any discussion of what danger to the nation was being avoided by this requirement—or why Congress was singling out recipients of Federal loans for educational purposes and not those who receive old age benefits, crop loans, or other unrelated payments.

The loyalty oath has no place in a program designed to encourage education. It is at variance with the declared purpose of the Act in which it appears; it acts as a barrier to prospective students; and it is distasteful, humiliating and unworkable to those who must administer it....

Source: National Archives and Records Administration, <http://www.nara.gov/cgi-bin/starfinder/27002/images.txt>

SENATOR J. WILLIAM FULBRIGHT (D-AR), "OUR CURRENT CRISIS—THE NEED FOR EDUCATION" (JANUARY 23, 1958)

...from what administration sources have already put out about their program, it is, at bottom, a program calling for a minimal instead of a maximum effort on the part of the United States. For the ruling principle to which it is tailored—as administration sources have made clear in conferences with Congressional leaders—is this: That the Soviet Union—our challenger—is a warped society, wracked by internal strains, and fated for an early and inglorious collapse. In the circumstances, all we have to do is the very little that is required to keep our own motors idling until the inevitable crackup occurs to the Soviet Union...

It is, in fact, precisely in the field of education and basic research that the Russians have apparently made their greatest progress. Why should this be so? How is it that they recognized some years ago that trained minds were indispensable to modern technology, modern weapons, and modern methods of subversion? How is it that they had the vision to upgrade the pay and status of educators and scientists?...

Right now, even in the hour of our so-called awakening to danger, the evidence offered by the administration that it is alive to the most difficult of all the challenges we face is discouraging in the extreme. There is little doubt that we will meet the immediate problem of missiles and satellites. But the real challenge we face involves the very roots of our society. It involves our educational system, the source of our knowledge and cultural values. And here the administration's program for a renaissance of learning is disturbingly small minded....

As things now stand in America, there is not particular incentive for young people to exert themselves to achieve excellence in intellectual attainment. Our students can leave school with a minimum of learning and still be reasonably sure of a life of relative ease and luxury.... A man's success of status is measured not so much by the ideas he may have developed or his service to the community. It is measured, rather, by the value of his house, the number and the vintage of the cars he owns, and where he spends his vacation. . . .

There will be those among us who say "But education takes too long, we do not have the time; our efforts need be devoted to missiles and outer space." This is truly the counsel of despair and disaster. The start toward improvement in education must be now; it should have been yesterday. . . .

One other observation, aside from the actual tangible effect: If Congress would do something which even recognized the importance of education as such, and recognized the importance of the teaching profession; if we were to give a little sign that we think it is important, it would provide a most beneficial shot in the arm, so to speak, to the teaching profession. . . . The teachers have the impression—and correctly so—that Congress cares nothing about teaching, although it cares about other things. . . .

Not only should we provide more money for education as a whole, but we should also reform our basic ideas about elementary and secondary education. We must emphasize the rigorous training of the intellect, rather than the gentle cultivation of the personality, which has been so popular in recent years.

If we are to play the role of a leader among nations, in truth, if we are to retain our independence, we must have men and women who can read, write, and speak effectively and who understand thoroughly the world in which we live. Courses in life adjustment and coed cooking will not do the job. Mathematics, languages, the natural sciences, and history must once again become the core of the curriculum, and a way must be found to induce the students to study, preferable by inducing a desire to learn. . . .

Source: *Congressional Record*, Vol. 104, Pt. 1, 870–877.

THE BEGINNINGS OF THE U.S. SPACE PROGRAM

In contrast to his interest in defense and education, President Eisenhower's position on the U.S. space program has been described as "reluctant." In keeping with his prevailing philosophy of balancing the budget, minimizing the expansion of the federal government, and strengthening national security, Eisenhower only agreed to devote significant funding to the U.S. space program after much hesitation. The successful launch of the Soviet capsule Sputnik on October 4, 1957, sent shock waves of anxiety through the nation, as Americans interpreted the event as signaling the inferiority of the U.S. national security program. Although government officials in the United States initially tried to dismiss the launching of Sputnik as a "stunt," an event that, according to Eisenhower "should not raise apprehensions one iota," the fact that Americans could well have Russian satellites looming over their own houses and backyards altered the attitudes many Americans held about space exploration. Quickly, many Americans came to believe that space was one of several battlefields in the Cold War, a frontier not unlike the territory of the Third World or the minds of those deciding between democracy and capitalism and dictatorship and communism. Thus, the Soviet presence in outer space dealt a blow to the confidence of Americans, and served as a wake-up call of sorts, prompting a renewed diligence not only in the U.S. space program, but also in American education, government spending, and military preparedness.

Although national security was a top priority for Eisenhower, he fought against those who called for reckless spending in the name of national security. He brought the same philosophy to the debate over the U.S. space program, frequently using the term "crash program" to describe the kind of response to Sputnik he wanted to avoid. Confident in his own estimates of the superiority of U.S. nuclear preparedness, Eisenhower asked the pragmatic questions: What will be achieved by sending capsules into space? Toward what other, higher-priority causes might monies devoted to the space program be otherwise directed? What, in fact, are the domestic political consequences, and international repercussions, of failing to "keep up with" the Soviet Union in space? Eisenhower's "New Look" foreign policy asked the same questions about nuclear weapons, increased military spending, and American forays into developing countries.

Perhaps the biggest consideration confronting Eisenhower and Americans after Sputnik was that of American prestige. On the Cold War playing field, many allotted an important role to prestige. And what, many asked, could be a greater symbol of a successful national economic and political program than catapulting an object into space and having it orbit the earth? Not only did a successful space launch represent technological and perhaps political and economic achievement, it also suggested that the Soviets were probably applying a similar work ethic and know-how to their missile programs. Consequently, following Sputnik, Americans criticized the Eisenhower program, claiming that his fiscal conservatism cleared the way for the Soviets to beat the United States into space, and making the United States appear weak and vulnerable.

Immediately after Sputnik, Eisenhower launched a public education campaign to reassure Americans that Sputnik neither indicated that the Soviets possessed Intermediate Continental Ballistic Missiles (ICBMs) nor represented any kind of military threat to the United States. Eisenhower insisted publicly that the United States was ahead of the Soviet Union in the nuclear field, and that incipient U.S. efforts to develop a space program were for scientific research rather than for "racing" the Soviet Union. Still, some, like Senator Olin Johnson (D-SC), argued that Eisenhower's response to the space program was embarrassing and dangerous. The President's critics argued that the failure to develop a significant space program jeopardized America's national security and international reputation. Over time, Eisenhower himself became more concerned about the psychological ramifications of Soviet advances in space and missile development. By October of 1959, Eisenhower had relegated the scientific aspects of the space program to the lowest priority and elevated defensive concerns and international prestige. Although he was still convinced that economic growth and stability were the most important factors in the international reputation of the United States, by January of 1960 he admitted that it may be important to "exceed Soviet accomplishments" in some areas in order to "achieve a psychological advantage."[1] Nonetheless, Eisenhower and most of his top advisors on space agreed that national security, not national image, should be the primary focus of the government's programs and, at the same time, that the United States could ultimately "prevail" in space without entering into a "race" with the Soviets.

Facing increasing pressure in the months immediately following the Soviet launch of Sputnik and its early successors, Eisenhower and his science advisors realized that a redoubled effort and expanded space program was both necessary and inevitable. Senate Majority Leader Lyndon Johnson delivered a speech that persuaded many Americans that a dramatic expansion of American efforts in space was needed; some have credited this speech as the most important event in the development of the American space program. Many policymakers began to argue for an executive agency specifically devoted to the space program. The debate centered around two questions. One related to timing and resources, that is, the speed and the size of the program. The second involved whether civilian or military authorities would control the program. Characteristically, Eisenhower initially opposed a new bureaucracy, preferring that the space program, even if expanded, remain in the Defense Department. However, Eisenhower had tried all along to keep politics out of the debate over space, and when a nonpartisan group of science advisors recommended the creation of a new, independent agency to administer the American space program, he conceded. Even after Eisenhower created this new agency, some still insisted that he had not gone far enough to create an American space program that could compete with the Russians.

The creation of the National Aeronautics and Space Administration (NASA) on July 29, 1958 did not end debate. Questions still persisted about the budget and goals of this program. The President declared, for example, that NASA would remain small, with a budget of less than $500,000; when he left office, NASA's budget exceeded $1 billion. Eisenhower also thought that getting a man into space should not be the single highest priority of the American space initiative, yet this became the major immediate goal of the space program once John F. Kennedy arrived in office.

NOTE

1. Quoted in David Callahan and Fred I. Greenstein, "Eisenhower and U.S. Space Policy," in Roger D. Launius and Howard M. McCurdy, *Spaceflight and the Myth of Presidential Leadership* (Urbana: University of Illinois Press, 1997), 30.

PRESIDENT DWIGHT D. EISENHOWER, MESSAGE TO CONGRESS (APRIL 2, 1958)

Recent developments in long-range rockets for military purposes have for the first time provided man with new machinery so powerful that it can put satellites into orbit, and eventually provide the means for space exploration. ... The early enactment of appropriate legislation will help assure that the United States takes full advantage of the knowledge of its scientists, the skill of its engineers and technicians, and the resourcefulness of its industry in meeting the challenges of the space age. ...

In statement which I released on March 26, 1958 the Science Advisory Committee has listed four factors which in its judgment give urgency and inevitability to advancement in space technology. These factors are: (1) the compelling urge of man to explore the unknown; (2) the need to assure that full advantage is taken of the military potential of space; (3) the effect on national prestige of accomplishment in space science and exploration; and (4) the opportunities for scientific observation and experimentation which will add to our knowledge of the earth, the solar system, and the universe.

The factors have such a direct bearing on the future progress as well as on the security of our Nation that an imaginative and well-conceived space program must be given high priority to carry it out. ...

I recommend that aeronautical and space science activities sponsored by the United States be conducted under the direction of a civilian agency, except for those projects primarily associated with military requirements. I have reached this conclusion because space exploration hold promise of adding importantly to our knowledge of the earth, the solar system, and the universe, and because it is of great importance to have the fullest cooperation of the scientific community at home and abroad in moving forward in the fields of space science and technology. Moreover, a civilian setting for the administration of space function will emphasize the concern of our Nation that outer space be devoted to peaceful and scientific purposes. ...

Source: *Congressional Record*, Vol. 104, Pt. 5, 61331–6132.

SENATOR OLIN JOHNSON (D-SC), "LAGGING UNITED STATES SATELLITE PROGRAM" (MAY 26, 1958)

It is with deepest concern and fear that I view the failure of the present administration's satellite program and its many dark ramifications. I hope that my fears will be unfounded....

Apart from the grim implications of this latest Soviet fear [the launching of the third Sputnik satellites], think of its propaganda value. Sputnik III can be seen practically anywhere in the world at dawn and at dusk with the unaided eye—it is a tremendous advertisement for Soviet science. Moreover, any ham operator can pick up its signal....

Soviet satellite successes as compared with America's meager accomplishments are not only humiliating but dangerous. What are neutral nations going to think when they weigh the comparative performances? Imagine the influence Sputnik III will have on public opinion in all quarters of the globe.... This whole outer space situation is fraught with serious implications. We can no longer proceed casually with our space program. Our survival as a free people is involved in this activity....

We need a new look at our satellites program. We simply cannot go on the way we have been—this way leads to ultimate disaster....

We must have planning that will place us first in the missile and space race—and keep us there.

There is need for a leapfrog type program—something beyond out present thinking and planning....

The first thing we need is a change of attitude. We must realize the threat that confronts us. We are not playing for marbles. We are engaged in an all-out, no-holds-barred battle for the preservation of western civilization, for survival as a free and independent nation....

Source: *Congressional Record*, Vol. 104, Pt. 7, 9477–9481.

THE MIDDLE EAST AND THE EISENHOWER DOCTRINE

While China and Guatemala called for specific diplomatic and military action, the tumult in the Middle East proved a far more complicated foreign policy affair for the Eisenhower administration. A complex region of the world, it was home in the 1950s to historic religious and ethnic tensions and to a complex web of political and military alliances. These involved not only the traditional Cold War ideological partisans, but also Arab and Jewish sympathies, as well as members of the so-called "nonaligned" movement. Nonaligned nations were trying to carve out their own niche in the Cold War, independent of the two superpowers and manipulating the tensions between them. Moreover, the Middle East served, as it does today, as a major source of oil for Western economies. Although scholars of the period have yet to direct the attention to this area that it deserves, the Middle East was a crucial area for the United States during the Eisenhower years. Throughout the decade, Americans worked both overtly and covertly to advance national interests in the region. The CIA assisted in the overthrow of the Iranian Prime Minister in 1953, and American Marines went to Lebanon to help restore political stability to the country amid internal strife. In addition, the French and British revisited nineteenth-century imperialist practices by bombing Egypt in order to wrestle back control of Suez Canal from Egyptian President Gamal Abdel Nasser, putting the Eisenhower foreign policy team in an awkward spot. Turmoil in the region led, by 1957, to the promulgation of the Eisenhower Doctrine, a congressional resolution clearing the way for the president to assist countries threatened by "armed aggression from any nation controlled by international communism."

The establishment of Israel as a state in 1948 had led to increased tension that confronted American foreign policymakers with unprecedented diplomatic questions. A recent book on relations between the United States and Israel defines the origins of that relationship as a struggle within the American foreign policy establishment between a "special interest paradigm" and an "American national interest paradigm."[1] American statesmen had to manage a complex relationship with Israel under the umbrella of Cold War tensions. Who were to be American allies in the region, and how would these alliances be forged? American sympathies clearly rested with the new Jewish state, but this friendship threatened to alienate Arab states in the region, who, like Israel, were working to establish themselves as viable and important states on the world stage in the wake of the retreat of colonialism.

American activities in the region during the Eisenhower years suggest that, as in all other areas of the world, American national interest guided by containment policy took priority. In the Middle East, American foreign policymakers used a variety of tactics to keep communism out of the region. Amid instability in Iran, and with a government that threatened to move against U.S. interests by nationalizing American corporations, in 1953 the CIA orchestrated a coup d'etat to remove the unfriendly Mohammad Mossadegh and install in his place the Shah Reza Pahlavi, who remained a close ally of the United States until his own overthrow in 1979 by the fundamentalist Ayatollah Ruhollah Khomeini. Just as in other regions of the world during the Cold War, Americans feared not only what was happening in Iran itself, but also that hostility to American interests might spread from Iran to its neighbors. Thus, removing the left-leaning Mossadegh was deemed essential. Iran then became a stable ally, but more serious issues loomed in Egypt and Lebanon.

Although the United States played only a secondary role in the Suez crisis, the Egyptian seizure of the canal in 1956 and the European and Israeli responses partly set the stage for future American action in the region. With the Suez crisis, American policymakers were confronted with a choice: support traditional allies, Britain and France, in their effort preserve the vestiges of colonialism by taking back control of the Canal from Egypt, and perhaps alienate Arab countries, or side against Britain and France by showing support for the unpredictable pan-Arabist movement led by the Egyptian President Nasser. Of course, Americans most wanted to prevent doing anything that would invite or encourage the entry of Russia into the region, either through the forging of an alliance, or by direct military action. The situation was complex. Britain and France conspired with Israel, and all three planned a coordinated attack on Egypt. The Cold War alliance structure suggested that the United States should have sided with these three powers, all friends of the United States. Yet, to do so likely would lead the Egyptians to call on Arab countries to enter the fray against Israeli aggression, and to invite the Soviets to support the Arabs against western imperialism.

Ultimately, the United States utilized the power of dollar diplomacy and international organizations to influence the outcome of the Suez crisis. Behind-the-scenes negotiating occurred throughout 1956, amid Eisenhower's reelection campaign. Despite the advice of some members of his campaign team, Eisenhower set aside domestic "special interests" in his handling of the Middle East crises that year. Despite their best efforts, American diplomats could not get cooperation from the British, French, or Israelis. All put their militaries into action against Egypt in October. Eisenhower harshly criticized the actions, calling on Americans and the world to enforce international law. "There can be no peace—without law," Eisenhower instructed Americans in a national television address. "And there can be no law—if we were to invoke one code of international conduct for those who oppose us—and another for our friends."[2] The threat of Russian intervention finally brought a conclusion to the crisis. Nasser appealed to the Soviets for assistance, and the Russians notified Paris and London of their willingness to aid the Egyptians. Fearing this, and having underestimated Eisenhower's resolve to stay out of the affair, the British and the French decided to pull back from their invasion of Egypt, without having repossessed the canal. The Israelis followed suit, withdrawing their troops from the Sinai peninsula, and a United Nations peacekeeping force arrived in the Sinai.

Although the threat of Soviet intervention had put an end to a crisis in which even the United States could not influence its own allies, the specter of strengthened Soviet ties with Egypt and other nations in the Middle East was not comforting to Americans—the "American national interest" in the region was not secure. Moreover, the Soviets had looked with great disfavor on what the Soviet government called the "colonist" behavior of the United States in the region. Consequently, in January 1957 Eisenhower asked the Congress for presidential powers that would become known as the Eisenhower Doctrine, which would give the president the authority to dispatch troops to the Middle East in the case of armed aggression by a country influenced by international communism. The president could only act, however, if threatened countries requested such assistance, and if the threat was an external one, not a civil concern. Although there was little serious domestic opposition to the new "doctrine" in American foreign policy, the Soviets issued a terse response to the promulgation of the Eisenhower Doctrine, and warned that the Soviet Union would not allow undue American influence in the region. Nonetheless, Congress put up little resistance to passage of the Eisenhower Doctrine, and, within a year, Eisenhower used the Doctrine to justify the deployment of Marines to help stabilize a volatile situation in Lebanon.

Unrest arose in Lebanon in the mid-1950s in the wake of the Suez crisis, with Nasser's emergence as the leader of the Arab world, and following the creation of the United Arab Republic (UAR), a union between Egypt, Yemen, and Syria that placed Lebanon in a awkward political and geographic position. These external developments added to the already tenuous balancing act that Lebanese politicians had to perform in order to maintain stability in a country where the population included substantial populations of both Christians, who were in the majority and held all of the most important government positions, and Muslims. Tensions between these populations mounted as Muslims in Lebanon favored Nasser and his pan-Arab movement, while Christians, fearing that Lebanon might be engulfed by the UAR, believed that a friendly relationship with the West was the only hope for continued Lebanese independence and even autonomy.

After a presidential election in Lebanon in 1957 in which the incumbent, Camille Shamun, won a sizable majority, violence erupted. Muslims who opposed the Christian Shamun protested that the election was corrupt. Confident that his Islamic agitators were receiving money and direction from Syria, Shamun called for help from the Western powers to put down the riots around the election. A cool-headed and pragmatic Eisenhower preferred to let the situation play itself out. The intensity of the situation was heightened in July 1958, when the royal government of Iraq succumbed to a coup d'etat, which included the murder of the royal family and the Prime Minister and brought the Baath Party of Saddam Hussein to power. Opponents of Shamun euphorically proclaimed that he would be the next Arab leader to suffer a similar fate. Fearing that Syria would invade Lebanon to take advantage of the internal instability, Shamun again called for U.S. assistance, invoking the terms of the Eisenhower Doctrine. Shamun argued that Lebanon was in fact threatened by international communism, as represented by Syrian aid to Lebanese Muslims, because Syria had itself received military assistance from the Soviet Union.

Although the situation did not clearly suggest the use of the Eisenhower Doctrine, the President nonetheless sent American Marines to Lebanon, although these forces played a minimal role in the Lebanese civil war. Not only concerned about stability and local American concerns in the Middle East, Eisenhower also worried that if the United States did not respond to the Lebanese call for assistance under the newly promulgated Eisenhower Doctrine, the world would see that policy as impotent. Eisenhower and his foreign policy team thought that American action in Lebanon was needed to reassure allies in the region, such as Turkey and Iran, and display American resolve to the Soviet Union and its Arab sympathizers.

The Marines were gone within months, as the dispute found its way to the United Nations, which agreed to a resolution whereby Arab nations pledged noninterference in the internal affairs of their neighbors. The resolutions also called for the withdrawal of Western troops from the Middle East (Britain had sent its own troops to Jordan to protect that country from foreign invasion). Although the deployment of U.S. troops to Lebanon was thus largely symbolic in 1958, it typified American foreign policy in the Cold War, which defined "American national interest" broadly and often without regional considerations. In an election-year speech to the Zionists of America Convention, then candidate John F. Kennedy would cite the Eisenhower Doctrine as a failure that encouraged Middle Eastern nations to think that America's only interest in their well-being stemmed from the nation's fear of communism. The American role in the Lebanese civil war of 1958, and the attempts of American statesmen to mediate disputes between Arab, Israeli, and Christian populations of the Middle East, marked only the beginning of a process that continues to the current day. As these three populations continue to square off against each other, disputing territory, political power, and cultural supremacy, Americans struggle to define their interests in the region and seek to play a constructive role in the region both in the name of American national security and in the name of peace.

NOTES

1. Abraham Ben-Ziv, *Decade of Transition: Eisenhower, Kennedy, and the Origins of the American-Israeli Alliance* (New York: Columbia University Press, 1998).

2. *Public Papers of the Presidents, 1956*, 1064–1066, cited in Herbert S. Parmet, *Eisenhower and the American Crusades* (New Brunswick, NJ: Transaction Publishers, 1991), 485.

PRESIDENT DWIGHT D. EISENHOWER, MESSAGE TO CONGRESS (JANUARY 5, 1957)

We have shown, so that none can doubt, our dedication to the principle that force shall not be used internationally for any aggressive purpose and that the integrity and independence of the nations of the Middle East should be inviolate. Seldom in history has a nation's dedication to principle been tested as severely as ours during recent weeks.

There is general recognition in the Middle East, as elsewhere, that the United States does not seek either political or economic domination over any other people. Our desire is a world environment of freedom, not servitude. On the other hand many, if not all, of the nations of the Middle East are aware of the danger that stems from International Communism and welcome close cooperation with the United States to realize for themselves the United National goals of independence, economic well being and spiritual growth. . . .

The proposed legislation is primarily designed to deal with the possibility of Communist aggression, direct and indirect. There is imperative need that any lack of power in the area should be made good, not only by external or alien force, but by the increased vigor and security of the independent nations of the areas.

Experience shows that indirect aggression rarely if ever succeeds where there is reasonable security against direct aggression; where the government possesses loyal security forces, and where economic conditions are such as not to make Communism seems an attractive alternative. . . . It will also be necessary for us to contribute economically to strengthen those countries, or groups of countries, which have governments manifestly dedicated to the preservation of independence and resistance to subversion. Such measures will provide the greatest insurance against Communist inroads. Words alone are not enough.

Let me refer again to the requested authority to employ the armed forces of the United States to assist to defend the territorial integrity and the political independence of any nation in the area against Communist armed aggression. Such authority would not be exercised except at the desire of the nation attacked. Beyond this it is my profound hope that this authority would never have to be exercised at all.

In the situation now existing, the greatest risk, as is often the case, is that ambitious despots may miscalculate. If power-hungry Communists should either falsely or correctly estimate that the Middle East is inadequately defended, they might be tempted to use open measures of armed attack. If so, that would start a chain of circumstances which would almost surely involve the United States in military action. I am convinced that the best insurance against this dangerous contingency is to make clear now our readiness to cooperate fully with our friends of the Middle East in ways consonant with the purposes and principles of the United Nations. I intend promptly to send a special mission to the Middle East to explain the cooperation we are prepared to give.

The policy which I outline involves certain burdens and indeed risks for the United States. . . . Those who covet the area will not like what is proposed.

Already they are distorting our purpose. However, before this Americans have seen our nation's vital interests and human freedom in jeopardy, and their fortitude and resolution have been equal to the crisis. . . . In those momentous periods of the past the President and Congress have united, without partisanship, to serve the vital interests of the United States and of the free world. The occasion has come for us to manifest again our national unity in support of freedom and to show our deep respect for the rights and independence of every nation—however great, however small. We seek, not violence, but peace. To this purpose we must now devote our energies, our determination, ourselves.

Source: *The Department of State Bulletin*, XXXVI, 917 (January 21, 1957), 83–87.

SOVIET RESPONSE TO PROMULGATION OF EISENHOWER DOCTRINE, TASS NEWS AGENCY (JANUARY 14, 1957)

In his message to Congress the President of the United States speaks of the sympathy which, he claims, the United States entertains for the Arab countries. Life, however, shows that in actual fact the American ruling circles are setting themselves obviously selfish aims in that area. . . .

At present, when a favorable situation has developed in the Middle East and real possibilities for consolidating peace and settling outstanding issues in that area have been created, the government of the United States has come forward with a programme which envisages flagrant interference by the United States in the affairs of the Arab countries, up to and including military intervention. The aggressive trend of this programme and its colonist nature with regard to the Arab countries are so obvious that this cannot be disguised by any nebulous phrases about the love for peace and the concern claimed to be shown by the United States for the Middle East countries. . . .

Seeking to cover up gross intervention in the internal affairs of the Middle East countries and their aggressive policy with regard to these countries, the United States ruling circles resort to inventions about a threat to the Arab countries emanating from the Soviet Union. These slanderous assertions will deceive no one. The peoples of the Middle East have not forgotten that the Soviet Union has always defended the self-determination of peoples, the gaining and consolidating of their national independence. They have learned from experience that in relations with all countries the Soviet Union steadfastly pursues the policy of equality and non-interference in internal affairs. . . .

Authoritative Soviet circles hold that the steps with regard to the Middle East area outlined by the United States government, which envisage the possibility of employing United States armed forces in that area, might lead to dangerous consequences, the responsibility for which will rest entirely with the United States government.

Source: Soviet News, 354 (January 14, 1957), 33–34, in *Internet Modern History Sourcebook*, ed. Paul Halsall, Fordham University, <http://www.fordham.edu/halsall/mod/1957tass-eisenhower.html>

EISENHOWER DOCTRINE, CRITICISM BY JOHN F. KENNEDY (AUGUST 26, 1960)

When I talked with Prime Minister Ben-Gurion on his most recent visit to this country, he told me of dangerous signs of unrest beneath the deceptive quiet that has fallen over the Middle East. For there is no peace in that region today—only an embittered truce between renewed alarms.

American intervention, on the other hand, will not now be easy for the record is not one to which we can point with pride:

...

The series of incredible American blunders which led to the Suez crisis of 1956, events in which the role of our Government has never been fully explained;

The so-called Eisenhower doctrine, now repudiated by some of the very nations which accepted our aid, and the cause even at that time of widespread antagonism from Middle Eastern leaders who felt we were cynically trying to use them for our own cold war ends;

And, in general, a deterioration in our relations with all Middle Eastern nations, primarily because neither Israel nor the Arabs knew exactly what to expect from us. At times it must have appeared to many in the area that the shortest route to Washington was through Moscow. At times it must have appeared that champions of democracy and freedom were being punished for their virtues, by being taken for granted by a neglectful administration that suddenly showed concern only when it was displeased by their conduct.

Source: Speech by Senator John F. Kennedy, Zionists of America Convention, Statler Hilton Hotel, New York, August 26, 1960, <http://www.jfklink.com/speeches/jfk/aug60/jfk260860_zionists.html>

RECOMMENDED READINGS

Cummings, Bruce. *The Origins of the Korean War*. Princeton: Princeton University Press, 1990.

Gleijeses, Piero. *Shattered Hope: The Guatemalan Revolution and the United States, 1944–1954*. Princeton: Princeton University Press, 1991.

Greenstein, Fred I. *The Hidden-Hand Presidency: Eisenhower as Leader*. New York: Basic Books, 1982.

Halberstam, David *The Fifties*. Ballantine Books, 1994.

———. *John Foster Dulles and the Diplomacy of the Cold War*. Princeton: Princeton University Press, 1990.

Lewis, Tom. *Divided Highways: Building the Interstate Highways, Transforming American Life*. New York: Viking, 1997.

Lowe, Peter. *The Korean War*. New York: St. Martin's Press, 2000.

Office of the Chief of Military History. "The Army and the New Look," *American Military History*. Chapter 26. Washington, DC: Center of Military History, 198. <http://www.army.mil/cmh-pg/books/amh/AMH-26.htm>

Rabe, Stephen *Eisenhower and Latin America: The Foreign Policy of Anticommunism*. Chapel Hill: University of North Carolina Press, 1988.

Seely, Bruce E. *Building the American Highway System: Engineers as Policy Makers*. Philadelphia: Temple University Press, 1987.

Vestel, Theodoa *The Eisenhower Court and Civil Liberties*. New York: Praeger, 2002.

Yaqub, Salim *Containing Arab Nationalism: The Eisenhower Doctrine and the Middle East*. Chapel Hill: University of North Carolina Press, 2004.

2

JOHN FITZGERALD KENNEDY

(1961–1963)

INTRODUCTION

The election of 1960 was one of the closest presidential contests in American history. Senator John F. Kennedy of Massachusetts defeated Vice President Richard Nixon of California by a mere two-tenths of 1 percent of the popular vote. Although Kennedy won the Electoral College more definitively, Nixon won a greater number of states. Neither candidate proposed radical reforms nor exposed fatal flaws in his opponent. The election is famous as the first presidential election to incorporate televised debates between the candidates. Both candidates appealed to the center on issues related to the economy, foreign policy, and civil rights. Given such relative consensus, some historians argue that Nixon's unimpressive physical appearance in the first of the TV debates could well have lost him the election. Nixon was ill, refused to wear makeup, and perspired profusely during the debate, while the younger, more handsome Kennedy, who concealed most of his own health problems, appeared dapper, composed, and vigorous.

Although Eisenhower almost surely would have been reelected had he been the Republican candidate, Nixon did not necessarily represent a continuation of the 1950s for many Americans. He promised a more activist role as president than his predecessor had employed and appeared more positive on many domestic issues than had Eisenhower. However, Nixon had earned a more negative reputation dating as far back as his role on the House Un-American Activities Committee in the 1940s, where he served as the main protagonist in the "uncovering" of "Un-American" behaviors, ruthlessly berating witnesses before the committee with questions about their personal and professional lives.

Many viewed him as duplicitous and untrustworthy, an image that ultimately earned him the nickname "Tricky Dick."

Like many of politicians of the day, both Nixon and Kennedy were Cold Warriors. As in the election of 1952, the election of 1960 put the track record of the incumbent party on foreign policy to the test. Kennedy consistently criticized the Eisenhower Administration for allowing a "missile gap" to develop between the Soviet Union and the United States. Even though Kennedy did not chastise Eisenhower for "losing Cuba," as Eisenhower had lambasted Truman during the campaign of 1952 for "losing China," he discussed and supported an invasion of Cuba in order to remove Fidel Castro, the communist leader who assumed power on the island in 1959.

THE NEW FRONTIER

Ordinary Americans may have been more energized by the Kennedy victory in 1960 than were most intellectuals and politicians. Democrats lamented their loss of twenty seats in the House of Representatives that accompanied Kennedy's presidential win, and Republicans questioned whether Kennedy would be able to accomplish much. Kennedy's centrist campaign had hardly broached tough topics like civil rights, and offered little of substance during the campaign that predicted dramatic change. Still, the new president inspired a great many Americans. The youngest person ever elected to the American presidency, Kennedy, and his beautiful young wife, Jacqueline (Jackie), exuded charm and style. Kennedy's enthusiasm and idealism brought unprecedented energy and optimism to America. Moreover, he was confident. "Sure it's big job," he was quoted as saying after his election to the presidency, "but I don't know of anybody who can do it better than I can." Kennedy spoke of a "New Frontier" and brought with him to the presidency "new frontiersmen," young academics largely from the Ivy League and New England to help him lead America through the 1960s and expand and spread American idealism across the globe. Not withstanding the way in which Kennedy's affluence and elite education enhanced the image of the presidency, Kennedy connected with Americans more intimately than his two immediate predecessors. Kennedy televised his press conferences and talked about reform in the areas more immediate to common people than missiles and monetary policy. Kennedy spoke of tax reform to ignite economic recovery, and of education, wages, women's rights, health care, and training for workers in depressed regions of the country. In early 1961, optimism reigned in America, Kennedy enjoyed great popular support, and many Americans believed they were, in fact, on the verge of a "New Frontier."

In articulating the ideal of the New Frontier, Kennedy tapped into an idea popular since historian Frederick Jackson Turner promulgated his "frontier thesis" in 1893, contending that the frontier experience was central to American culture. From the beginning, frontiers had confronted American life in Appalachia, in the Northwest, and in the West, and the task of taming the frontier and bringing to it the American way of life had both rallied citizens throughout their history and shaped their culture. Efforts on the frontier required and epitomized those values Americans had long held dear—hard work, self-reliance, perseverance, and to a certain degree, egalitarianism. Moreover, Americans found the idea of conquering the frontier to be appealing. Thus, later historians explained, the American occupation of the Philippines, American economic imperialism, Charles Lindbergh's solo flight across the Atlantic, and America's later dominance in the Western world drew on the American desire for a frontier experience. Kennedy redefined the frontier both by extending it to include new regions of the world and by finding new frontiers at home. Kennedy suggested that just as Americans had brought the wilds of the West under control, so too they could apply science, hard work, and dedication to the problems of poverty at home and abroad. Similarly, just as American military and economic might had created allies out of enemies in Asia and Latin America, so too Americans could win the struggle against communism in the "frontiers" of Southeast Asia and Cuba. Americans could also combine their work ethic and determination with their superior technical knowledge and military supplies to conquer the newest frontier of all, outer space.

DOMESTIC POLICIES

Although the new president outlined a domestic agenda, foreign policy occupied Kennedy's attention from the outset, and his administration was not particularly successful in the domestic sphere. Kennedy proved unable to work effectively with Congress, even with the help of his vice president, Lyndon Johnson, whom Kennedy had partly selected as his running mate for his ability to cut deals and push bills through the legislative body. Few of Kennedy's major proposals for domestic policy made it successfully through the Congress. Kennedy was both ineffective and uninterested in domestic policy. He once told Nixon that a president's real concern was foreign affairs rather than more petty issues like the minimum wage. Furthermore, despite his calls for reforms in the tax code to benefit American corporations, Kennedy ran afoul of the American business community when he tried to bully the six American steel companies into holding steady on steel prices in April 1962. In that instance, concerned about inflation (and realizing a similar concern from powerful congressional leaders, like the anti-inflationist Democrat, Tennessee Senator Albert Gore, Sr.), Kennedy appealed to the major American steel companies not to increase the price of steel when renegotiating wages and benefits with the unions. Having held prices steady for four years while wages increased, the steel companies felt compelled to raise steel prices in order to maintain profits and recoup profits lost during the 1961 recession. Furious over the situation, Kennedy told U.S. Steel CEO that he had "double-crossed" the President, and quickly turned loose the Justice Department and Federal Trade Commission to investigate the six major steel companies that had announced price increases for antitrust violations. Ultimately, the steel companies rescinded their price increases, but the episode did not ingratiate the new president with the nation's business leaders.

THE COLD WAR: CUBA AND GERMANY

Despite the difficulties Kennedy faced in the domestic sphere, historians have only recently uncovered the degree to which Kennedy's desire to trump the Soviets in the Cold War shaped and set the agenda for his presidency with respect to both foreign and domestic policy. Indeed, the new president faced a plethora of foreign policy crises that served to divert his attention further from the domestic sphere. Lawrence Freedman has observed that throughout his presidency Kennedy faced a "familiar predicament" of being "torn between dismay over being 'humiliated' by a communist victory and alarm at the prospect of getting dragged into an unwinnable war."[1]

The problem of Communist Cuba confronted the Kennedy team immediately. Not only did Cuba's proximity to the United States make the situation crucial, but Eisenhower told Kennedy during the transition that the CIA was preparing for an invasion of the island by Cuban exiles. Thus, Kennedy had to come to terms with his hard-line stance on Cuba during the presidential campaign and decide whether or not to proceed with the operation. Only three months after Kennedy took office, he proceeded with the invasion at the Bay of Pigs. It proved disastrous, but Kennedy overcame both the botched attempt to land Cuban exiles on the shores of Cuba and the mismanagement of the public relations aspects of the invasion, to take on the Soviets directly in Germany in the summer of 1961. As in Cuba, Kennedy inherited a crisis situation in Berlin, where the Soviet and American militaries were squaring off and preparing none too cautiously for war. Mounting pressure on the post war arrangement in Europe threatened peace and stability in the region. Kennedy managed the situation, settling for a wall rather than war. Although war hawks criticized him for backing down to the Soviets, he emerged from the Berlin crisis in June 1961 with a renewed sense of credibility both at home and abroad. In Berlin the President saved face, and put the Bay of Pigs fiasco behind him.

The Soviets tested Kennedy again in October of 1962, this time using Cuba rather than Germany as the theater. As he had been in Berlin a year earlier,

Kennedy was again between a rock and a hard place when images from American surveillance planes revealed the presence in Cuba of Soviet nuclear missiles that would soon be able to strike the United States. During the famous "thirteen days" Kennedy and his advisors dealt with the prospects of projecting an American image of strength and will and the consequences of nuclear war. Again, aided by some behind-the-scenes negotiating by his brother Robert, the Attorney General, and Soviet diplomats, Kennedy emerged from the crisis with increased popular support for having again averted nuclear war while at the same time asserting the strength and power of the United States.

OTHER AREAS OF THE WORLD

Events in Cuba and Berlin certainly highlighted the foreign policy of the Kennedy years. Yet, Kennedy's foreign policy team devoted considerable attention to other parts of the world as well. The CIA worked in cahoots in Zaire, the former Belgian Congo, with Joseph Mobutu (Mobutu Sese Seko) to destabilize the newly independent nation and install a government sympathetic to the national security interests of the United States, even though Mobutu's regime was less sympathetic to American ideals of democracy than other, less powerful Congoese leaders would have been. In Southeast Asia, Kennedy escalated American financial and military support for the Diem regime in South Vietnam, and in Laos, Americans meddled in a civil conflict that eventually resulted in the formation of a "neutral government" there. The tenuous nature of that regime allowed both the Americans and the Vietnamese to manipulate that government as they struggled across the border.

In other regions of the world, Kennedy's foreign policy included less overt, but still powerful tactics. Kennedy pushed for the Alliance for Progress, aid program it attempted to improve relations between the United States and Latin America. It proposed to join Americans and Latin Americans in efforts to increase literacy, housing development, land reform, and other social and economic development measures at a cost of $20 billion over ten years. Similarly, the Peace Corps sent young Americans across the globe to promote education, sanitation, and other social and economic programs in the underdeveloped world. Although these initiatives endeavored to fulfill humanitarian interests, they cannot be separated from the prevailing anticommunist sentiment in the Kennedy administration and in America generally. Policymakers were happy to have their programs yield humanitarian results like improved literacy in Latin America, or public health in Africa. However, the inspiration for these efforts was not purely humanitarian. Rather, the Kennedy team viewed economic and social development in the Third World as important components in the forging of alliances and the fostering of stability.

Particularly in Latin America and in Africa, where drastic disparities in the distribution of wealth led to political instability, American foreign policy-makers believed that American economic and social assistance was equally as important as military aid in order to keep developing nations from choosing to look to the Soviet Union or other communist nations, like Cuba or Czechoslovakia, for help in growing their economies and improving the quality of life.

SUMMARY

Although Kennedy proved fairly successful in getting Congress to approve his requests for spending on defense and national security, his record on domestic policy is less impressive. Somewhat naïve about working with Congress when he took office, Kennedy figured large Democratic majorities in both houses would allow for the smooth sailing of his domestic agenda. However, many of those Democrats were southern conservatives, who did not sympathize with Kennedy's New England brand of liberalism. Kennedy had not been a particularly capable or popular congressman, and thus veteran Democrats did not respond as well as they might have to Kennedy as president. Moreover, Lyndon Johnson, who had been the Democratic leader in the Congress since the mid-1950s, and who was known for his skill in moving bills through the legislative body, was now with Kennedy in the White House. His colleagues like Mike Mansfield (D-MT), the new Democratic congressional leader, simply did not have Johnson's leadership ability.

During the "honeymoon" period of Kennedy's first year in office, the new president got congressional approval for a large housing bill, an expansion of the minimum wage, and more funding for federal highways. Supporters perceived housing and minimum wage legislation, as well as area redevelopment programs (federal government efforts to revitalize depressed areas of the country and integrate these regions into the national economy), as stimuli to help pull the nation out of a minor recession. Congress did not respond as positively to the big-ticket items that followed, such as health care and education. Congress also struck down Kennedy requests for legislation in his first year on farm aid, tax reform, and protecting natural resources. In fact, many of Kennedy's largest requests of Congress on domestic issues never even made it to the floor of the Congress for votes. Moreover, once settled into office, Kennedy moved more toward the center, favoring reductions in the tax rates rather than less dramatic tax reforms, and after the steel crisis in April 1962, working more closely with business leaders. He also became less interested in domestic policy both as he found it more difficult to get cooperation from Congress and as events in foreign policy consumed more of his attention.

NOTE

1. Lawrence Freedman, *Kennedy's Wars: Berlin, Cuba, Laos, and Vietnam* (New York: Oxford University Press, 2000), 297.

THE ALLIANCE FOR PROGRESS

In addition to bringing idealism to America's domestic agenda, John Kennedy assumed the presidency with an ambitious and optimistic outlook for foreign policy. Although several crises confronted Kennedy as president, most notably the failure of the Bay of Pigs invasion, the Berlin crisis, and the Cuban Missile crisis, Kennedy also inaugurated a number of his own initiatives in foreign affairs. His two most notable programs, the Peace Corps and the Alliance for Progress, both exemplify the idealism of the Kennedy Administration, appropriately dubbed as Camelot, and the underlying Cold War motives behind many of Kennedy's actions as president.

Although historians have largely credited Kennedy for proposing massive aid for Latin America under the Alliance for Progress, the origins of the program are really to be found in the Social Progress Trust Fund and the Inter-American Development bank. Eisenhower did not have a great interest in Latin America, but he did approve a $500 million aid program for the region in 1958, and financing for a development bank for the region was secured during his administration. After the Cuban revolution and the entrenchment of Fidel Castro in Cuba by 1960, Latin America became a focal point of U.S. foreign policy. Castro's effort to spread his revolution by exporting agents, arms, and ideology struck fear in the hearts of Americans, and many began to think that this region needed more than token assistance. Those concerned with the situation throughout the Americas determined that economic and social development, rather than military assistance, was the best way to combat the efforts of the Cuban government. Thus, humanitarian aid and economic assistance during the Cold War had a double purpose. Undoubtedly, many Americans, Peace Corps volunteers and those who participated in sister relationships between U.S. states and foreign countries (i.e., the California-Chile program), were genuinely interested in helping others improve their standard of living and quality of life. However, policymakers during the period also saw programs such as the Alliance for Progress, the Peace Corps, and development grants as part of the strategic conduct of foreign policy during the Cold War. With newly independent and developing nations around the world making choices about the kinds of economic and political systems they would implement, the United States and Soviet Union scrambled to make friends and allies in these regions through security alliances and development partnerships. "The situation in Cuba," observed Undersecretary of State

C. Douglas Dillon, "is a dramatic example of what happens when social progress is not keeping up in pace with general economic development."[1] Both the concern about democracy in Latin America and the emphasis on social and economic development carried over from the Eisenhower Administration to the Kennedy team. The Alliance for Progress, which sought to pick up the pace of social progress in Latin America, is perhaps the best example of the kind of Cold War foreign policy that had both a humanitarian and a strategic objective. Significantly, the Charter of the Alliance specifically outlined not only social and economic development goals for the program but the promotion and preservation of democratic governments as well.

The Alliance for Progress was one of the largest and most ambitious foreign policy packages in the history of American statecraft. Kennedy included Latin America in the "New Frontier." Together with all of the noncommunist nations in Latin America, American policymakers developed a program of mutual assistance and outlined a series of far-reaching, if not always realistic, goals for hemispheric development and cooperation. The American government pledged $20 billion to the program, $10 billion from the government itself and another $10 billion from the private sector. Among other objectives, the Charter of the Alliance included plans for full-scale agrarian reform throughout the region; an average 2.5 percent annual economic growth rate; the eradication of illiteracy; the building of houses, schools, hospitals, and infrastructure across Latin America; and improvements in sanitation and public health. Kennedy hoped to achieve all these goals by the end of the decade. Member states signed the Charter of the Alliance in April of 1961 at a Hemispheric Conference in Punta del Este, Uruguay, amid much euphoria and hope. In a declaration laced with American Cold War rhetoric, Kennedy proclaimed that the Alliance for Progress would not only heal wounds and misunderstandings of the past, but that it would also "demonstrate to the entire world that man's aspiration for economic progress and social justice can best be achieved by free men and women working within a framework of democratic institutions."[2]

Most Americans in the early 1960s were game for just about anything aimed at keeping communism out of the hemisphere so relatively few opposed the Alliance, but some did express concern over some of its aspects. Naturally, the question of financing arose. Although he supported the Alliance, Senator Leverette Saltonstall (R-MA) identified a number of problems, including "the question of self-help among our friends in Latin America, the funds that should be appropriated ... for that purpose, and the extent of the participation of the governments involved."[3] Others, such as Kennedy advisor Arthur Schlesinger, Jr., worried not about the Alliance itself, but about the administration of the program and the philosophy behind it on the part of American policymakers. Schlesinger feared that Americans would see the program as a fix-all effort focused on throwing money at the problems in Latin America. Schlesinger believed Latin America's problems extended beyond the need for capital, and he argued both that the public presentation of the program and the administration of the program should be true to the promulgations of President Kennedy and to the Charter of Punta del Este. Similarly, Undersecretary of State Chester Bowles feared that the Alliance was so overly "dedicated to financial and technical measures" that the more crucial "human elements [would be] lost in the shuffle." Finally, there were those who supported the Alliance but argued that the Alliance alone was not sound economic policy because it did not address directly the question of communism in Cuba. Representative Armistead Seldon (D-AL), the Chairman of the House Inter-American Affairs Subcommittee on Foreign Affairs, criticized Kennedy's Latin America policy for being "one of drift rather than drive, of response rather than initiative." Seldon, along with Representatives. Dante Fascell and Paul Rogers (both D-FL), decried the Administration's lack of action against Cuba and railed against the continuation of American trade with Cuba, arguing that Cuba posed a imminent threat to the United States and was a scourge that the United States should deal with immediately, either in conjunction with nations of the hemisphere, or single-handedly.[4]

Even among opponents, few would have predicted at the time that the initiative would have yielded so few results ten years later. There were some positive results. For example, the Chilean government, especially after 1965, accomplished substantial agrarian reform. Some schools, hospitals, and airports had been constructed. Colombia experienced an export boom and a temporary abatement of the internecine violence that had plagued the country since the nineteenth century. But by and large, the region did not experience the rapid and profound transformation that policymakers had envisioned. By decade's end, only $4.6 billion of the $20 billion projected in the Alliance charts in 1961 had been spent in countries in Latin America. U.S. government officials had been unable to mobilize the business community behind the effort, and by mid-decade the U.S. government had redirected its attention and resources from Latin America to Vietnam. In 1970 a small number of wealthy families still controlled most of the land in Latin America, and few countries there enjoyed sustained economic growth and social progress. Conservative forces across the region had resisted and frustrated reform efforts. Efforts to promote change clashed with efforts to stymie reform and led to perhaps the most significant disappointment of the Alliance, at least for many who had had a role in the origins of the initiative. The effort to foster democracy in Latin America had failed. By 1969, military dictatorships had replaced democratic governments in Argentina, Brazil, Peru, Ecuador, Guatemala, Honduras, and the Dominican Republic, Chile was on the verge of electing (albeit democratically) a socialist president whom a military coup d'etat toppled three years later, and Nicaragua, Haiti, and Paraguay remained under the dictatorships under which they had entered the decade. Thus, 1970 was not a year to celebrate the culmination of the ten-year Alliance but a time to reconsider the nature of U.S. policy toward the region.

NOTES

1. Cited in Rabe, *Eisenhower and Latin America: The Foreign Policy of Anti-communism* (Chapel Hill: University of North Carolina Press, 1988), 141.
2. Cited in Edward M. Kennedy, forward to *The Alliance for Progress: A Retrospective*, ed. L. Ronald Scheman (New York: Praeger, 1988), xv.
3. *Congressional Record*, Vol. 107, Pt. 3, 3858.
4. *Congressional Record*, Vol. 107, Pt. 9, 11914–11916.

PRESIDENT JOHN F. KENNEDY, ADDRESS TO MEMBERS OF CONGRESS AND DIPLOMATIC CORPS OF LATIN AMERICAN REPUBLICS (MARCH 13, 1961)

We meet together as firm and ancient friends, united by history and experience and by our determination to advance the value of American civilization. For this New World of ours is not a mere accident of geography. Our continents are bound together by a common history, the endless exploration of new frontiers. Our nations are the product of a common struggle, the revolt from colonial rule. And our people share a common heritage, the quest for the dignity and the freedom of man....

As a citizen of the United States let me be the first to admit that we North Americans have not always grasped the significance of this common mission, just as it is also true that many in your own countries have not fully understood the urgency to the need to lift people from poverty and ignorance and despair. But we must turn from these mistakes—from the failures and the misunderstandings of the past not to a future full of peril, but bright with hope.

Throughout Latin America, a continent rich in resources and in the spiritual and cultural achievements of its people, millions of men and women suffer the daily degradations of poverty and hunger. They lack decent shelter or protection from disease. Their children are deprived of the education or the jobs which are the gateway to a better life. And each day the problems grow more urgent. Population growth is outpacing economic growth—low living standards are further endangered and discontent—the discontent of a people who know that abundance and the tools of progress are at last within their reach—that discontent is growing. In the words of [former Costa Rican president] Jose Figueres, "once dormant peoples are struggling upward toward the sun, toward a better life."

If we are to meet a problem so staggering in its dimensions, our approach must itself be equally bold—an approach consistent with the majestic concept of Operation Pan America. Therefore I have called on all people of the hemisphere to join in a new Alliance for Progress—Alianza para Progreso—a vast cooperative effort, unparalleled in magnitude and nobility of purpose, to satisfy the basic needs of the American people for homes, work and land, health and schools—techo, trabajo y tierra, sauld y escula.

First, I propose that the American Republics begin on a vast new Ten Year Plan for the Americas, a plan to transform the 1960's into a historic decade of democratic progress.

These 10 years will be the years of maximum progress—maximum effort, the years when the greatest obstacles must be overcome, the years when the need for assistance will be the greatest.

And if we are successful, if our effort is bold enough and determined enough, then the close of this decade will mark the beginning of a new era in the American experience. The living standards of every American family will be on the rise, basic education will be available to all, hunger will be a forgotten experience, the need for massive outside help will have passed, most nations will have entered a period of self-sustaining growth, and though there will be still much to do, every American Republic will be the master of its own revolution and its own hope and progress.

Let me stress that only the most determined efforts of the American nations themselves can bring success to this effort. They, and they alone, can mobilize their resources, enlist the energies of their people, and modify their social patterns so that all, and not just a privileged few, share in the fruits of growth. If this effort is made, then outside assistance will give vital impetus to progress; without it, no amount of help will advance the welfare of the people.

Thus if the countries of Latin America are ready to do their part, and I am sure they are, then I believe that United States, for its part, should help provide resources of a scope and magnitude sufficient to make this bold development plan a success—just as we helped to provide, against equal odds nearly, the resources adequate to help rebuild the economics of Western Europe. For only an effort of towering dimensions can ensure fulfillment of our plan for a decade of progress....

To achieve this goal, political freedom must accompany material progress. Our Alliance for Progress is an alliance of free governments, and it must work to eliminate tyranny from a hemisphere in which it has no rightful place. Therefore let us express our special friendship to the people of Cuba and the Dominican Republic—and the hope that they will soon rejoin, the society of free men, uniting with us in common effort....

And so I say to the men and women of the Americas—to the campesino in the fields, to the obrero in the cities, to the estudiante in the schools—prepare your mind and heart for the task ahead—call forth your strength and let each devote his energies to the betterment of all, so that your children and our children in this hemisphere can find an ever richer and a freer life.

Let us once again transform the American continent into a vast crucible of revolutionary ideas and efforts—a tribute to the power of the creative energies of free men and women—an example to all the world that liberty and progress walk hand in hand. Let us once again awaken our American revolution until it guides the struggle of people everywhere—not with an imperialism of force or fear—but the rule of courage and freedom and hope for the future of man.

Source: John F. Kennedy Presidential Library, <http://www.cs.umb.edu/jfklibrary/jfk_alliance_for_progress.html>

MEMORANDUM FROM UNDERSECRETARY OF STATE, CHESTER BOWLES, TO SECRETARY OF STATE RUSK (JULY 25, 1961)

I am concerned lest the momentum generated by the Act of Bogota and the Alliance for Progress be dissipated by a conference at Montevideo which is so heavily dedicated to financial and technical measures that the human element gets lost in the shuffle.

Expectations are very high in Latin America. Yet if the primary test of the Alliance's success is to be the number of dollars that are made available by the U.S.A. we may end up with every country dissatisfied with its share of our necessarily limited funds.

Since our financial capabilities are not inexhaustible, we must seek constantly to identify the United States with other less costly aspects of the process of economic and social change which are of equal or even greater importance to the development of prosperous, stable, democratic societies.

It seems to me, speaking in the most general terms, that we can identify three major elements in the development complex where we can be most effective.

The first of these is providing resources for economic growth. We have many instruments for doing this, most of which are expensive. Moreover, massive investments in infrastructure and industrial facilities, essential though we know them to be, may in fact create additional tensions within a society by failing to meet immediate consumer expectations and by increasing the disparity between the wealthy and the poor.

Greater emphasis, therefore, should be applied to bringing about basic reforms in the distribution of wealth. This means promoting social justice through changes in tax systems, land tenure patterns, credit arrangements, which in addition to their obvious political implications, can help release domestic resources and talents for more productive utilization.

For the United States this is a dramatic, necessary and yet virtually costless exercise. Moreover, such reforms will make sense to the American people because they stem from such well-accepted convictions as to the proper nature of society as that a man should own his land and home and that the burden of taxation should be distributed on the basis of ability to pay. Sometimes there are suggestions that pushing for social reform abroad means espousing some "radical," un-American doctrine; in fact quite the opposite is true.

A third area where we can assist, also at relatively little financial expense, is in promoting the welfare of the rural areas, where 70 percent of the people of Latin America live. An integrated approach to rural poverty through extension services, cooperatives, land reform, self-help schools, roads, and so forth, can yield an enormous return not only in better living conditions but in the immeasurable elements of hope and self respect which are the strongest bulwarks against Castro-Communism. Yet for all of Northeast Brazil, probably the most poverty-stricken part of Latin America, the dollar needs are estimated at only $76 million over the next five years.

Integration, it seems to me, must be the essential element of our efforts to stimulate rural development not only in Latin America but throughout the underdeveloped world. . . .

I hope that our delegation to Montevideo will bear constantly in mind these three inter-related aspects of United States involvement in Latin American economic and social progress and will lose no opportunity to reemphasize our concern with the last two elements as well as the first. It will help re-inspire many of our Latin American friends as well as reassure our own citizens that "foreign aid" need not consist solely of an ever-increasing stream of dollars.

Source: *Foreign Relations Series of the United States, 1961–1963*, Vol. XII, *American Republics*, 44–45.

THE PEACE CORPS

Kennedy's creation of the Alliance for Progress, and his formation of the Peace Corps soon after, exemplify the contradictions of the Kennedy presidency and of American life in the 1960s. Both programs projected a sense of altruism as America entered into partnerships with less-developed countries to stimulate economic development and initiate political, social, and cultural improvements. With both programs, American policymakers in the early 1960s sought to win friends for the United States by joining the energies, skills, and resources of Americans with those of the peoples of the Third World in an attempt to transform the quality of life, as one historian has written, by "making them like us." On the surface, the Alliance and the Peace Corps did not focus on political or military issues, but rather on the standard of living of the world's people.

This was particularly true in the case of the Peace Corps, which drew on the volunteer spirit of Americans, rather than the bureaucrats and technocrats integral to the operation of the Alliance. The Peace Corps employed the energies and good intentions of thousands of young Americans, who deployed across the globe, from Ghana in West Africa to Micronesia in the South Pacific, in the name of bringing improved health care, education, sanitation, and pure drinking water to developing regions of the world. According to its first director, Sargent Shriver, the purpose of the Peace Corps was to help people help themselves. Yet, the same people who had put the Alliance for Progress into action designed the Peace Corps, and as in the case of the Alliance, their designs for the Peace Corps were twofold. The "best and the brightest" clearly had a sincere interest in improving the quality of life for the millions who resided in or near poverty in Latin America, Africa, Asia, and the Pacific. As they worked to "develop" a "new frontier" at home, they hoped, through the Peace Corps, to civilize "new frontiers" all over the world. Just as domestic consensus and development were integral aspects of containment, so too containment informed the goals and objectives of the Peace Corps. Kennedy expressed this objective in his speech announcing his intent to create the Corps, which he delivered in San Francisco in November 1960 in conjunction with criticisms of perceived weaknesses in American foreign policy. He noted that Soviet doctors, engineers, and teachers were working across Asia and Africa and suggested that it would be essential for Americans to match this sort of Soviet activity in those areas of the world, in order to build "goodwill" and "peace." Thus, by bringing "development" to Africa, Latin America, and Asia, U.S. policymakers hoped also to counter the influence of the Soviets, and to win the support of the peoples of the Third World in the Cold War. By introducing the merits of capitalism and democracy as they worked for America, Peace Corps workers would convince the peoples of the less-developed world that these systems, not communism, would lead them to the standard of living and quality of life they desired.

Just as the designers of the Peace Corps accomplished two objectives with the program, so too the volunteers who implemented the programs of the Corps satisfy their own needs in a twofold way. Restive in this "age of consensus," young Americans in the early 1960s were looking for a way to bring meaning to their lives; it is no coincidence that Kennedy heavily promoted the idea of the Peace Corps during his presidential campaign at stump speeches on university campuses. At home, students supported Kennedy's idealism, and many joined Students for a Democratic Society and other such groups to protest the conservatism of their parents and other adults who, they thought, stifled creativity, progress, and harmony in American life. Many during the 1960s embraced challenging cultural developments, and expressed themselves, or sought to placate their search for meaning, through rock music, sex, drugs, eastern religions, and other "alternative" cultures. Likewise many joined the Peace Corps in order to bring the values and ideas of the civil rights movement, the "New Frontier," and later, the "Great Society" to those across the world who needed their help. According to Sargent Shriver, the first director of the Peace Corps, the Corps offered Americans "meaningful work worthy of free men."[1]

Just as the Corps helped young Americans find a sense of purpose and meaning in their lives, the Corps also offered a purpose for America foreign policy. In this way, the Peace Corps served to counter the image of the "ugly American" abroad with that of the beneficent American. Through the activities of the Peace Corps, people throughout the world would see America as racially tolerant, yearning to work with people of different races, ethnicities, and backgrounds. This might help to overcome the blatantly contradictory messages coming out of America in the early 1960s, pledging friendship and assistance to the newly independent countries of Africa but revealing deep-seated racial intolerance for blacks residing in the United States. In addition, Americans received language training so that they could communicate with their hosts in the vernacular. The first deployment of Peace Corps volunteers symbolized this effort when, upon arriving in Accra, the capital of Ghana, they promptly lined up on the airport tarmac and erupted in song, belting out the national anthem of Ghana in the native language, Twi.

Kennedy established the Peace Corps by executive order in early 1961, and appointed his brother-in-law, Sargent Shriver, to head the new organization. Named in part because of his "get things done" mentality, Shriver created an ambitious and massive program. By July of 1961, the Corps planned projects in Ghana, Tanzania, the Philippines, Chile, and St. Lucia. Young Americans responded enthusiastically, signing up in large numbers. By 1966, there were 15,000 Peace Corps volunteers working in 46 countries across the globe. Congress approved legislation authorizing the Peace Corps in September 1961, establishing for it the mission to "promote world peace and friendship." The Corps would work to carry out three main goals: to train workers to accommodate the development needs of host countries; to help promote a better relationship between Americans and the people of the host country; and to foster a better understanding of foreign peoples by Americans. Countries received the Corps enthusiastically, as evidenced by the large number of countries inviting the Corps to aid in village development, assist in modernizing agriculture, and participate in the education of future national leaders. Moreover, the Corps helped improve the image of the United States abroad. In his monumental tome on the Kennedy presidency, *A Thousand Days*, Kennedy advisor Arthur Schlesinger recalls that the foreign minister of Thailand told him that the Corps demonstrated that the ideas, and not just the economy and military, of the United States, were powerful.

While Kennedy was able to create the program on his own, he ran into some opposition when he approached Congress for money. Some members of Congress worried about the independence of the Peace Corps. Only after intense lobbying by Shriver and his aides did Congress authorize the Peace Corps as an autonomous agency. Others, notably and perhaps ironically, Senators. J. William Fulbright (D-Ark.) and Bourke Hickenlooper (R-Iowa), worried about the size and expense of the program. And then there were those who opposed the program outright, supportive of its intent, but concerned about its implementation and its consequences. Representative W.J. Bryan Dorn (R-SC) worried that Peace Corps volunteers would not receive proper training and would seem imperialistic by imposing American practices on foreign cultures. Senator Barry Goldwater (R-AZ), like Dorn, considered himself a "friend of the program" but feared that the haphazard creation of the program could lead it "to do more harm than good." Some of the nation's leading journalists weighed in with similar concerns. Earnest K. Lindley opined in *Newsweek* that "local difficulties may frustrate even the best people and the most useful projects," while Marquis Childs argued in the *Washington Post*: "Those who see themselves in the role of messiahs had better stay home. They will only be frustrated, while they alienate those they are seeking to help. The ideal candidate must have the patience of Job, the forbearance of a saint and the digestive system of an ostrich." Finally, an editorial in the *Wall Street Journal* criticized the Peace Crops as a weapon in the Cold War. "Perhaps the worst feature of [the Corps] is its gimmick-type approach to the deep and intractable problems of cold war. It purports to offer a dramatic solution to problems which simply are not susceptible to easy solutions."[2]

Despite objections to the administration of the Peace Corps, the program initially enjoyed great popularity with volunteers. However, since that time, the numbers of those participating has declined. An opponent of the program from the outset, as President, Richard Nixon cut its funding, initiating annual reductions in appropriations for the Peace Corps that continued until the election of Jimmy Carter. The Peace Corps is still active today, however, operating mostly in Africa and Latin America with the same mission for which it was created. Its legacy also inspired a domestic version, known as AmeriCorps,[3] which President Bill Clinton created in the 1990s. Like the Peace Corps, AmeriCorps organizes college graduates to volunteer to foster interaction between communities that otherwise might not come in contact with each other with the common goal of improving the quality of life. Today, while Peace Corps participants find themselves abroad, AmeriCorps volunteers work in the inner cities and rural areas of America.

NOTES

1. Cited in Elizabeth Cobbs Hoffman, *All You Need Is Love: Peace Corps and the Spirit of the 1960s*, (Cambridge, MA: Harvard University Press), 23.

2. *Congressional Record*, Vol. 107, Pt. 5, 5926–5927.

3. It should be noted that during discussions creating the Peace Corps, there were those, including Eleanor Roosevelt, who argued that a domestic version of the Peace Corps should be developed and implemented along with the Peace Corps, to target impoverished areas of the United States.

JOHN F. KENNEDY ANNOUNCEMENT OF THE SIGNING OF EXECUTIVE ORDER 10924 ESTABLISHING THE PEACE CORPS (MARCH 1, 1961)

I have today signed an Executive Order providing for the establishment of a Peace Corps on a temporary pilot basis. I am also sending to Congress a message proposing authorization of a permanent Peace Corps. This Corps will be a pool of trained American men and women sent overseas by the U.S. Government or through private institutions and organizations to help foreign countries meet their urgent needs for skilled manpower.

It is our hope to have 500 or more people in the field by the end of the year.

The initial reactions to the Peace Corps proposal are convincing proof that we have, in this country, an immense reservoir of such men and women—anxious to sacrifice their energies and time and toil to the cause of world peace and human progress.

In establishing our Peace Corps we intend to make full use of the resources and talents of private institutions and groups. Universities, voluntary agencies, labor unions and industry will be asked to share in this effort—contributing diverse sources of energy and imagination—making it clear that the responsibility for peace is the responsibility of our entire society.

We will only send abroad Americans who are wanted by the host country—who have a real job to do—and who are qualified to do that job. Programs will be developed with care, and after full negotiation, in order to make sure that the Peace Corps is wanted and will contribute to the welfare of other people. Our Peace Corps is not designed as an instrument of diplomacy or propaganda or ideological conflict. It is designed to permit our people to exercise more fully their responsibilities in the great common cause of world development.

Life in the Peace Corps will not be easy. There will be no salary and allowances will be at a level sufficient only to maintain health and meet basic needs. Men and women will be expected to work and live alongside the nationals of the country in which they are stationed—doing the same work, eating the same food, talking the same language.

But if the life will not be easy, it will be rich and satisfying. For every young American who participates in the Peace Corps—who works in a foreign land—will know that he or she is sharing in the great common task of bringing to man that decent way of life which is the foundation of freedom and a condition of peace.

Source: John Fitzgerald Kennedy Library, <http://www.jfklibrary.org/jfk_peace_corps.html>

REPRESENTATIVE W. J. BRYAN DORN (D-SC), COMMENTARY ON THE PEACE CORPS (SEPTEMBER 7, 1961)

This proposal would send novices and amateurs to perform the most delicate human relationship known to man. A Peace Corps man sent to perform any task in a so-called underdeveloped country must be thoroughly familiar with the traditions, superstitions, religion, history, language, culture, philosophy, politics, and psychology of the people....

Before our extension service representatives go out into the field in a highly developed country like our own, they have years of thorough training and then work years under experienced extension leaders.... Our people going into the Peace Corps are to be commended for their patriotism, enthusiasm, and idealism. However, the cold war is a ruthless death struggle with a highly skilled professional enemy. We cannot jeopardize the prestige of the United States with inadequately trained and inadequately indoctrinated personnel. The times require professionals rather than idealistic novices. The stakes are too high.... If this bill passes, the Peace Corps will expand into a gigantic international bureaucracy bleeding the US taxpayers of hundreds of millions of dollars annually. It will destroy our remaining prestige abroad and accelerate the onward march of socialism throughout the world.

Source: *Congressional Record*, Vol. 107, Pt. 14, 18596.

REPRESENTATIVE W. J. BRYAN DORN, COMMENTARY ON THE PEACE CORPS (SEPTEMBER 11, 1961)

Mr. Speaker, no one connected with our Foreign Service could officially and openly oppose the creation of a Peace Corps, particularly since it is already in being by Executive order. No one connected with our foreign-aid program could officially and openly oppose the Peace Corps under such circumstances; but, Mr. Speaker, everyone, connected with our Foreign Service could or our mutual security program with whom I have conferred privately express grave concern and misgivings about this hastily assembled organization of amateurs. Likewise, no official of a friendly nation is going to openly oppose the Peace Corps. As the recipient of our aid, it would be most expedient for them to do so. But the reports I receive from abroad indicate there is extreme skepticism of the Peace Corps and there is fear that it could cause serious damage to friendly relations with the United States. As a member of this House, you would not welcome amateur reformers into your district to tell your people what is wrong with their way of life. This is a dangerous, psychological approach to foreign, internal, and domestic problems. This House will make a grave mistake if we pass HR 7500 without a thorough investigation at home and abroad of the need and effect of this organization. The establishment of the Peace Corps was a political decision made during the heat of a national political campaign without thorough investigation of its operation at the grassroots level in foreign lands. As a duplication of many of our foreign activities, it cannot possibly do any good, but may without thorough training do irreparable harm. The time to prevent empire building is before it starts. The time to rid the world of this ill-advised Peace Corps is now. Our foreign friends are tired of this superior than thou attitude of swarms of Americans roving around the world telling them what is wrong with their way of life.

Source: *Congressional Record*, Vol. 107, Pt. 14, 18812.

CUTTING TAXES

Domestic economic strength was essential to funding the massive foreign affairs programs that the Kennedy team envisioned, but, as Kennedy entered office, the nation was mired in its third recession in a decade. Even though as a congressman Kennedy had favored surplus budgets to deficit spending, during the campaign he had criticized Eisenhower's intransigent insistence on a balanced budget, and he pledged to address the high level of unemployment, which was hovering between 6 and 7 percent in 1960–61, including a spike to 8.1 percent just before the election of 1960. During the campaign, Kennedy otherwise left his ideas on the economy vague.

Once he took office in 1961, Kennedy's selection of economic advisors did not clarify the direction he planned to take on economic policy. As Secretary of Treasury, he chose C. Douglas Dillon, a fiscally conservative Republican who had served as Eisenhower's Undersecretary of State. Yet to chair the Council of Economic Advisors, Kennedy named Walter Heller, the liberal Keynesian economist of the University of Minnesota, who professed little worry about budget deficits and focused on increasing purchasing power in the economy. Heller, like all Keynesians, believed that, in order to get out of recessions, governments should pump money into the economy—even if that meant running a government budget deficit—thereby stimulating consumer spending (demand), in turn stimulating production and employment.

Although Heller pushed for a tax cut from the beginning, Kennedy initially questioned the urgency of his arguments. The atmosphere in 1961 was probably not right for proposing major tax reductions. During the campaign Kennedy had called on Americans to make sacrifices to "get the country moving again." A tax cut, he reasoned, was not the policy exemplar of sacrifice. Moreover, increased military spending and allocations for the space program already signaled the onset of a budget deficit in the first year of Kennedy's administration. Even though Kennedy and Dillon did not fear deficit spending, neither believed that foreign investors or business leaders would respond well to a substantial imbalance between government revenue and government spending. In addition, as Arthur Schlesinger notes, Kennedy believed that popular sentiment favored cautious spending and a balanced budget as the tools of a prosperous economy. Kennedy believed that Eisenhower's insistence on balanced budgets had convinced Americans that spending was "sinful," and that spending and deficits equaled inflation. Moreover, by the middle of 1961, the economy was recovering, and the impetus for government intervention in the economy was thus far less urgent.

Kennedy only proposed reforms in the tax code for 1962, but by the end of that year he was ready to call for major tax reductions and to begin a campaign to convince the nation that budget deficits would not be the evil blight on the economy that Eisenhower had suggested. Several factors combined in the summer of 1962 to sway Kennedy's thinking in favor of a major tax cut proposal. Perhaps most important, economists were predicting recession. On May 28, the stock market experienced its worst single day decline since 1929, and it continued to slide throughout the summer. Kennedy had also grown increasingly annoyed with the leaders of the nation's business community. A major confrontation occurred when Kennedy could not get the heads of the major steel corporations to work with him to keep prices for the commodity stable. The press began to quote businessmen who claimed the Kennedy administration was turning to socialism. Not only that, but, mostly due to Heller's teachings, Kennedy had come to believe that a deficit was inevitable if the nation were unable to control unemployment and inflation, Kennedy's two main economic concerns. With the Cold War's emphasis on projecting an image of power and stability, Kennedy told the nation that the choice was not between deficit or surplus, but rather between two deficits: one the result of waste and weakness due to poor fiscal policy, the other incurred as "we build strength" through military and defense spending. As he told the Economic Club of New York in December of 1962, Kennedy was convinced that a tax cut would stimulate spending in the private sector, thereby increasing demand and concomitantly production and profits. He not only expected that the economy would recover, but that government revenue would actually increase thanks to the tax burden on increased profits and an expanded tax base.

More than a few disagreed with Kennedy and Heller on tax reductions. John Kenneth Galbraith, a leading academic economist, argued in his book *The Affluent Society* that as much as 25 percent of the population lived in poverty. He strongly opposed tax cuts, favoring instead increased spending on social services and job training, arguing that the country needed cleaner air and water, and more schools and hospitals, rather than more consumer goods. Moreover, Galbraith claimed, tax cuts would not provide assistance to the uneducated, the underskilled, or to blacks and others who found it hard to break into the job market. Senator Albert Gore, Sr. (D-TN) argued that tax cuts would destroy the social programs created by the New Deal. Moreover, Gore told Kennedy, once the president cut taxes, he would find it nearly impossible to increase them when needed. Dan Throop Smith, the leading tax man in the Treasury Department during the Eisenhower administration, told the Senate Finance Committee in October of 1963 that a tax cut would be foolhardy and would not address the problem of structural unemployment. Eisenhower came out against lower taxes as well, in a *Saturday Evening Post* article in May of 1963. Treasury Secretary Douglas Dillon himself still hoped for a balanced budget. Desiring to keep the administration's relation with the business community from souring even more, he was more interested in reforms to the tax code than in massive tax cuts for individuals. Congressional Republicans, like Senator Barry Goldwater (of Arizona), also objected both to some of Kennedy's proposals and to his rhetoric. They argued that Kennedy's efforts were aimed at increasing the tax burden on businesses and promoted, rather than diminished, inequities in the system. They further thought that Kennedy's claim that government revenue would increase as a result of changes in the tax code and reduced tax rates was only an attempt to win support for government spending programs. On the other hand Republican Representative Marion Snyder of Kentucky argued that the tax cuts Kennedy proposed did not go deep enough, and insisted on accompanying tax cuts with spending cuts. Gallup polls further indicated that 72 percent of the American people opposed tax reductions if they increased the public debt.

Although proposals for tax reform were derailed in Congress both in 1961 and 1962, and the House Ways and Means Committee debated the tax cut bill of 1963 for seven months, both Houses of Congress eventually passed the Kennedy tax cut. Unfortunately, this delay prevented Kennedy from having the chance to sign his tax bill into law. It did not emerge from

Congress until November 27, 1963, less than a week after the president was assassinated. Johnson signed the law days later. The law reduced tax rates for individuals from 91 to 70 percent at the highest level and from 20 to 14 percent at the lowest. It slightly lowered corporate tax rates as well. As James T. Patterson points out, Kennedy's resilience in his fight for the tax cut, against substantial opposition, marks a significant episode in the history of economic policy and the presidency. Keynesian economic ideas influenced the programs and policies of the New Deal, but no president had publicly favored Keynesian economic theory in its entirety until Kennedy argued that a fiscal policy that increased purchasing power, even at the expense of short-term public debt, could lead to economic growth.[1] This is why Arthur Schlesinger, in his book *A Thousand Days*, designated Kennedy as "the first Keynesian president." Many factors in addition to the Kennedy tax cuts contributed to the phenomenon, but the American economy witnessed the greatest period of sustained economic growth in its history from 1961 to 1968. Only the prosperous decade of the 1990s surpassed it in length.

The taxation debate did not end in 1963. It has continued, passionately. Ever since the founding of the nation, politicians, presidents, and the public have struggled with the question of taxation. From the Whiskey Rebellion of 1795 to the Tax Relief legislation of 2001, tax rates, the equity of the system of taxation, and the balance among taxation, deficits, and spending have been central questions. Since the Kennedy tax cut in 1963, Americans have witnessed a general decline in tax rates, the highest rate dropping from 91 percent before Kennedy took office, to 35 percent in 2005.

NOTE

1. James T. Patterson, *Grand Expectations: The United States, 1945–1975* (New York: Oxford University Press, 1996), 465.

PRESIDENT JOHN F. KENNEDY, ADDRESS AT THE ECONOMIC CLUB OF NEW YORK (DECEMBER 14, 1962)

... Less than a month ago this Nation reminded the world that it possessed both the will and the weapons to meet any threat to the security of free men.... But in the long run, that security will not be determined by military or diplomatic moves alone....

You will recall that Chairman Khrushchev has said that he believed that the hinge of world history would begin to move when the Soviet Union outproduced the United States. Therefore, the subject to which we address ourselves tonight concerns not merely our own well-being, but also very vitally the defense of the free world.... The economic health of this Nation has been and is now fundamentally sound....

... I know you share my conviction that, proud as we are of its progress, this Nation's economy can and must do even better than it has done in the last 5 years. Our choice, therefore, boils down to one of doing nothing and thereby risking a widening gap between our actual and potential growth in output, profits, and employment—or taking action, at the Federal level, to raise our entire economy to a new and higher level of business activity....

... the most direct and significant kind of Federal action aiding economic growth is to make possible an increase in private consumption and investment demand—to cut the fetters which hold back private spending.... The final and best means of strengthening demand among consumers and business is to reduce the burden on private income and the deterrents to private income which are imposed by our present tax system; and this administration pledged itself last summer to an across-the-board, top-to-bottom cut in personal and corporate income taxes to be enacted and become effective in 1963.

I am not talking about a "quickie" or a temporary tax cut, which would be more appropriate if a recession were imminent. Nor am I talking about giving the economy a mere shot in the arm, to ease some temporary complaint. I am talking about the accumulated evidence of the last 5 years that our present tax system ... exerts too heavy a drag on growth in peace time; that it siphons out of the private economy too large a share of personal and business purchasing power; that it reduces the financial incentives for personal effort, investment, risk-taking....

... in general, any new tax legislation enacted next year should meet the following three tests:

First, it should reduce net taxes by a sufficiently early date and sufficiently large amount to do the job required ... Too large a tax cut, of course, could result in inflation and insufficient future revenues—but the greatest danger is a tax cut too little or too late to be effective.

Second, the new tax bill must increase private consumption as well as investment.... When consumers purchase more goods, plants use more of their capacity, men are hired instead of laid off, investment increases and profits are high. Corporate tax rates must also be cut to increase incentives and the availability of investment capital.... For all these reasons next year's tax bill should reduce personal as well as corporate income taxes, for those in the lower brackets, who are certain to spend their additional take-home pay, and for those in the middle and upper brackets, who can thereby be encouraged to undertake additional efforts and enabled to invest more capital.

Third, the new tax bill should improve both the equity and the simplicity of our present tax system. This means the enactment of long-needed tax reforms, a broadening of the tax base and the elimination or modification of many special tax privileges.... These various exclusions and concessions have been justified in part as a means of overcoming oppressively high rates in the upper brackets—and a sharp reduction in those rates, accompanied by base-broadening, loophole-closing measures, would properly make the new rates not only lower but also more widely applicable. Surely this is more equitable on both counts. . . .

This administration is determined to protect America's security and survival and we are also determined to step up its economic growth. I think we must do both. . . .

Our true choice is not between tax reduction, on the one hand, and the avoidance of large Federal deficits on the other. It is increasingly clear that . . . an economy hampered by restrictive tax rates will never produce enough revenue to balance our budget just as it will never produce enough jobs or enough profits. Surely the lesson of the last decade is that budget deficits are not caused by wild-eyed spenders but by slow economic growth and periodic recessions. . . . In short, it is a paradoxical truth that tax rates are too high today and tax revenues are too low and the soundest way to raise the revenues in the long run is to cut the rates now. . . .

I do not underestimate the obstacles which the Congress will face in enacting such legislation. . . . A high order of restraint and determination will be required if the possible is not to wait on the perfect. But a nation capable of marshaling these qualities in any dramatic threat to its security is surely capable, as a great free society, of meeting a slower and more complex threat to our economic vitality. This Nation can afford to reduce taxes, we can afford a temporary deficit, but we cannot afford to do nothing. For on the strength of our free economy rests the hope of all free nations. We shall not fail that hope, for free men and free nations must prosper and they must prevail. Thank you.

Source: *Public Papers of the Presidents, John F. Kennedy*, 1962 (Washington, DC: Government Printing Office, 1963), 875–881.

SENATOR BARRY GOLDWATER (R–AZ) ON THE AMERICAN TAX SYSTEM, SENATE (AUGUST 11, 1961)

The president has made some recommendations and promised far-reaching proposals for next year. The purpose of this drive is to create the impression that vast governmental programs can be financed without raising taxes on the general taxpayer. It is suggested that the cost of new programs could be obtained by taxing somebody else who is now getting away without paying his fair share.

This drive is merely a maneuver to sell more welfare programs. . . . Dr. Roger A. Freeman [Institute for Studies in Federalism, Claremont Men's

College[... pointed out that "a substantial reduction in tax rates or a substantial increase in collections through the closing of 'loopholes' is not a hope but a mirage." ...

If "loophole" be the word used, these things do exist in the present tax structure, and they have been put there by acts of Congress, and signed by the President. If a desire exists to do away with these things, I think an honest effort can be made in that direction, but I do not agree for one instant that if these so-called loopholes were all plugged up it would provide one-tenth of the money needed to finance the New Frontier.

I shall state ... one example. With respect to all the so-called loopholes of which we have heard the President talk, I have never heard the President suggest a complete taxation of the cooperative movement which, in itself, would provide amounts of money ranging up to $3 billion, merely by provision that the cooperatives pay the same taxes as any other group.... I think we ought to make it abundantly clear that people who use the devices which are provided by law are not violating the law, are not acting illegally, but are merely acting in accordance with what the tax laws provide they can do. If our opposition wishes to call these things loopholes, and to attach some stigma to them, that is their own choice, but I think it is a mistake.

Source: *Congressional Record*, Vol. 107, Pt. 12, 15522–15527.

REPRESENTATIVE MARION SNYDER (R-KY), "TAX REFORM" (JANUARY 29, 1963)

Under a new and cleaver smokescreen of apparently soaking the rich, the administration now desires to impose greater tax hardships on its middle and lower income taxpayers than at any time in history. It is time for genuine tax reform all right, but one that will restore some balance and fiscal sanity to a situation that is on the verge of getting out of control....

Those who pretend that taxes are aimed only or mostly at the other fellow had better take a hard look at the facts, namely, 91.6 percent of all taxable income falls below the $6000 level.

Unless the line is drawn and a halt is called, it is obvious where the present tax system will lead us. It is already pinching the low and middle income groups, but a tax reduction that increases the debt will not aid the situation. It will compound the felony.

The advocacy of greater and greater deficits aggravates the crime being perpetrated on the people. To advocate a tax reduction with an increased deficit is like giving a worker a weekly pay increase of a few dollars while at the same time increasing his debt at the department store by many times the amount of the weekly increase in pay.

Despite the high graduation that is already applied at the upper income levels, taxpayers in the brackets below $10,000 pay about 60 percent of the personal income tax revenues being collected. . . . Our tax system soaks the rich alright, but it also soaks the little man too. . . .

The administration talks about various kind of deficits such as "deficits of weakness" and "deficits of strength" and "transitional deficits." I take the latter to be that momentary transitional period between insolvency and bankruptcy.

Whenever additional revenue is made available by any growth of the American economy, the New Frontiersmen have plans for spending it by the time the ink dries on the new estimates. Obviously it is time for a tax cut, but also it is time for a spending cut. . . .

The logical question then arises as to where the new money would come from, assuming continuation of present level of expenditures. The growth created by release of additional funds for people to save and spend for business establishments to invest in expansion would generate enough new revenue to offset it . . . .

It would be of specific help to the wage earner. It would be of significant help to his employer. It would be an encouragement to the investor. It would help everyone; it is punitive against no one . . . .

It is not only time to ask what we can do for our Nation but also time to ask what America can do for itself. I urge all citizens of good will and intelligence in both parties to back a sensible tax reduction, and to see that it is tied to a balanced budget.

Source: *Congressional Record*, Vol. 109, Pt. 1, 1265–1266.

VIETNAM

Despite the intensity and brinkmanship of the standoffs that Kennedy inherited in Berlin and Cuba, they were flash-in-the-pan events that he resolved through compromise, and they did not plague Americans for years on end. The Vietnam conflict, which Kennedy also found on his plate in 1961, was different. Although it did not pose the threat of nuclear war, the United States was on the verge of committing its people and resources to a long-lasting conflict that would have a devastating and profound impact on American politics and culture. By the time the United States withdrew in 1975, the war in Vietnam had taken the lives of more than 58,000 Americans, wounded tens of thousands more, and psychologically affected millions, both at home and on the ground in Vietnam, in ways that still influence U.S. military, political, and cultural thinking.

The situation in Vietnam was difficult. After the French colonialists withdrew in 1955, Vietnam was divided into North Vietnam and South Vietnam. North Vietnam quickly won Chinese support and installed a communist government under Ho Chi Minh, the Vietnamese leader who had led independence efforts since the First World War. The political scene in South Vietnam was chaotic. Many factions vied for control of the new country. Ultimately, Ngo Dinh Diem, the leader of a powerful Roman Catholic family, consolidated control of political affairs in South Vietnam. Diem was not a democrat; he dealt harshly and violently with his opposition, and corruption infected his administration. However, Diem's hatred of communism attracted U.S. favor. Kennedy's letter to President Diem in December of 1961, indicates that in keeping with the containment policy guiding American foreign policy during the Cold War, American policymakers considered Diem an important ally who was determined to prevent the expansion of communism from North to South Vietnam. North Vietnamese leaders, meanwhile, made no secret of their intention to reunite Vietnam under a North Vietnamese government, and the Vietcong, communist forces fighting a guerilla war in South Vietnam, agitated throughout the countryside to win the support of South Vietnamese peasants. Eisenhower had begun efforts to support Diem politically and militarily. U.S. policy in South Vietnam from 1956 to 1961 was predicated on keeping Diem in power and developing the South Vietnamese army, known as ARVN (Army of the Republic of Vietnam) into a viable and capable fighting force that could repel an invasion by North Vietnamese troops. During these years, the United States sent over $1.6 billion to South Vietnam, most of which was used for military supplies and training.

Despite events on the ground in Vietnam, and the seeming importance of the escalating conflict, Vietnam was neither an important campaign issue nor part of transition discussions between Kennedy and Eisenhower.[1] From the start, Vietnam was an important matter of debate for those in the Kennedy Administration, but they did not achieve consensus. Some, such as the Chairman of the Joint Chiefs of Staff, General Lyman L. Lemnitzer, and Special Assistant to the President for National Security Affairs, McGeorge Bundy, urged aggressive U.S. action in South Vietnam. They argued that a substantial commitment of ground troops could crush the attempts of Ho Chi Minh and the North Vietnamese to expand the influence of communism in Southeast Asia. Others, like retired General Douglas MacArthur, were more cautious, contending that the United States would not fare well in a ground war in Southeast Asia. George Ball, Undersecretary of State for Economic Affairs, warned that aggressive bombing campaigns proposed by hard-liners would be ineffective and cautioned that any deployment of American ground troops would inevitability lead to a further commitment. Once engaged, Ball suggested, the United States would be unable to limit its involvement. Moreover, Ball did not believe that a stable, politically and economically viable South Vietnam was possible; he predicted the infamous "quagmire" that ultimately ensued. Chester Bowles and W. Averell Harriman, both of the State Department, urged Kennedy to reach a diplomatic solution to the Vietnam conflict, based on compromise between the North and South Vietnamese, similar to the one just concluded in Laos.

With the disaster of the Bay of Pigs on his resume, and Nikita Khrushchev publicly and euphorically proclaiming Soviet support for "wars of national liberation" around the world, Kennedy did not want to appear weak. At the same time his own advisors and the press were sending mixed information about the situation in South Vietnam, and Kennedy was not convinced that a deployment of 8,000 American troops, which General Maxwell Taylor had requested after a visit to Southeast Asia, was proper. Although he believed that American military men could handle the Vietcong in South Vietnam, Kennedy was uncertain what kind of response that action would provoke from the North Vietnamese government.

As a consequence, Kennedy decided to pursue a middle road. Instead of employing American troops, Kennedy sent more American "advisors" to South Vietnam to assist the Diem regime with military training and economic development. Kennedy continued this strategy throughout his presidency. Nine hundred American "advisors" were in South Vietnam when Kennedy took office; 3,200 were working with the Diem government and ARVN in November 1961. These advisors had a very specific agenda; they were not simply teaching sharp-shooting skills and tactical knowledge. At the urging of General Maxwell Taylor, who became Chairman of the Joint Chiefs of Staff after 1961, Kennedy implemented a policy of counterinsurgency based on what he believed to be the realities of the situation. The enemy in South Vietnam employed untraditional tactics and was not easily identified. The Vietcong wore no uniforms, used makeshift weaponry, and traveled individually or in small groups, often via a network of underground tunnels that spanned South Vietnam. The Vietcong planned to win the war not with bombs and bullets, but by winning the hearts and minds of the peasants of South Vietnam. As a result, Americans and the South Vietnamese would need nontraditional methods to defeat the Vietcong, both with respect to military tactics and to managing the war in the countryside.

These circumstances led Kennedy and his aides to implement the Strategic Hamlet Program. Because it was so difficult to distinguish friends from enemies, the Hamlet Program would surround peasant villages with barbed wire and mine fields. Peasants could be kept inside the hamlets, which contained schools, a hospital, and other community needs. With tight control over access to the hamlets, American forces could protect South Vietnamese peasants from the influence of the Vietcong, and the military could assume that those outside the hamlets were Vietcong.

Although the conflict in South Vietnam continued to become more intense, more violent, and more of a quagmire throughout his administration, Kennedy consistently received conflicting reports from the field. In late 1962 after a visit to South Vietnam, Senator Mike Mansfield (D-MT) delivered a report criticizing U.S. policy in Vietnam and expressing little hope for the achievement of U.S. objectives. Mansfield continued to oppose U.S. involvement in Vietnam throughout the ordeal. But at the same time military leaders, including Taylor and Secretary of Defense Robert McNamara, were telling Kennedy that the United States and ARVN were winning the war, and that things were going so well in South Vietnam that all U.S. troops could be withdrawn from South Vietnam by the end of 1965. Despite evidence of peasant discontent in South Vietnam, signs of instability and lack of control within the Diem regime, increasing numbers of Vietcong in South Vietnam, and a disastrous encounter between ARVN and the Vietcong at Ap Bac in December 1962, Kennedy also put a positive spin on events in Vietnam. Although American journalists described the altercation as a victory for the Vietcong, military leaders and policymakers in Washington, including the President in his State of the Union address, exuded optimism and confidence, and predicted quick success.

Throughout 1963, however, the situation in Vietnam continued to deteriorate. The degree of instability in the Diem regime manifested itself in a national confrontation between Vietnamese Buddhists and Diem's oppressive regime, which Roman Catholics supported. During the summer of 1963, Buddhists staged protests across the country as Diem's unofficial police squads raided Buddhist temples, killing hundreds and arresting many more. This set the stage for the gruesome self-immolation of Buddhist monk Thich Quang Duc on June 11, 1963 in Saigon to protest the tactics of the Diem government. Six other Buddhist monks inflicted the same fate on themselves, further highlighting the horror and confusion there. David Halberstam, reporting on the Vietnam conflict for the *New York Times*, wrote of Thich Quang Duc's immolation, which he witnessed, "I was too shocked to cry, too confused to ask questions, too bewildered to even think."

Diem no longer had any significant support among the South Vietnamese population, and his control of the country was precarious; but, haunted by the fear of losing Vietnam, Kennedy continued to pledge American support for the Diem regime. In a television interview on the Huntley-Brinkley Report on September 9, 1963, Kennedy indicated that United States stood firmly behind the South Vietnamese government. "If you reduce your aid, it is possible you could have some effect upon the government structure there," Kennedy admitted, when a reporter asked if diminishing economic assistance might persuade Diem to employ a less authoritarian style. But, the President cautioned, "strongly in our mind is what happened in the case of China at the end of World War II, where China was lost [when] a weak government became increasingly unable to control events. We don't want that."

The issue of the Diem regime's tactics soon became moot. In November 1963, assassins killed both Diem and Kennedy. Diem died during a coup attempt, which Diem appears to have initiated in order to create a heroic role for himself and regain the support of the South Vietnamese people. An assassin Lee Harvey Oswald, killed Kennedy while he was riding in a parade in Dallas, Texas. More than 16,000 American military "advisors" found themselves in Vietnam in November 1963. During the three years of Kennedy's presidency, America had spent over $1 billion in Vietnam. Americans—military, policymakers, civilians—were involved in a quagmire, and Lyndon Johnson would have to decide how to get them out.

NOTE

1. James S. Olson and Randy Roberts, *Where the Domino Fell: America and Vietnam 1945–1990* (New York: St. Martin's Press, 1991), 72.

JOHN F. KENNEDY, LETTER TO NGO DINH DIEM, PRESIDENT OF SOUTH VIETNAM (DECEMBER 14, 1961)

Dear Mr. President:

I have received your recent letter in which you described so cogently the dangerous conditions caused by North Vietnam's effort to take over your country. The situation in your embattled country is well known to me and to the American people. We have been deeply disturbed by the assault on your country. Our indignation has mounted as the deliberate savagery of the Communist programs of assassination, kidnapping, and wanton violence became clear.

Your letter underlines what our own information has convincingly shown—that the campaign of force and terror now being waged against your people and your Government is supported and directed from outside by the authorities at Hanoi. They have thus violated the provisions of the Geneva Accords designed to ensure peace in Vietnam and to which they bound themselves in 1954.

At that time, the United States, although not a party to the Accords, declared that it "would view any renewal of the aggression in violation of the Agreements with grave concern and as seriously threatening international peace and security." We continue to maintain that view.

In accordance with that declaration, and in response to your request, we are prepared to help the Republic of Vietnam to protect its people and to preserve its independence. We shall promptly increase our assistance to your defense effort as well as help relieve the destruction of the floods which you describe. I have already given the orders to get these programs underway.

The United States, like the Republic of Vietnam, remains devoted to the cause of peace and our primary purpose is to help your people maintain their independence. If the Communist authorities in North Vietnam will stop their campaign to destroy the Republic of Vietnam, the measures we are taking to assist your defense efforts will no longer be necessary. We shall seek to persuade the Communists to give up their attempts to force and subversion. In any case, we are confident that the Vietnamese people will preserve their independence and gain the peace and prosperity for which they have sought so hard and so long....

Source: *The American Experience*, "The Presidents," Kennedy, Foreign Affairs, <http://www.pbs.org/wgbh/amex/presidents/frames/featured/featured. html>

REPORT TO THE CONGRESS BY THE SENATE MAJORITY LEADER MIKE MANSFIELD UPON RETURNING FROM A TRIP TO SOUTHEAST ASIA, WASHINGTON (DECEMBER 18, 1962)

We have problems of varying complexity with all of the nations in Southeast Asia. Clearly, however, the critical focus is south Vietnam. Developments there in the next two or three years may well influence greatly the trends in the whole region for the following ten or twenty....

We have now had for some months new concepts and a new American approach in Vietnam. But the purpose of both remains, in essentials, what the purpose of other approaches have been from the outset. Indeed, it was distressing on this visit to hear the situation described in much the same terms as on my last visit although it is seven years and billions of dollars later.... In short, it would be well to face the fact that we are once again at the beginning of the beginning.

But as noted there are now new concepts and a new American approach. The new concepts, as undoubtedly you are aware, center on the strategic hamlets.... Although the first results have scarcely been registered, the evaluations of the new approach—Vietnamese and American—in Saigon are extremely optimistic. Those bearing responsibility—Vietnamese and American—speak of success in the solution of the problem in terms of a year or two.

Having heard optimistic predictions of this kind ... certain reservations seem to me to be in order.... Reservations are in order because in the first place, the rapid success of the concept of the strategic hamlet would seem to depend on the assumption that the Vietminh will remain wedded to their present tactics and will be unable to devise significant and effective revisions to meet the new concepts and the new highly mobile firepower of the American-trained forces. That may be the case but it would be unwise to underestimate the resourcefulness of any group which has managed to survive years of the most rugged kind of warfare. In the second place, rapid success of the new concepts depends upon the assumption that the great bulk of the people in the countryside sustain the Vietminh merely out of fear or, at best, indifference. There is really no effective measure of the accuracy of this assumption. It may indeed contain a good deal of truth but the critical question is how much truth. The temptation to extrapolate our own reactions on to the Vietnamese peasant in this kind of a situation is as obvious as it is dangerous....

This is not to say that even a serious error in this assumption renders success impossible. If we were prepared to increase the commitment of men and military aid to compensate for the error it is not impossible that the concept of the strategic hamlet could still be brought into existence, in time, despite widespread support of the peasants for the Vietcong.... But it would be well to recognize that any such reorientation involves an immense job of social engineering, dependent on great outlays of aid on our part for many years and a most responsive, alert and enlightened leadership in the government of Vietnam.

... The success of the new approach in Vietnam presupposes a great contribution of initiative and self-sacrifice from a substantial body of Vietnamese with capacities for leadership at all levels. Whether that contribution can be obtained remains to be seen. For in the last analysis it depends upon a diffusion of political power, essentially in a democratic pattern. The trends in the political life of Vietnam have not been until now in that direction despite lip service to the theory of developing democratic and popular institutions "from the bottom up" through the strategic hamlet program.

... As noted, there is optimism that success will be achieved quickly. My own view is that the problems can be made to yield to present remedies, provided the problems and their magnitude do not change significantly and provided that the remedies are pursued by both Vietnamese and Americans (and particularly the former) with great vigor and self-dedication.

Certainly, if these remedies do not work, it is difficult to conceive of alternatives, with the possible exception of a truly massive commitment of American military personnel and other resources—in short going to war fully ourselves against the guerrillas—and the establishment of some form of neocolonial rule in south Vietnam. That is an alternative which I most emphatically do not recommend. On the contrary, it seems to me most essential that we make crystal clear to the Vietnamese government and to our own people that while we will go to great lengths to help, the primary responsibility rests with the Vietnamese. Our role is and must remain secondary in present circumstances. It is their country, their future which is most at stake, not ours.

To ignore that reality will not only be immensely costly in terms of American lives and resources but it may also draw us inexorably into some variation of the unenviable position in Vietnam which was formerly occupied by the French. We are not, of course, at that point at this time. But the great increase in American military commitment this year has tended to point us in that general direction and we may well begin to slide rapidly toward it if any of the present remedies begin to falter in practice.

As indicated, our planning appears to be predicated on the assumption that existing internal problems in south Vietnam will remain about the same and can be overcome by greater effort and better techniques. But what if the problems do not remain the same? . . .

This sort of anticipatory thinking cannot be undertaken with respect to the situation in Vietnam alone. The problem there can be grasped, it seems to me, only as we have clearly in mind our interests with respect to all of Southeast Asia. If it is essential in our interests to maintain a quasi-permanent position of power on the Asian mainland as against the Chinese then we must be prepared to continue to pay the present cost in Vietnam indefinitely and to meet any escalation on the other side with at least a commensurate escalation of commitment of our own. This can go very far, indeed, in terms of lives and resources. Yet if it is essential to our interests then we would have no choice.

But if on the other hand it is, at best, only desirable rather than essential that a position of power be maintained on the mainland, then other courses are indicated. We would, then, properly view such improvement as may be obtained by the new approach in Vietnam primarily in terms of what it might contribute to strengthening our diplomatic hand in the Southeast Asian region. And we would use that hand as vigorously as possible and in every way possible not to deepen our costly involvement on the Asian mainland but to lighten it. . . .

The real question which confronts us, therefore, is how much are we ourselves prepared to put into Southeast Asia and for how long in order to serve such interests as we may have in that region? Before we can answer this question, we must reassess our interests, using the words "vital" or "essential" with the greatest realism and restraint in the reassessment. When that has been done, we will be in a better position to estimate what we must, in fact, expend in the way of scarce resources, energy and lives in order to preserve those interests. We may well discover that it is in our interests to do less rather than more than we are now doing. If that is the case, we will do well to concentrate on a vigorous diplomacy which would be designed to lighten our commitments without bringing about sudden and catastrophic upheavals in Southeast Asia.

Source: Senate Document 93-11. Printed in U.S. Senate 93d Congress, 1st session, *Two Reports on Vietnam and Southeast Asia to the President of the United States by Senator*

Mike Mansfield (Washington: Government Printing Office, April 1973), 7–14.

PRESIDENT KENNEDY ON THE U.S. ROLE IN VIETNAM, INTERVIEW ON THE HUNTLEY-BRINKLEY REPORT (SEPTEMBER 9, 1963)

Mr. Huntley: Mr. President, in respect to our difficulties in South Vietnam, could it be that our Government tends occasionally to get locked into a policy or an attitude and then finds it difficult to alter or shift that policy?

THE PRESIDENT: Yes, that is true. I think in the case of South Vietnam we have been dealing with a Government which is in control, has been in control for 10 years. In addition, we have felt for the last 2 years that the struggle against the Communists was going better. Since June, however, the difficulties with the Buddhists, we have been concerned about a deterioration, particularly in the Saigon areas, which hasn't been felt greatly in the outlying areas but may spread. So we are faced with the problem of wanting to protect the area against the Communists. On the other hand, we have to deal with the Government there. That produces a kind of ambivalence in our efforts which exposes us to some criticism. We are using our influence to persuade the Government there to take those steps which will win back support. That takes some time, and we must be patient, we must persist.

Mr. Huntley: Are we likely to reduce our aid to South Vietnam now?

THE PRESIDENT: I don't think we think that would be helpful at this time. If you reduce your aid, it is possible you could have some effect upon the government structure there. On the other hand, you might have a situation which could bring about a collapse. Strongly in our mind is what happened in the case of China at the end of World War II, where China was lost [when] a weak government became increasingly unable to control events. We don't want that.

Mr. Brinkley: Mr. President, have you had any reason to doubt this so-called "domino theory," that if South Vietnam falls, the rest of Southeast Asia will go behind it?

THE PRESIDENT: No, I believe it. I believe it. I think that the struggle is close enough. China is so large, looms so high just beyond the frontiers, that if South Vietnam went, it would not only give them an improved geographic position for guerrilla assault on Malaya but would also give the impression that the wave of the future in Southeast Asia was China and the Communists. So I believe it....

...

Mr. Brinkley: With so much of our prestige, money, so on, committed in South Vietnam, why can't we exercise a little more influence there, Mr. President?

THE PRESIDENT: We have some influence. We have some influence and we are attempting to carry it out. I think we don't...we can't expect these countries to do everything the way we want to do them. They have their own interest, their own personalities, their own tradition. We can't make everyone in our image, and there are a good many people who don't want to go in our image. In addition, we have ancient struggles between countries. In the case of India and Pakistan, we would like to have them settle Kashmir. That is our view of the best way to defend the subcontinent against communism. But that struggle between India and Pakistan is more important to a good many people in the area than the struggle against the Communists.... We can't make the world over, but we can influence the world. That fact of the matter is that with the assistance of the United States and SEATO, Southeast Asia and indeed all of Asia has been maintained independent against a powerful force the Chinese Communists. What I am concerned about is that Americans will get impatient and say, because they don't like the events in Southeast Asia or they don't like the Government in Saigon, that we should withdraw. That only makes it easy for the Communists. I think we should stay. We should use our influence in as effective a way as we can, but we should not withdraw.

Source: *Public Papers of the Presidents of the United States, John F. Kennedy, 1963* (Washington, DC: United States Government Printing Office, 1964), 658–60.

THE SPACE RACE

Just as Kennedy feared a loss of American prestige in Vietnam, he could not allow the Russians to better America in space. While President Eisenhower had resisted what he called a "crash" space program and downplayed the significance of Soviet space advances, Kennedy used what he called the "space gap" against Richard Nixon in 1960, claiming that the Eisenhower-Nixon team had not responded aggressively enough to Sputnik. Kennedy argued that the U.S. position in the space race represented failings in military strength, economic power, and international prestige. The Soviet

Premier, Nikita Khrushchev, bolstered Kennedy's position with his own proclamations to the same effect. He bragged that Soviet successes in space showed that they had achieved both military and economic superiority over the U.S., thus allowing Kennedy to play off his rhetoric. Moreover, Kennedy entered office with momentum and idealism. As with other programs, Kennedy defended his space initiatives in the name of fighting the Cold War. Arguing that the nation should spare no expense, in his first year in office, Kennedy asked for a 30 percent increase in Eisenhower's space budget.

Presidential historian Michael Beschloss has pointed to two events in April 1961 that propelled the space program to one of the highest priorities of the Kennedy Administration. On April 12, the Soviets sent Yuri Gargarin into orbit around the earth, and days later, Fidel Castro foiled the efforts of U.S.-backed Cuban exiles to invade Cuba by sea and overthrow him. Like the flight of the first Sputnik in 1957, both episodes were frightening reminders of Cold War perils that implied a position of weakness and failure for the United States. At this point Kennedy decided that the United States had to find a "program which promises dramatic results in which we could win." A space station, laboratory, or moon shot, anything would do. Kennedy thought the latter was preferable, but the key was that he believed superiority in space would signal the potential for dominance on earth.[1]

Kennedy sent Vice President Lyndon Johnson, the chairman of his Space Council, who had championed and expanded the space program as Senate Majority Leader in the 1950s, to survey the political landscape and the technical feasibility of getting a man to the moon and back. Johnson fostered bipartisan support in the Congress. He discovered not only that the engineers and scientists believed that a manned mission to the moon was possible before the end of the decade, but also that Secretary of Defense Robert McNamara fully supported such a project and accepted Kennedy's view that the question of prestige was of utmost importance. Some within NASA itself resisted, fearing that military and political objectives might undermine the scientific purposes of the space program.

The goal of landing a man on the moon drove the U.S. space program until the end of the decade. It involved massive spending. Thus, the 1962 budget for the program exceeded all of the pre-1961 space budgets combined. Kennedy considered the program to be so grand and important that he delivered an unprecedented "second" State of the Union address on May 25 to announce the decision to commit the United States to putting a man on the moon by the end of the decade and to call for the full support of the nation and of Congress. Without dedication and a total commitment, Kennedy warned, the effort would be pointless. His remarks signaled the relegation of space exploration for scientific purposes to the back burner; the urgency of his language suggests that Kennedy believed that international prestige was now the primary reason Americans should work to put a man on the moon. Kennedy's speech ushered in the unprecedented Apollo Project aimed at sending an American to the moon and returning him safely.

Kennedy's initiative won a great deal of support. He had not, however, built a complete consensus. Many policymakers and even some outside of government worried that the expense of the space program would balloon out of control. Others were unable to comprehend the rationale behind the Apollo Project. Eisenhower, who had resisted a crash program in response to the Soviet space program during his own administration, called Kennedy's program "a stunt," which was "almost hysterical." NASA's administrator under Eisenhower, T. Keith Glennan, also disapproved of Kennedy's proposal. He predicted that neither Kennedy, nor anyone else for that matter, could predict the costs, not just of getting a man to the moon, but doing it before the Russians did. He told a colleague that he did not believe Kennedy was being honest with Americans when he told them that the Apollo Project could be undertaken without new taxes, and, indeed, in the wake of a tax reduction. Glennan, like others, also thought that Kennedy's claim that prestige would come with manned lunar exploration was unfounded. "I cannot bring myself to believe that we will gain lasting 'prestige' by a shot we may make six to eight years from now," he informed Kennedy's NASA director. Senator Mike Mansfield (D-MT) expressed a similar view in the Senate on the occasion of celebrating Alan Shepard's voyage as the first American to journey into space. Although Mansfield called the flight of Shepard's vessel, the "Freedom VII," an "important step toward maintaining both freedom in outer space and earthly freedom," he also called for "less talk about prestige" in favor of "a better understanding of the significance of space exploration for our way of life."[2] Representative Thomas Pelly (R-WA) went further in his objections to Kennedy's proposals, describing the "crash moon trip" as "a spectacular piece of nonsense." Senator Gordon Allott (R-CO) also questioned both the costs and the purpose of Kennedy's space program, arguing that America's defense, rather than prestige, should be the primary objective of its space program.

The Apollo Project succeeded in placing a man on the moon in 1969, but support for the project waned over the decade. Taxpayers and policymakers began to complain about the high costs of the program. Americans have continued to venture into space, exploring in the last four decades not only other planetary objects, but even the farthest reaches of the solar system. Americans still debate the practicality of manned space exploration and the public benefit of the expenditure on the space program.

NOTES

1. Michael R. Beschloss, "Kennedy and the Decision to go to the Moon," in Roger D. Launius, and Howard M. McCurdy, *Spaceflight and the Myth of Presidential Leadership* (Urbana: University of Illinois Press, 1997), 55–57.

2. *Congressional Record*, Vol. 107, Pt. 6, 7465.

KENNEDY, SPECIAL MESSAGE TO CONGRESS ON URGENT NATIONAL NEEDS (MAY 25, 1961)

... Finally, if we are to win the battle that is now going on around the world between freedom and tyranny, the dramatic achievements in space which occurred in recent weeks should have made clear to us all, as did the Sputnik in 1957, the impact of this adventure on the minds of men everywhere, who are attempting to make a determination of which road they should take. Since early in my term, our efforts in space have been under review. ... Now it is time to take longer strides—time for a great new American enterprise—time for this nation to take a clearly leading role in space achievement, which in many ways may hold the key to our future on earth. ...

Recognizing the head start obtained by the Soviets with their large rocket engines, which gives them many months of leadtime, and recognizing the likelihood that they will exploit this lead for some time to come in still more impressive successes, we nevertheless are required to make new efforts on our own. For while we cannot guarantee that we shall one day be first, we can guarantee that any failure to make this effort will make us last. We take an additional risk by making it in full view of the world, but as shown by the feat of astronaut Shepard, this very risk enhances our stature when we are successful. But this is not merely a race. Space is open to us now; and our eagerness to share its meaning is not governed by the efforts of others. We go into space because whatever mankind must undertake, free men must fully share.

I therefore ask the Congress, above and beyond the increases I have earlier requested for space activities, to provide the funds which are needed to meet the following national goals:

First, I believe that this nation should commit itself to achieving the goal, before this decade is out, of landing a man on the moon and returning him safely to the earth. No single space project in this period will be more impressive to mankind, or more important for the long-range exploration of space; and none will be so difficult or expensive to accomplish. We propose to accelerate the development of the appropriate lunar space craft. We propose to develop alternate liquid and solid fuel boosters, much larger than any now being developed, until certain which is superior. We propose additional funds for other engine development and for unmanned explorations—explorations which are particularly important for one purpose which this nation will never overlook: the survival of the man who first makes this daring flight. But in a very real sense, it will not be one man going to the moon—if we make this judgment affirmatively, it will be an entire nation. For all of us must work to put him there.

Secondly, an additional 23 million dollars, together with 7 million dollars already available, will accelerate development of the Rover nuclear rocket.

This gives promise of some day providing a means for even more exciting and ambitious exploration of space, perhaps beyond the moon, perhaps to the very end of the solar system itself.

Third, an additional 50 million dollars will make the most of our present leadership, by accelerating the use of space satellites for world-wide communications.

Fourth, an additional 75 million dollars—of which 53 million dollars is for the Weather Bureau—will help give us at the earliest possible time a satellite system for world-wide weather observation.

Let it be clear—and this is a judgment which the Members of the Congress must finally make—let it be clear that I am asking the Congress and the country to accept a firm commitment to a new course of action, a course which will last for many years and carry very heavy costs: 531 million dollars in fiscal '62—an estimated seven to nine billion dollars additional over the next five years. If we are to go only half way, or reduce our sights in the face of difficulty, in my judgment it would be better not to go at all. . . .

This decision demands a major national commitment of scientific and technical manpower, materiel and facilities, and the possibility of their diversion from other important activities where they are already thinly spread. It means a degree of dedication, organization and discipline which have not always characterized our research and development efforts. It means we cannot afford undue work stoppages, inflated costs of material or talent, wasteful interagency rivalries, or a high turnover of key personnel.

New objectives and new money cannot solve these problems. They could in fact, aggravate them further—unless every scientist, every engineer, every serviceman, every technician, contractor, and civil servant gives his personal pledge that this nation will move forward, with the full speed of freedom, in the exciting adventure of space.

Source: John Fitzgerald Kennedy Presidential Library, <http://www.cs.umb.edu/jfklibrary/j052561.htm>

SENATOR GORDON ALLOTT (R-CO) (JUNE 28, 1961)

. . . This means that in the next 10 years . . . for each man, woman, and child in the United States it will be necessary to expend upon the soft shot on the moon—that is, landing three men on the moon—the sum of $100. That is the present estimate. In my opinion . . . within the next ten years the cost of the project will rise at least 50 percent. So when we consider the project, we will have to consider the cost ratio of $150 for every man, woman, and child in the United States.

This brings us to the question which no man, however wise, can answer today. . . . The problem is whether the shot on the moon is the ultimate goal and the thing which will reap the most benefits for the United States. In other words, if we are to do this for the mere sake of propaganda, the shot will not be worth $20 billion—or even $30 billion, as I maintain it will cost. . . .

On the basis of only the propaganda value, I do not believe this course is justified. I wish to make perfectly clear that I do not believe in engaging in a useless contest with the Russians; I do not believe such a contest can be worth what I believe will be the cost . . . to the American people.

The only question I raise . . . is whether the real interests of the United States would be far better served by the development of an ultimate orbital instrument, a manned space vehicle, which, in effect, will have complete supervision of the earth, while it is in orbit, plus the antimanned orbital vehicle which could destroy one in the event we had to destroy one, of an enemy. I think this is the real problem and the real gist of the problem which we Americans must face.

I am not impressed completely by the arguments of the scientists who simply want more and more and more research, even though the research thus far engaged in has just about, to all practical effects, taken over the budget of the US Government; the research scientists have taken over in dozens of fields so that in every area in which we engage we find research, research, and more research—duplication and overlapping, and then more duplication and more overlapping, in place after place. . . .

I believe that one of the main things we have to achieve in this field . . . is the answer to the question of whether it is more important to develop a means of putting men on the moon or whether it is more important to develop . . . orbital, manned spaced shots around the earth, together with the antimanned orbital vehicle which we shall also have to develop as, first, a means of propaganda value, and second, a means of bringing to this country, by means of such surveillance and the other scientific data we could have acquired, the greatest amount of protection our country could get, together with, third, the greatest scientific value. . . .

The real concern I have is whether, in setting a moonshot as the goal, we may be setting a false goal rather than a goal . . . which will give the greatest results to mankind and to the United States.

Source: *Congressional Record*, Vol. 107, Pt. 9, 11626–11628.

THE BAY OF PIGS

In January of 1959 Fidel Castro and his band of revolutionaries supplanted the dictatorial regime of Fulgencio Batista in Cuba. Although the new Cuban leader did not initially pledge allegiance to either of the two Cold War superpowers, for many Americans, Castro's programs, which included literacy training, reform of the island's public health care system, nationalization of utilities and industry, and land redistribution, looked too similar to the socialist programs of the Eastern Bloc. Americans, policy-makers and the public alike, were concerned with what was taking shape in Cuba. By 1960, Castro began to nationalize properties, land, and industry, which Americans owned, and he had concluded several trade agreements with socialist countries of Eastern Europe. Moreover, Castro made over-tures of friendship to the U.S.S.R. when the United States began embargoing Cuban sugar, and restricting trade generally with Cuba. This was all too much for Americans to take—policymakers decided Castro could not stay, and they began to develop plans for his ouster.

CIA officials had a model to follow for the overthrow of unwanted governments. Seven years earlier, the United States had engineered such a coup in Guatemala. In that case the "danger" was a freely elected president; in Castro's case, he had forced his way into power. Nonetheless, in 1954 the CIA trained and supplied a group of Guatemalan "exiles." With the assistance and support of Nicaraguan president Anastasio Somoza, the United States "encouraged" the exiles' invasion of their homeland and the removal of Guatemalan President Jacobo Arbenz Guz man. Because a general friendly to the United States had replaced Arbenz, the CIA now had ideal training grounds in Guatemala and Nicaragua for its next clandestine operation. This time, the United States would organize, train, and supply Cuban exiles. With sea and air support from the United States, the approximately 1,500 exiles would land at the Playa Giron (Bay of Pigs) on Cuba's southern coast. Richard Bissell, the CIA official who developed the program, believed that the Cuban people would rally behind the Cuban exiles to force Castro from power. Should this fail to happen on their initial landing, he further believed that the exiles would be able to regroup and function as a guerilla force, agitating Castro's regime from the mountains, as Castro had done to the Batista regime after Castro's own initial failed attempt to unseat that government in 1953. Eisenhower initiated plans for the invasion of the Bay of Pigs in late 1960. Cuban exiles willing to fight for the freedom of Cuba gathered in Guatemala and Florida to be trained and armed by the CIA. By April 1961, President Kennedy, Secretary of State Dean Rusk, Secretary of Defense Robert McNamara, and the Joint Chiefs of Staff all were convinced that the exiles, and the CIA, could overthrow Castro's government.[1] Kennedy was among those who feared that the United States would be discovered. Because the United States projected itself as the defender of freedom rather than a malevolent meddler in the affairs of other nations, Kennedy insisted that U.S. military stay out of the fray. U.S. seafaring vessels were to maintain a minimum distance of five miles from the Cuban coast. More importantly, the Administration scrapped the provision in the original plans for the invasion that called for substantial air cover from the U.S. military, this after an initial bombing run by unmarked CIA-operated planes alerted the Cuban military and provoked Cuba to complain to the United Nations.

Few within the Administration opposed the plans to invade Cuba. Among his close aides, only Kennedy's special assistant, Arthur Schlesinger, Jr. advised against the Bay of Pigs invasion, warning that the United States would be implicated for its role in aiding and supporting the Cuban exiles, regardless of the role of U.S. forces in the actual invasion. But there were others, like advisors Thomas Mann and Chester Bowles, who adamantly opposed the plan as well. In a thorough and eloquent message to the Secretary of State, Mann outlined his reasons for believing that the invasion was both unnecessary and unwise. Likewise, Bowles expressed his concern that those supporting the plan were overestimating the threat posed by Castro and warned that the Bay of Pigs scheme was needlessly jeopardizing the international reputation of the United States. Kennedy decision-makers pressed ahead, pledging U.S. support, and encouraging the Cuban exiles to proceed with their plan.

American historians have called the Bay of Pigs invasion a "failure," a "disaster," and a "fiasco." Castro called it a "triumph." Castro had been fully aware of the activities of the CIA and the Cuban exiles in Florida and Guatemala. Cuban government documents show that Cuban government officials were privy to details as specific as how many men were being trained and how many aircraft were involved in training exercises.[2] The invasion began on April 17 and was over by April 19. Almost every one of the exiles who landed on the beach was either killed or arrested. Ignoring calls from the beach to lend aid, ammunition, or even evacuation services, American military personnel avoided any commitment to the scuffle between the exiles and Cuban forces, taking every precaution given the "need for concealing involvement of U.S. forces."[3]

At first, the U.S. government denied involvement in the affair at every opportunity. In the United Nations, American Ambassador Adlai Stevenson aggressively refuted claims of U.S. involvement and condemnations by other countries. "Everyone, of course, friend or foe, believes we have engineered this revolution and no amount of denials will change their minds," he wrote back to Kennedy and Rusk. (Stevenson denied U.S. involvement sincerely. Only later would he discover that he too had been kept in the dark about CIA activities relating to Cuba).[4] Kennedy made no statement to the American people acknowledging the CIA role in the affair until days after the event concluded. Kennedy even rebuffed the allegations of U.S. involvement made by Nikita Khrushchev in private correspondence between the two leaders, telling the Soviet premier that he was "under a serious misapprehension in regard to events in Cuba."[5]

Despite repeated denials of U.S. involvement during and in the immediate aftermath of the Bay of Pigs invasion, international condemnation forced the issue. With U.S. credibility at stake, Kennedy came clean, admitting CIA support for the exiles and taking personal responsibility for the role played by the United States. At the same time though, Kennedy insisted on the support of the United States for freedom and pledged that Americans would not relent in the struggle to contain communism. The disaster at the Playa Giron was devastating for Kennedy. The President was disappointed both in the advice he had been given about the chances for success and with himself for relying too much on the advice of others. Just as Schlesinger had warned, the Bay of Pigs cast an ominous shadow over the new administration throughout the world. Even Latin American allies like Mexico and Colombia condemned the United States in the United Nations. The Bay of Pigs debacle did not rid the Western Hemisphere of a potential communist foe. Instead, in its aftermath Cuba and the Soviet Union forged an alliance, and Castro proclaimed himself a Marxist-Leninist. Historian Warren I. Cohen observes that "with Washington's assistance, Castro transformed revolutionary Cuba from an irritant to a powder keg."[6]

NOTES

1. See National Security Interview with Robert McNamara: <http://www.gwu.edu/~nsarchiv/coldwar/interviews/episode-10/mcnamara1.html>

2. Republica de Cuba, Ministerio de las Fuerzas Armadas Revolucionarios, Informe sobre las campamentos y las bases de mercenarios en Guatemala, Nicaragua, y la Florida, 12 de enero de 1961, <http://www.gwu.edu/~nsarchiv/bayofpigs/19610112-trans.pdf>

3. Telegram, Commander in Chief, Atlantic (Dennison) to Commander of Special Task Group (Clark), April 19, 1961, *Foreign Relations of the United States (FRUS), 1961–1963*, Volume X, *Cuba 1961–1962*, 137.

4. Telegram, Mission to the United Nations to the Department of State, April 19, 1961, *Foreign Relations of the United States, 1961–1963*, Volume X, *Cuba 1961–1962*, 148.

5. Letter, Kennedy to Khrushchev, April 18, 1961, *Foreign Relations of the United States*, Volume VI, *Kennedy-Khrushchev Exchanges*, 10.

6. Warren I. Cohen, *America in the Age of Soviet Power, 1945–1991* (Cambridge: Cambridge University Press, 1993), 131.

JOHN F. KENNEDY, ADDRESS BEFORE THE AMERICAN SOCIETY OF NEWSPAPER EDITORS (APRIL 20, 1961)

... I have decided in the last 24 hours to discuss briefly at this time the recent events in Cuba.

On that unhappy island, as in so many other arenas of the contest for freedom, the news has grown worse instead of better. I have emphasized before that this was a struggle of Cuban patriots against a Cuban dictator. While we could not be expected to hide our sympathies, we made it repeatedly clear that the armed forces of this country would not intervene in any way.

Any unilateral American intervention, in the absence of an external attack upon ourselves or an ally, would have been contrary to our traditions and to our international obligations. But let the record show that our restraint is not inexhaustible. Should it ever appear that the inter-American doctrine of non-interference merely conceals or excuses a policy of nonaction—if the nations of this Hemisphere should fail to meet their commitments against outside Communist penetration—then I want it clearly understood that this Government will not hesitate in meeting its primary obligations which are to the security of our Nation! . . .

Mr. Castro has said that these were mercenaries. According to press reports, the final message to be relayed from the refugee forces on the beach came from the rebel commander when asked if he wished to be evacuated. His answer was: "I will never leave this country." That is not the reply of a mercenary. He has gone now to join in the mountains countless other guerrilla fighters, who are equally determined that the dedication of those who gave their lives shall not be forgotten, and that Cuba must not be abandoned to the Communists. And we do not intend to abandon it either!

The Cuban people have not yet spoken their final piece . . .

Meanwhile we will not accept Mr. Castro's attempts to blame this nation for the hatred which his onetime supporters now regard his repression. But there are from this sobering episode useful lessons for us all to learn. Some may be still obscure, and await further information. Some are clear today.

First, it is clear that the forces of communism are not to be under-estimated, in Cuba or anywhere else in the world. . . .

Secondly, it is clear that this Nation, in concert with all the free nations of this hemisphere, must take an ever closer and more realistic look at the menace of external Communist intervention and domination in Cuba. The American people are not complacent about Iron Curtain tanks and planes less than 90 miles from their shore. But a nation of Cuba's size is less a threat to our survival than it is a base for subverting the survival of other free nations throughout the hemisphere. It is not primarily our interest or our security but theirs which is now, today, in the greater peril. It is for their sake as well as our own that we must show our will.

The evidence is clear—and the hour is late. We and our Latin friends will have to face the fact that we cannot postpone any longer the real issue of survival of freedom in this hemisphere itself. On that issue, unlike perhaps some others, there can be no middle ground. Together we must build a hemisphere where freedom can flourish; and where any free nation under outside attack of any kind can be assured that all of our resources stand ready to respond to any request for assistance.

Third, and finally, it is clearer than ever that we face a relentless struggle in every corner of the globe that goes far beyond the clash of armies or even nuclear armaments. The armies are there, and in large number. The nuclear armaments are there. But they serve primarily as the shield behind which subversion, infiltration, and a host of other tactics steadily advance, picking off vulnerable areas one by one in situations which do not permit our own armed intervention. . . .

We dare not fail to see the insidious nature of this new and deeper struggle. . . . The message of Cuba, of Laos, of the rising din of Communist voices in Asia and Latin America—these messages are all the same. The complacent, the self-indulgent, the soft societies are about to be swept away with the debris of history. Only the strong, only the industrious, only the determined, only the courageous, only the visionary who determine the real nature of our struggle can possibly survive.

No greater task faces this country or this administration. No other challenge is more deserving of our every effort and energy. Too long we have fixed our eyes on traditional military needs, on armies prepared to cross borders, on missiles poised for flight. Now it should be clear that this is no longer enough—that our security may be lost piece by piece, country by country, without the bring of a single missile or the crossing of a single border.

We intend to profit from this lesson. We intend to reexamine and reorient our forces of all kinds—our tactics and our institutions here in this community. We intend to intensify our efforts for a struggle in many ways more difficult than war, where disappointment will often accompany us.

For I am convinced that we in this country and in the free world possess the necessary resource, and the skill, and the added strength that comes from a belief in the freedom of man. And I am equally convinced that history will record the fact that this bitter struggle reached its climax in the late 1950's and the early 1960's. Let me then make clear as the President of the United States that I am determined upon our system's survival and success, regardless of the cost and regardless of the peril!

Source: *Public Papers of the President of the United States, John F. Kennedy, 1961* (Washington, DC: United States Government Printing Office, 1962), 304–396.

MEMORANDUM FROM THE UNDERSECRETARY OF STATE (BOWLES) TO SECRETARY OF STATE RUSK ARGUING AGAINST AN INVASION OF CUBA (MARCH 31, 1961)

. . . In considerable degree, my concern stems from a deep personal conviction that our national interests are poorly served by a covert operation of this kind at a time when our new President is effectively appealing to world opinion on the basis of high principle.

Even in our imperfect world, the differences which distinguish us from the Russians are of vital importance. This is true not only in a moral sense but in the practical effect of these differences on our capacity to rally the non-Communist world in behalf of our traditional democratic objectives.

In saying this, I do not overlook the ruthless nature of the struggle in which we are involved, nor do I ignore the need on occasion for action which is expedient and distasteful. Yet I cannot persuade myself that means can be wholly divorced from ends—even within the context of the Cold War.

Against this background, let me suggest several points which I earnestly hope will be fully taken into account in reaching the final decision.

1. In sponsoring the Cuban operation, for instance, we would be deliberately violating the fundamental obligations we assumed in the Act of Bogota establishing the Organization of American States. . . .

   To act deliberately in defiance of these obligations would deal a blow to the Inter-American System from which I doubt it would soon recover. The suggestion that Cuba has somehow "removed itself" from the System is a transparent rationalization for the exercise of our own will.

   More generally, the United States is the leading force in and substantial beneficiary of a network of treaties and alliances stretching around the world. That these treaty obligations should be recognized as binding in law and conscience is the condition not only of a lawful and orderly world, but of the mobilization of our own power.

   We cannot expect the benefits of this regime of treaties if we are unwilling to accept the limitations it imposes upon our freedom to act.

2. Those most familiar with the Cuban operation seem to agree that as the venture is now planned, the chances of success are not greater than one out of three. This makes it a highly risky operation. If it fails, Castro's prestige and strength will be greatly enhanced. . . .

3. Under the very best of circumstances, I believe this operation will have a much more adverse effect on world opinion than most people contemplate. It is admitted that there will be riots and a new wave of anti-Americanism throughout Latin America. It is also assumed that there will be many who quietly wish us well and, if the operation succeeds, will heave a sigh of relief.

   Moreover, even if the reaction in Latin America is less damaging than we expect, I believe that in Europe, Asia, and Africa, the reaction against the United States will be angry and the fresh, favorable image of the Kennedy Administration will be correspondingly dimmed. It would be a grave mistake for us to minimize this factor and its impact on our capacity to operate effectively in cooperation with other nations in other parts of the world.

4. If the operation appears to be a failure in its early stages, the pressure on us to scrap our self-imposed restriction on direct American involvement will be difficult to resist, and our own responsibility correspondingly increased.

5. A pertinent question, of course, is what will happen in Cuba if this operation is cancelled and we limit ourselves to small and scattered operations?

    There is the possibility that the Castro effort will be a failure without any further intervention from us. It is not easy to create a viable Communist state on an island, totally dependent upon open sea lanes, with a large population, and inadequate resources. As Castro applies more and more pressure, the spirit of rebellion is likely to grow.

6. It appears more likely that Castro will succeed in solidifying his political position. Although this would be sharply contrary to our national interest, it does not mean that we would be impotent to deal with him.

    If the Soviets should attempt to provide Castro with substantially larger amounts of arms, including naval vessels, we have the power to throw a blockade around Cuba and to extend it, if necessary, to petroleum supplies. This could bring the Cuban economy to a grinding halt within a few months.

    Technically, this would be an act of war. However, I believe we would find it vastly easier to live with direct action of this kind in the face of what we could fairly describe as an open Soviet move to establish Cuba as a military base than with the covert operation now under consideration.

7. Another possibility is that Castro, once he has created sufficient military power, will move against a neighboring area, such as Haiti, the Dominican Republic, or perhaps into Central America. If this occurs, we can move to block him with whatever force is required, presumably through the Organization of American States and with the full support of the people in Latin America and elsewhere. . . .

I believe it would be a grave mistake for us to jeopardize the favorable position we have steadily developed in most of the non-Communist world by the responsible and restrained policies which are now associated with the President by embarking on a major covert adventure with such very heavy built-in risks. . . .

Source, U.S. Department of State, *Foreign Relations of the United States, 1961–1963*, Volume X, *Cuba, 1961–1962.*

MEMORANDUM FROM THE ASSISTANT SECRETARY OF STATE FOR INTER-AMERICAN AFFAIRS (MANN) TO SECRETARY OF STATE RUSK ARGUING AGAINST AN INVASION OF CUBA (FEBRUARY 15, 1961)

I
The March 1960 Plan

What is proposed is the landing of a brigade of approximately 800 men from bases in Guatemala and Nicaragua, supported by an air strike from the same bases either simultaneously with the landing or 24 hours preceding it. Naval craft, with some "contracted" United States nationals aboard, would transport the brigade and supply logistic support. It is planned that the brigade, if unopposed and if surprise were achieved, would be able to consolidate their position and hold a beachhead for a limited number of days. If internal support does not materialize, it is planned that the brigade could either march directly to nearby mountains or be withdrawn from the beach to other nearby beaches from whence they could move into the mountains. Once in the mountains they would operate as a guerrilla unit.

My conclusions regarding this proposal are as follows:

1. The military evaluation of this proposal is that "ultimate success will depend upon political factors, i.e., a sizeable popular uprising or substantial follow-on forces." It is unlikely that a popular uprising would promptly take place in Cuba of a scale and kind which would make it impossible for the Castro regime to oppose the brigade with superior numbers of well armed troops.

2. It therefore appears possible, even probable, that we would be faced with the alternative of a) abandoning the brigade to its fate, which would cost us dearly in prestige and respect or b) attempting execution of the plan to move the brigade into the mountains as guerrillas, which would pose a prolonged problem of air drops or supplies or c) overt U.S. military intervention; a JCS staff officer has estimated there is at least a 10% chance that U.S. forces would be required unless alternative (a) were adopted.

3. Execution of the proposed plan would be in violation of Article 2, paragraph 4, and Article 51 of the Charter of the United Nations, Articles 18 and 25 of the Charter of the Organization of American States, and Article 1 of the Rio Treaty, which, in general, proscribe the use of armed force with the sole exception of the right of self-defense "if an armed attack occurs."

The Castro regime could be expected to call on the other American States (Article 3, paragraph 1 of the Rio Treaty) to assist them in repelling the attack, and to request the Security Council (Chapter 7 of the UN Charter) to take action to "maintain and restore international peace and security." The chances of promptly presenting both international organizations with a fait accompli are, in my opinion, virtually nil. It would therefore be extremely difficult to deal with Castro demarches of this kind. We could not disassociate ourselves from our complicity with Guatemala and Nicaragua; and if we tried to do so, both [Guatemalan President] Ydigoras and [Nicaraguan President] Somoza are in possession of sufficient information to implicate the United States in the eye of reasonable men.

4. Since the proposal comes closer to being a military invasion than a covert operation of the Guatemala type, account must be taken of the possibility that the execution of this proposal would attract to Castro additional support within Cuba. More important, a majority of the people of Latin America would oppose the operation, and we would expect that the Communists and Castroites would organize and lead demonstrations designed to bring about the overthrow of governments friendly to us. At best, our moral posture throughout the hemisphere would be impaired. At worst, the effect on our position of hemispheric leadership would be catastrophic.

5. Time is running against us in Cuba in a military sense since it is probable Castro soon will acquire jet aircraft, since he may acquire missiles and since Castro needs time to train his army and militia. Nevertheless, Defense does not currently consider Cuba to represent a threat to our national security. If later it should become a threat we are able to deal with it. . . .

6. The intelligence community was, and probably still is, unanimously of the opinion that time is running against us in Cuba in the sense that a declining curve of Castro popularity is offset by a rising curve of Castro control over the Cuban people. Nevertheless, it is not impossible that rifts between leaders in the Castro regime, mounting economic difficulties and rising resentment with terrorist methods will lead to the eventual over-throw of the Castro regime by the Cubans themselves, aided only by the more "conventional" type of covert activities now being carried out. In any case, time is not currently running against us in terms of Latin American public opinion; there has already been a significant decline in Castro's popularity in Latin America, a trend which we have reason to hope will continue, assuming Castro continues to employ the same methods. If one

looks at the Castro problem in the context of the struggle between the East and the West for Latin America, if one assumes the success or failure of the Castro policies to achieve a better life for the masses will significantly influence future hemisphere thought and action, and if one assumes that discipline and austerity will be hallmarks of Castroism, the political advantages to us of letting Latin America see for itself the practical results of applying communist theory in a Latin American country could well give us a decisive advantage in the ideological hemisphere struggle ahead of us.

7. I therefore conclude it would not be in the national interest to proceed unilaterally to put this plan into execution.

8. I also conclude that in spite of the difficulty maintaining or re-creating our Cuban "asset," we should consider proceeding as planned only if we receive strong support for collective action by the two-thirds majority required by the Rio Treaty. The chances of obtaining this agreement within the time limits imposed on us by the plan are not good. . . .

9. To determine whether Latin American support will be forthcoming it will be necessary discreetly to make soundings. There is no chance of obtaining Latin American support for a resolution authorizing the use of armed force against Cuba. Our best chance of getting support would be to propose a resolution for the collective recognition of a rebel government. The Latin Americans would understand the relationship between recognition of a rebel government and the Cuban "asset" in Central America without being told, i.e., that the recognition of the government would give at least a color of legality to support the proposed operation. . . .

. . . In any case, we will be much better off in the UN and the OAS if we are debating this issue than if we are debating the issue of whether the proposed operation constitutes an armed attack. It would offer the additional advantage of converting our posture from covert to overt, a posture which is in keeping with the American tradition. . . .

Source: U.S. Department of State, *Foreign Relations of the United States, 1961–1962,* Volume X, *Cuba,* 1961–1962.

MESSAGE FROM SOVIET PREMIER NIKITA KHRUSHCHEV TO JOHN F. KENNEDY, APRIL 19, 1961

Mr. President: I address this message to you at an alarming hour which is fraught with danger against universal peace. An armed aggression has been started against Cuba. It is an open secret that the armed bands which have invaded that country have been prepared, equipped, and armed in the United States. . . .

All this arouses in the Soviet Union...an understandable feeling of indignation.... Your statement a few days ago to the effect that the United States of America would not participate in military actions against Cuba created an impression that the leading authorities of the United States are aware of the consequences which aggression against Cuba could have for the whole world and the United States of America itself.

How are we to understand what is really being done by the United States now that the attack on Cuba has become a fact?...

As for the USSR, there must be no mistake about our position. We will extend to the Cuban people and its Government all the necessary aid for the repulse of the armed attack on Cuba. We are sincerely interested in the relaxation of international tension, but if others go in for its aggravation, then we will answer them in full measure....

I hope that the US Government will take into consideration these reasons, dictated only by concern that steps should not be permitted which might lead the world to a catastrophe of war.

Source: *Department of State Bulletin*, May 8, 1961, 662.

COMMUNIQUE ISSUED BY THE PRIME MINISTER OF CUBA FIDEL CASTRO (APRIL 15, 1961)

At 6 A.M., B-26 planes of the United States simultaneously bombed points in the city of Havana, San Antonio de los Baños and Santiago, according to reports received up to now.

Our anti-aircraft batteries opened fire on the attacking planes, hitting several, one of which withdrew enveloped in flames.

Cuban Air Force planes left immediately to pursue the enemy.

Up to the moment this report is being drafted explosions continue because the ammunition dump of the Cuban Air Force is in flames.

Up to the moment there are no dead although there are numerous wounded. The attack was a surprise and cowardly.

Our country has been the victim of a criminal imperialist aggression which violates all norms of international law.

The Cuban delegation to the United Nations has received instructions to accuse the United States Government directly of aggression.

The order has been given for mobilization of all combat units of the revolutionary army and the national revolutionary militia. All posts have been alerted.

If this air attack is a prelude to an invasion, the country, on a war basis, will resist and destroy with an iron hand any force which attempts to disembark upon our land.

The people will be amply informed of everything.

Every Cuban must occupy the post to which he has been assigned in military units and work centers without interrupting production of the anti-illiteracy campaign or a single revolutionary task.

The fatherland will resist with firm footing, serenely, an enemy attack assured of its victory.

The fatherland or death.

Source: *New York Times*, April, 16, 1961 in *American Foreign Policy: Current Documents*, 1961, 289.

BERLIN

The fiasco of the Bay of Pigs was only the first of a series of foreign relations crises that confronted Kennedy during his years in office. Not long after the dust had settled from the failed CIA operation in Cuba, tension that had been boiling in Europe over the division of Germany and the status of Berlin finally came to a head. After World War II, the Allies had jointly occupied Germany, but, by 1948, they had divided it into two parts. West Germany was accountable to the Western allies and NATO members, and East Germany fell within the Soviet sphere of influence in Eastern Europe. The Allies had also partitioned the German capital, located in the center of East Germany, into western and eastern spheres. This situation posed two problems for the Soviets. First, they were concerned about the presence of U.S. troops within a city in Eastern Europe, which the Soviets regarded as their sphere of influence. Second, the flourishing West Berlin economy, aided by economic reforms that the Western allies implemented in West Berlin, stood in stark contrast to the economic circumstances surrounding it in East Germany, struggling to implement the Soviet economic model. As a consequence, 30,000 East Germans a month were fleeing East Germany to West Berlin. West Berlin began to attract capital and skilled manpower from East Germany, threatening its collapse and undermining Soviet efforts to implement their own economic system there.

The Soviets had long been pressing for a formal resolution of the status of Germany. As early as 1958, Khrushchev had informed the Western allies that in the absence of a four power agreement on Germany, the Soviets would sign an independent treaty with the East German government, recognizing its legitimacy, yielding control of Berlin to the East German government, and thus cutting off Western access to West Berlin. Eisenhower had been willing to discuss the status of Germany and Berlin, though not the issue of Western presence in the latter. Eisenhower accomplished little on this issue though, and by early 1961, Khrushchev had decided to press the issue again. He took it up with the new president at a conference in Vienna in June. Khrushchev again threatened that if America did not remove its troops from West Berlin, making Berlin a "free city," the U.S.S.R. would sign a treaty with East Germany that would subject Western access to West Berlin to the whim of the East German government.

Kennedy had prepared to confront the Berlin issue. Although the German question did not play a major role in his campaign, from the beginning of his administration the Kennedy team debated the proper U.S. stance on Germany and Berlin. The discussion centered on the willingness to negotiate. Hard-liners, led by former Secretary of State Dean Acheson, McGeorge Bundy, and Vice President Lyndon Johnson, believed that American credibility was on the line in Berlin. They feared that if the United States backed down from the Soviets in Germany, America would project a position of weakness rather than strength in other parts of the world. U.N. Ambassador Adlai Stevenson, U.S. Ambassador to the Soviet Union Averill Harriman, and Senator Mike Mansfield (D-MT) advocated a more flexible position. They thought that Berlin was not worth the risk of war, that the commitment to a reunified Germany was impractical and only added fuel to the fire, and that the United States should be open to an alternative status for Berlin, such as a "free city." Senator J. William Fulbright (D-AK) even suggested making Berlin the permanent headquarters for the United Nations.

Reeling from the humiliation of the Bay of Pigs, and seeing Berlin as an important test of his mettle in foreign policy, Kennedy returned from the Vienna conference less receptive to the soft-liners. Buoyed by the support of the over 80 percent of Americans who favored the status quo in Berlin,[1] Kennedy was determined to convince the Soviet leader that he was not to be bullied. He strongly rebuffed the Soviet premier's threat, insisting that the position of the West on access to West Berlin, and ultimately to a reunified Germany, was not subject to debate. The president asked Congress for an emergency increase in defense spending, an increase in the size of the army of more than 10 percent by expanding the draft, and the mobilization of reservists. Kennedy called Berlin "the great testing place of Western courage and will."[2] For the first time, the Cold War was on the verge of becoming hot. Kennedy even called for the initiation of a coordinated fallout shelter program in the United States.

The situation escalated in August, when the East German government erected a cement and barbed wire "wall" dividing East and West Berlin. The wall worked in more ways than one. It halted the tide of East German refugees. Khrushchev accepted the wall, fearing that any more aggressive maneuvers would provoke the United States. Kennedy also backed down, calling the wall "a hell of a lot better than a war."[3] The crisis had not yet ended however. While the leaders of the two superpowers formulated responses to the building of the wall, military personnel on the ground in Germany implemented their own response. American General Lucius Clay equipped U.S. tanks with bulldozing mechanisms and prepared to bring down the wall. When the Soviet government learned of these actions, it sent its tanks to meet them. On October 27, 1961 American and Soviet tanks stood nose to nose, with the potential that one false move could precipitate a war that could result in millions of deaths and untold destruction. Behind the scenes, using a private "back channel" that Khrushchev had requested be established between Kennedy and him, the two leaders agreed to withdraw the tanks. The crisis in Germany was over, but the issue did not die. Both sides continued attempts to formalize the division of Germany and the question of "access" for at least another year. One historian even has called the Cuban Missile crisis, which followed in the fall of 1962, "the final phase of the Berlin crisis." Two Germanys and two Berlins remained until 1989, when the Berlin Wall finally crumbled as the Cold War era ended.

NOTES

1. George H. Gallup, *The Gallup Poll*, Vol. 3 (New York, 1972), 1729, cited in Thomas Allan Schwatz, "Victories and Defeats in the Long Twilight Struggle: The United States and Western Europe in the 1960s" in *The Diplomacy of the Crucial Decade*, ed. Diane Kunz (New York: Colombia University Press, 1994), 123.

2. *Public Papers of the Presidents, Kennedy, 1961* (Washington, DC: Government Printing Office, 1962), 534.

3. Cited in Michael Beschloss, *The Crisis Years* (New York: Harper Collins, 1991), 278.

LETTER FROM SOVIET PREMIER NIKITA KHRUSHCHEV TO U.S. PRESIDENT JOHN F. KENNEDY (SEPTEMBER 29, 1961)

I have given much thought of late to the development of international events since our meeting in Vienna, and I have decided to approach you with this letter. The whole world hopefully expected that our meeting and a frank exchange of views would have a soothing effect, would turn relations between our countries into the correct channel and promote the adoption of decisions which could give the peoples confidence that at last peace on earth will be secured. To my regret—and, I believe, to yours—this did not happen....

But you will agree with me, Mr. President, that the present international situation and its tension can hardly be assessed as a simple arithmetical sum total of unsolved issues.... Instead of confidence we are turning to an even greater aggravation. Far from bringing the possibility of agreement between us on disarmament closer, we are, on the contrary, worsening the situation still further. That is another important reason why the Soviet Union is now attaching such exclusive significance to the German question. We cannot escape the fact that there has been a second world war and that the problems we have inherited from the last war—first and foremost the conclusion of a German peace treaty—require their solution. . . .

If you were to come to the Soviet Union now—and this incidentally is something I am hoping for—you would surely convince yourself that not a single Soviet citizen will ever reconcile himself to the peace, which was won at such great cost, being under constant threat. But that will be the case until the countries that participated in the war recognize and formalize the results of the war in a German peace treaty. Yes, that is what our people are demanding, and they are right. . . . The position of the Soviet Union is shared by many. The impression is formed that understanding of the need to conclude a German peace treaty is growing in the world. I have already told you, Mr. President, that in striving for the conclusion of a German peace treaty we do not want somehow to prejudice the interests of the United States and their bloc allies. Neither are we interested in exacerbating the situation in connection with the conclusion of a German peace treaty. What need have we of such exacerbation? It is in the Western countries that they create all sorts of fears and allege that the socialist States intend well-nigh to swallow up West Berlin. You may believe my word, the word of the Soviet Government that neither we nor our allies need West Berlin.

I do not doubt that, given good will and desire, the Governments of our countries could find a common language in the question of a German peace treaty too. Naturally in the solution of that question it is necessary to proceed from the obvious fact, which even a blind man cannot fail to see, that there exist two sovereign German States. . . .

There remains the question of West Berlin which must also be solved when a German peace treaty is concluded. From whatever side we approach the matter, we probably will not be able to find a better solution than the transformation of West Berlin into a free city. And we shall proceed towards that goal. If, to our regret, the Western Powers will not wish to participate in a German peace settlement and the Soviet Union, together with the other countries that will be prepared to do so, has to sign a treaty with the German Democratic Republic (East Germany) we shall nonetheless provide a free city status for West Berlin.

Your statements, Mr. President, as well as the statements of other representatives of Western Powers not infrequently show signs of concern as to whether freedom for the population of West Berlin will be preserved, whether it will be able to live under the social and political system of its own choosing, whether West Berlin will be safeguarded against interference and outside pressure. I must say we see no difficulties in creating such conditions, the more so since the assurance of the freedom and complete independence of West Berlin is also our desire, is also our concern. . . .

It goes without saying that the occupation regime in West Berlin must be eliminated. Under the allied agreements occupation is a temporary measure and, indeed, never in history has there been a case of occupation becoming a permanent institution. But sixteen years have already elapsed since the surrender of Germany. For how long then is the occupation regime to be preserved?

A more stable status should be created for West Berlin than existed under the occupation. If the occupation regime has lived out its time and has become a source of strife among States it means the time has come to discard it. It has completely exhausted itself, has become a burden in relationships among nations and does not meet the interests of the population of West Berlin....

Of course, no one can be satisfied with half-measures which superficially would seem to erase from the surface differences among States while in effect they would be preserving them under cover and driving them in deeper. What use would there be if we barely covered up this delayed action landmine with earth and waited for it to explode. Indeed, no, the countries which are interested in consolidating peace must render that landmine completely harmless and tear it out of the heart of Europe.

The representatives of the United States sometimes declare that the American side is not advancing its concrete proposals on the German question because the Soviet Union allegedly is not striving for agreed solutions and wants to do everything by itself regardless of what other States may say. It is hard for me to judge how far such ideas really tell on the actions of the United States Government, but they are based on a profoundly mistaken assessment of the position of the Soviet Union....

Source: Letter, Khrushchev to Kennedy, September 29, 1961, *Foreign Relations of the United States, 1961–1963*, Vol. VI, *Kennedy-Khrushchev Exchanges*, Document 21, Department of State (Washington DC: Government Printing Office, 1996).

LETTER FROM U.S. PRESIDENT JOHN F. KENNEDY TO SOVIET PREMIER NIKITA KHRUSHCHEV (OCTOBER 16, 1961)

I, too, have often thought of our meeting in Vienna and the subsequent events which worsened the relations between our two countries and heightened the possibilities of war. I have already indicated that I think it unfruitful to fill this private channel with the usual charges and counter-charges; but I would hope that, upon re-examination, you will find my television address of July 25th was more balanced than "belligerent," as it is termed by your letter, although there may have been statements of opinion with which you would naturally disagree. To be sure, I made it clear that we intended to defend our vital interests in Berlin, and I announced certain measures necessary to such a defense. On the other hand, my speech also made it clear that we would prefer and encourage a peaceful solution, one which settled these problems, in the words of your letter, "on a mutually acceptable basis." My attitude concerning Berlin and Germany now, as it was then, is one of reason, not belligerence. There is peace in that area now—and this government shall not initiate and shall oppose any action which upsets that peace.

You are right in stating that we should all realistically face the facts in the Berlin and German situations—and this naturally includes facts which are inconvenient for both sides to face as well as those which we like. And one of those facts is the peace which exists in Germany now. It is not the remains of World War II but the threat of World War III that preoccupies us all. Of course, it is not "normal" for a nation to be divided by two different armies of occupation this long after the war; but the fact is that the area has been peaceful—it is not in itself the source of the present tension—and it could not be rendered more peaceful by your signing a peace treaty with the East Germans alone.

On the contrary, there is very grave danger that it might be rendered less peaceful, if such a treaty should convince the German people that their long-cherished hopes for unification were frustrated, and a spirit of nationalism and tension should sweep over all parts of the country. From my knowledge of West Germany today, I can assure you that this danger is far more realistic than the alleged existence there of any substantial number of Hitlerites or "revanchists." The real danger would arise from the kind of resentment I have described above; and I do not think that either of us, mindful of the lessons of history, is anxious to see this happen. Indeed, your letter makes clear that you are not interested in taking any step which would only be "exacerbating the situation." And I think this is a commendable basis on which both of us should proceed in the future.

The area would also be rendered less peaceful if the maintenance of the West's vital interests were to become dependent on the whims of the East German regime. Some of Mr. Ulbricht's statements on this subject have not been consistent with your reassurances or even his own—and I do not believe that either of us wants a constant state of doubt, tension and emergency in this area, which would require an even larger military build-up on both sides.

So, in this frank and informal exchange, let us talk about the peace which flows from actual conditions of peace, not merely treaties that bear that label. I am certain that we can create such conditions—that we can, as you indicate, reach an agreement which does not impair the vital interests or prestige of either side—and that we can transform the present crisis from a threat of world war into a turning-point in our relations in Europe. . . .

Whatever action you may take with East Germany, there is no difficulty, it seems to me, in your reserving your obligations and our rights with respect to Berlin until all of Germany is unified. But if you feel you must look anew at that situation, the real key to deciding the future status of West Berlin lies in your statement that the population of West Berlin must be able to "live under the social and political system of its own choosing." On this basis I must say that I do not see the need for a change in the situation of West Berlin, for today its people are free to choose their own way of life and their own guarantees of that freedom. If they are to continue to be free, if they are to be free to choose their own future as your letter indicates in the phrase quoted above, I take it this includes the freedom to choose which nations they wish to station forces there (limited in number but with unrestricted access) as well as the nature of their own ties with others (including, within appropriate limits, whatever ties they choose with West Germany). Inasmuch as you state very emphatically that you have no designs on West Berlin—and I am glad to have this assurance, for it makes the prospects of negotiation much brighter—I am sure you are not insisting on the location of Soviet troops in that portion of the city.

Thus, although there is much in your letter that makes me doubtful about the prospects in Germany, there are many passages which lead me to believe that an accommodation of our interests is possible. . . .

The alternative is so dire that we cannot give up our efforts to find such a settlement. . . .

Source: Letter, Kennedy to Khrushchev, October 16, 1961, *Foreign Relations of the United States, 1961–1963*, Vol. VI, *Kennedy-Khrushchev Exchanges*, Document 22, Department of State (Washington DC: Government Printing Office, 1996).

THE CUBAN MISSILE CRISIS

Although Kennedy managed to avoid war in Berlin in the summer of 1961, he faced an even more serious test the next year. By 1962 Soviet Premier Nikita Khrushchev was feeling pressure at home and abroad. The United States had shown during the Bay of Pigs that it would employ almost any measure to derail the expansion of communism. Even after the failed invasion, the United States continued to formulate plans to oust Castro, including the development of renewed contingency plans to invade the island. America was conducting drills off the coast of the Carolinas, dubbed "Orstac," and both Soviet and Cuban intelligence knew of these plans. Furthermore, in a speech in October 1961, the U.S. Deputy Secretary of Defense ended the perception that a "missile gap" existed between the Soviet Union and the United States when he confirmed that the United States could absorb the "first strike" in a nuclear exchange with the Soviets and retaliate with sufficient force to destroy the Soviet Union. Some in the Soviet Union expressed disappointment with Khrushchev's handling of the Berlin crisis, feeling that he backed down to the United States by failing to insist on the removal of Western troops from Berlin. Worse for the Soviets, in April of 1962, American Jupiter missiles poised on the Soviet-Turkish border, armed with nuclear warheads, became operational. Just as Kennedy was determined to preserve Western access to Berlin in order to keep the West in a "position of strength," Khrushchev now turned his attention to ensuring that the world, and the United States in particular, viewed the Soviet position as one of strength as well.

The Kennedy administration had been receiving intelligence reports since August of 1962 suspecting the installation of offensive Soviet missiles in Cuba, just ninety miles of the coast of South Florida. Kennedy, Rusk, and others initially discounted the reports, arguing that no evidence existed to indicate that Soviet weapons systems in Cuba were anything more than defensive installations (intelligence reports had confirmed that surface-to-air missiles were present in Cuba). The Soviets too maintained that they would refrain from placing offensive missiles in Cuba, and in mid-October 1962 National Security Advisor McGeorge Bundy informed the American public through a national television address that the American government had no reason to believe that the Soviets were installing an offensive arsenal in Cuba. However, at the same time as Bundy delivered his message to the American people, American spy planes over Cuba captured images from the island showing the development of massive missile complexes and the presence of medium-range ballistic missiles that could be fired from Cuba to the United States, with a range including all of Central America, Houston, Washington, DC, and New York City. On October 17, U-2 spy planes took pictures of intermediate-range ballistic missiles in Cuba. They had a strike zone that included all of the continental United States except for the extreme Pacific Northwest.

On October 15 Kennedy met with his top twelve security advisors, known as EXCOMM, commencing a series of top-secret discussions about the crisis that lasted for several days, practically unabated. They deliberated three possible American responses to the discovery of the Soviet missiles in Cuba. One option was an American air strike on the missile sites. Another was for the U.S. military to invade Cuba. Military leaders strongly supported these options. Joint Chiefs Chairman Maxwell Taylor argued that the United States needed to act quickly in order to ensure that the Soviets and their Cuban allies did not interpret a passive American response to the arrival of the missiles as American indifference to this development. The General also argued that a limited military response—striking the missile bases alone, for example—would leave Cubans with the capacity to retaliate. Taylor argued that U.S. air attacks should seek to destroy both the Soviet missiles and Cuban MIG fighter planes. Kennedy ruled out these aggressive actions. Khrushchev might react aggressively if Americans killed Soviet soldiers. Moreover, an American attack in Cuba might provoke a Soviet attack in Berlin or Turkey.

Nonetheless, Kennedy and everyone else in EXCOMM believed that the American response had to signal that the United States would not tolerate this kind of Soviet challenge. EXCOMM ultimately decided on a third option, a naval blockade of Cuba. Because American policymakers believed at the time, albeit incorrectly, that the Soviet missiles were not yet armed with nuclear warheads, EXCOMM figured that missiles could only threaten the United States once they became operational. By preventing Soviet ships from reaching Cuba with nuclear warheads, the missiles would be little more than empty tubes of steel. This would commit American seamen to confront and prevent, by force if necessary, Soviet ships from making deliveries to Cuba, and such confrontations could lead to disaster.

Not everyone in Kennedy's administration supported this strategy. In a letter to Kennedy on October 17, UN Ambassador Adlai Stevenson urged the President not to threaten action that would suggest U.S. unwillingness to negotiate a resolution to the crisis. "I feel you should have made it clear that the existence of nuclear bases anywhere is negotiable before we start anything," he lamented. More dramatically, commentator Walter Lippman criticized the blockade. In a *New York Herald Tribune* article, he opined that these actions signified the abandonment of diplomacy and thus put the country closer, rather than further, from war.

Historian Warren I. Cohen described the grim mood that prevailed when on October 22, President Kennedy for the first time informed Americans and the rest of the world of the presence of the Soviet missiles in Cuba and the American-imposed quarantine of the island. "To Americans—and knowledgeable people everywhere—there came an awareness that they hovered on the edge of extinction."[1] For the next five days, the world was "on the brink," or, in Attorney General Robert Kennedy's words, "one step away" from nuclear war.

Neither Khrushchev nor Kennedy wanted war, but both were trying to protect their images with domestic and global audiences. The prestige, credibility, and status of their respective countries hung in the balance. For five tense days, the entire Cuban military mobilized for war, Russia placed its military in a state of readiness, and the United States placed its military in the highest state of alert it would ever experience during the Cold War. Negotiations between the U.S.S.R. and the United States took place on several levels: Kennedy and Khrushchev exchanged private and public letters; Attorney General Robert Kennedy and Soviet ambassador to the United States, Alexander Dobrynin, engaged in private talks; both nations advanced proposals and received rebuffs in the United Nations; and John Scali, of ABC news, and Alexander Fomin, the KGB chief in Washington, who acted as ex officio representatives of the American and Soviet governments, engaged in unofficial communications. The Americans wanted the Soviets to withdraw their missiles from Cuba. The Soviet Union wanted the United States to issue a public declaration respecting the integrity of the Cuban government and pledging not to invade the island, as well as the removal of U.S. nuclear missiles from the Turkish-Russian border. Cubans were largely excluded from the negotiations. Fortunately, even though he continued to call the quarantine an "act of war," Khrushchev instructed Russian ships not to challenge U.S. naval vessels blockading Cuba.

On October 27, officials from the two governments agreed to terms to resolve the crisis, albeit initially on an informal basis. The Soviets would remove missiles from Cuba in exchange for a U.S. pledge not to invade Cuba. Behind the scenes, Kennedy also agreed to remove U.S. missiles from Turkey. This aspect of the deal though had to remain secret. Kennedy did not want Americans believing that he had exchanged American security interests in Turkey for the cessation of Soviet missile programs in Cuba. With his image as a Cold Warrior again on the line, he could not accept a situation that could make him seem vulnerable to the bullying tactics of the Soviet Union. Moreover, because Turkey was a member of NATO, Europeans might regard America's removal of the Jupiter Missiles as backing away from its commitments in Europe and Soviet. Thus, Kennedy's message to Khrushchev on October 27, agreeing to an outline of terms for a resolution of the crisis, made no mention of the missiles in Turkey. Robert Kennedy and Ambassador Dobrynin concluded that aspect of the deal privately.

The Cuban Missile crisis ended, and the threat of nuclear war subsided. In the aftermath of this brinksmanship, Kennedy and Khrushchev began work on, and eventually concluded, a Nuclear Test Ban Treaty. They also arranged to install a telephone "hot line" providing communications between the White House and the Kremlin. Although neither side in the crisis won a clear victory, the episode served throughout the Cold War as a reminder of the dangers of the bipolar balance of power in the nuclear age.

NOTE

1. Warren I. Cohen, *America in the Age of Soviet Power, 1945–1991* (New York: Cambridge University Press, 1996), 140.

PRESIDENT JOHN F. KENNEDY, "RADIO AND TELEVISION REPORT TO THE AMERICAN PEOPLE ON THE SOVIET ARMS BUILDUP IN CUBA" (OCTOBER 22, 1962)

This Government, as promised, has maintained the closest surveillance of the Soviet Military buildup on the island of Cuba. Within the past week, unmistakable evidence has established the fact that a series of offensive missile sites is now in preparation on that imprisoned island. The purpose of these bases can be none other than to provide a nuclear strike capability against the Western Hemisphere....

This action... contradicts the repeated assurances of Soviet spokesmen, both publicly and privately delivered, that the arms buildup in Cuba would retain its original defensive character, and that the Soviet Union had no need or desire to station strategic missiles on the territory of any other nation....

Neither the United States of America nor the world community of nations can tolerate deliberate deception and offensive threats on the part of any nation, large or small. We no longer live in a world where only the actual firing of weapons represents a sufficient challenge to a nation's security to constitute maximum peril. Nuclear weapons are so destructive and ballistic missiles are so swift, that any substantially increased possibility of their use or any sudden change in their deployment may well be regarded as a definite threat to peace....

In that sense, missiles in Cuba add to an already clear and present danger—although it should be noted the nations of Latin America have never previously been subjected to a potential nuclear threat.

But this secret, swift, and extraordinary buildup of Communist missiles ... is a deliberately provocative and unjustified change in the status quo which cannot be accepted by this country, if our courage and our commitments are ever to be trusted again by either friend or foe....

Acting, therefore, in the defense of our own security and of the entire Western Hemisphere, and under the authority entrusted to me by the Constitution as endorsed by the resolution of the Congress, I have directed that the following initial steps be taken immediately:

First: To halt this offensive buildup, a strict quarantine on all offensive military equipment under shipment to Cuba is being initiated. All ships of any kind bound for Cuba from whatever nation or port will, if found to contain cargoes of offensive weapons, be turned back.... We are not at this time, however, denying the necessities of life as the Soviets attempted to do in their Berlin blockade of 1948.

Second: I have directed the continued and increased close surveillance of Cuba and its military buildup.... Should these offensive military preparations continue, thus increasing the threat to the hemisphere, further action will be justified. I have directed the Armed Forces to prepare for any eventualities; and I trust that in the interest of both the Cuban people and the Soviet technicians at the sites, the hazards to all concerned in continuing this threat will be recognized.

Third: It shall be the policy of this Nation to regard any nuclear missile launched from Cuba against any nation in the Western Hemisphere as an attack by the Soviet Union on the United States, requiring a full retaliatory response upon the Soviet Union.

Fourth: As a necessary military precaution, I have reinforced our base at Guantanamo, evacuated today the dependents of our personnel there, and ordered additional military units to be on a standby alert basis.

Fifth: We are calling tonight for an immediate meeting of the Organ of Consultation under the Organization of American States, to consider this threat to hemispheric security and to invoke articles 6 and 8 of the Rio Treaty in support of all necessary action. The United Nations Charter allows for regional security arrangements—and the nations of this hemisphere decided long ago against the military presence of outside powers. Our other allies around the world have also been alerted.

Sixth: Under the Charter of the United Nations, we are asking tonight that an emergency meeting of the Security Council be convoked without delay to take action against this latest Soviet threat to world peace. Our resolution will call for the prompt dismantling and withdrawal of all offensive weapons in Cuba, under the supervision of U.N. observers, before the quarantine can be lifted.

Seventh and finally: I call upon Chairman Khrushchev to halt and eliminate this clandestine, reckless and provocative threat to world peace and to stable relations between our two nations. I call upon him further to abandon this course of world domination, and to join in an historic effort to end the perilous arms race and to transform the history of man. He has an opportunity now to move the world back from the abyss of destruction—by returning to his government's own words that it had no need to station missiles outside its own territory, and withdrawing these weapons from Cuba—by refraining from any action which will widen or deepen the present crisis—and then by participating in a search for peaceful and permanent solutions....

Many times in the past, the Cuban people have risen to throw out tyrants who destroyed their liberty. And I have no doubt that most Cubans today look forward to the time when they will be truly free—free from foreign domination, free to choose their own leaders, free to select their own system, free to own their own land, free to speak and write and worship without fear or degradation. And then shall Cuba be welcomed back to the society of free nations and to the associations of this hemisphere.

My fellow citizens: let no one doubt that this is a difficult and dangerous effort on which we have set out. No one can see precisely what course it will take or what costs or casualties will be incurred. Many months of sacrifice and self-discipline lie ahead—months in which our patience and our will will be tested—months in which many threats and denunciations will keep us aware of our dangers. But the greatest danger of all would be to do nothing....

Our goal is not the victory of might, but the vindication of right—not peace at the expense of freedom, but both peace and freedom, here in this hemisphere, and, we hope, around the world. God willing, that goal will be achieved.

Source: John F. Kennedy Library, <http://www.cs.umb.edu/jfklibrary/j102262.htm>

JOINT CHIEFS OF STAFF CHAIRMAN
MAXWELL TAYLOR, EXCHANGE WITH
PRESIDENT KENNEDY DURING EXCOM MEETING
(OCTOBER 16, 1962)

Taylor: This is a point target, Mr., uh, President. You're never sure of having, absolutely of getting everything down there. We intend to do a great deal of damage because we can [words unintelligible]. But, as the Secretary says here, there was unanimity among all the commanders involved in the Joint Chiefs, uh, that in our judgment, it would be a mistake to take this very narrow, selective target because it invited reprisal attacks and it may be detrimental. Now if the, uh, Soviets have been willing to give, uh, nuclear warheads to these missiles, there is every, just as good reason for them to give nuclear capability to these bases. We don't think we'd ever have a chance to take 'em again, so that we lose this, the first strike surprise capability. Our recommendation would be to get complete intelligence, get all the photography we need, the next two or three days, no, no hurry in our book. Then look at this target system. If it really threatens the United States, then take it right out with one hard crack.

JFK: That would be taking out the, uh, some of those fighters, bombers and . . .

Taylor: Fighters, the bombers, uh, IL-28s may turn up in this photography. It's not all that unlikely there're some there.

JFK: Think you could do that in one day?

Taylor: Uh, we think that the first strike, we'd get a great majority of this. We'll never get it all, Mr. President. But we then have to come back day after day for several days—we said, uh, five days perhaps—to do the complete job. Uh, meanwhile, we could then be making up our mind as to whether or not to go on and invade the island. I'm very much impressed with the need for a time something like five to seven days for this air purpose because of the parachute aspect of the in-, proposed invasion. You can't take parachute formations, close formations of, uh, troop carrier planes in the face of any air opposition really. So the first job, before the, any land, uh, attack, including [parachutes or para-troops?], is really cleaning out the, the MIGs and the, uh, the accompanying aircraft. . . .

Source: U.S., Department of State, *Foreign Relations of the United States, 1961–1963,* Volume XI, *Cuban Missile Crisis and Aftermath.*

WALTER LIPPMANN, "BLOCKADE PROCLAIMED,"
NEW YORK HERALD TRIBUNE
(OCTOBER 25, 1962)

It is Wednesday morning as I am writing this article and the President's proclamation of a selective blockade has just gone into effect. We are now waiting for the other shoe to drop....

...we can only speculate as to whether the Soviets will engage themselves at sea on the way to Cuba, will submit to the blockade and retaliate elsewhere, or will limit themselves to violent statements without violent action. There are those for whose judgment I have profound respect who think that it is now too late for this country to influence the decisions of the Soviet Union and that the President is now irretrievably committed to a course which can end only with a total blockade or an invasion of Cuba.

They may be right. But I have lived through two world wars, and in both of them, once we were engaged, we made the same tragic mistake. We suspended diplomacy when the guns began to shoot. In both wars as the result we achieved a great victory but we could not make peace. There is a mood in this country today which could easily cause us to make the same mistake again. We must in honor attempt to avoid it....

There are three ways to get rid of the missiles in Cuba. One is to invade and occupy Cuba. The second way is to institute a total blockade, particularly of oil shipments, which would in a few months ruin the Cuban economy. The third way is to try, I repeat to try, to negotiate a face-saving agreement....

The only place that is truly comparable with Cuba is Turkey. This is the only place where there are strategic weapons right on the frontier of the Soviet Union....

There is another important similarity between Cuba and Turkey. The Soviet missile base in Cuba, like the U.S.-NATO base in Turkey, is of little military value. The Soviet military base in Cuba is defenseless, and the base in Turkey is all but obsolete. The two bases could be dismantled without altering the world balance of power....

For all these reasons I say that an agreement of this sort may be doable and that there may exist a way out of the tyranny of automatic and uncontrollable events.

Source: Vincent Ferraro, <http://www.mtholyoke.edu/acad/intrel/cuba/lippmann.htm>

LETTER FROM SOVIET PREMIER NIKITA KHRUSHCHEV
TO U.S. PRESIDENT JOHN F. KENNEDY (OCTOBER 26, 1962)

You are mistaken if you think that any of our means on Cuba are offensive. However, let us not quarrel now. It is apparent that I will not be able to convince you of this. But I say to you: You, Mr. President, are a military man and should understand: Can one attack, if one has on one's territory even an enormous quantity of missiles of various effective radiuses and various power, but using only these means. These missiles are a means of extermination and destruction. But one cannot attack with these missiles, even nuclear missiles of a power of 100 megatons because only people, troops, can attack. Without people, any means however powerful cannot be offensive. . . .

I believe that you have no basis to think this way. You can regard us with distrust, but, in any case, you can be calm in this regard, that we are of sound mind and understand perfectly well that if we attack you, you will respond the same way. But you too will receive the same that you hurl against us. And I think that you also understand this. My conversation with you in Vienna gives me the right to talk to you this way. . . .

You have now proclaimed piratical measures, which were employed in the Middle Ages, when ships proceeding in international waters were attacked, and you have called this "a quarantine" around Cuba. Our vessels, apparently, will soon enter the zone which your Navy is patrolling. I assure you that these vessels, now bound for Cuba, are carrying the most innocent peaceful cargoes. Do you really think that we only occupy ourselves with the carriage of so-called offensive weapons, atomic and hydrogen bombs? Although perhaps your military people imagine that these (cargoes) are some sort of special type of weapon, I assure you that they are the most ordinary peaceful products. . . .

. . . If you stop the vessels, then, as you yourself know, that would be piracy. If we started to do that with regard to your ships, then you would also be as indignant as we and the whole world now are. One cannot give another interpretation to such actions, because one cannot legalize lawlessness. If this were permitted, then there would be no peace, there would also be no peaceful coexistence. We should then be forced to put into effect the necessary measures of a defensive character to protect our interests in accordance with international law. Why should this be done? To what would all this lead? . . .

Mr. President, I appeal to you to weigh well what the aggressive, piratical actions, which you have declared the USA intends to carry out in international waters, would lead to. You yourself know that any sensible man simply cannot agree with this, cannot recognize your right to such actions.

If you did this as the first step towards the unleashing of war, well then, it is evident that nothing else is left to us but to accept this challenge of yours. If, however, you have not lost your self-control and sensibly conceive what this might lead to, then, Mr. President, we and you ought not now to pull on the ends of the rope in which you have tied the knot of war, because the more the two of us pull, the tighter that knot will be tied. And a moment may come when that knot will be tied so tight that even he who tied it will not have the strength to untie it, and then it will be necessary to cut that knot, and what that would mean is not for me to explain to you, because you yourself understand perfectly of what terrible forces our countries dispose.

Consequently, if there is no intention to tighten that knot and thereby to doom the world to the catastrophe of thermonuclear war, then let us not only relax the forces pulling on the ends of the rope, let us take measures to untie that knot. We are ready for this. . . .

Source: Telegram, Khrushchev to Kennedy, October 29, 1962, *Foreign Relations of the United States, 1961–1963*, Vol. VI, *Kennedy-Khrushchev Exchanges*, Document 65, Department of State (Washington DC: Government Printing Office, 1996).

ARMS CONTROL AND THE LIMITED TEST BAN TREATY

With two crises in Berlin and Cuba putting the world on the brink of nuclear war, prudence suggested the need for arms control. Eisenhower had begun such a movement, and although no formal agreements were concluded in the 1950s, both the Soviets and the Americans ceased testing nuclear weapons for a brief period at the end of that decade. By the time Kennedy assumed office, nuclear tensions were on the rise again. For leaders on both sides, the development of nuclear policy was a risky, but necessary, proposition. Both sides recognized that a successful nuclear development program rested on at least a sense of parity in the nuclear arsenals of the two superpowers. Although more nuclear warheads existed than were necessary effectively to end modern civilization, Americans and Soviets alike feared allowing the other to achieve "superiority" in the nuclear arms race. Still, building more weapons than either nation could possibly use wasted resources that either country could better spend on other government programs. Until the Limited Test Ban Treaty cooled tensions a bit in 1963, the arms race not only added more and more powerful weapons to the world's supply of nuclear warheads, but seemed to make real war ever more imminent. The need to balance the national security interests of nuclear deterrence and the national security interests of preventing a nuclear exchange thus formed the crux of the defense policy at the super-power level, and the core of arms control considerations in particular.

Kennedy and most of his military and foreign policy advisors came to realize the importance of arms control in the aftermath of the Cuban

Missile crisis. Although quietly many realized that arms control was the wisest policy, Kennedy had campaigned on the premise of a "missile gap" and had pledged to remedy the deficiency in the stock of American nuclear weapons. Moreover, the Kennedy team initially proved unable to establish a position on arms control that everyone in the administration could support. However, after the two superpowers twice brought the world to the brink of nuclear disaster, Kennedy and his foreign policy advisors, like their Soviet counterparts, began to consider more seriously the need for bringing the production of nuclear weapons under control.

American and Soviet diplomats met in Geneva, but discussions were initially difficult. Americans wanted a comprehensive test ban agreement, prohibiting any kind of testing of nuclear weapons. Leary of the mechanisms required to ensure compliance, the Soviets resisted any such agreement. Inspection of testing sites, they reasoned, which would require bringing specialists from the other side of the East-West divide into the Soviet Union (or into the United States for that matter), raised suspicion and concern about the potential for spying. American diplomats tried to negotiate with the Soviets on the inspection issue to no avail. At the same time, some American foreign-policymakers worried about the very ability of American inspection mechanisms. The members of the Inspection Study Group, with the Arms Control and Disarmament Agency, for example, expressed their concern in a published report in July 1962, noting: "It appears to us that the resources of existing technology will allow an inspection system that will support an arms control agreement. We are impressed however, with the gap in our knowledge of such capabilities and therefore believe that a program of experiment and test is much needed to determine and perfect inspection equipment. . . ."[1]

When the inspection issue could not be resolved, testing underwater, in air, and in space became the focus of the talks, with underground testing a question Americans would not include so long as the Soviets resisted a rigorous inspection regime. At the same time, some Americans were becoming restless with the efforts to water-down the agreements in order to move the Soviets to acquiesce while others expressed concerns that any limitations on the U.S. nuclear program, with Soviet reciprocity or not, would inhibit improvements in the American arsenal that were necessary to the security of the United States. Moreover they argued, even if the Soviets agreed to a test ban, there was no guarantee that they would uphold their end of the bargain. According to Kennedy's national security advisor, McGeorge Bundy, what really put an arms control agreement on the fast track in the aftermath of the Missile Crisis was a speech President Kennedy delivered at American University committing the United States to limiting the testing of nuclear weapons. In Bundy's words, "what caused [the Test Ban Treaty] to become reality was the . . . development of confidence and readiness to dare on the part of one man—the President himself."[2] While

Kennedy's speech signaled his willingness to broker an arms limitation agreement, other factors were also important.

For one, by the summer of 1963 Khrushchev was no longer courting the Chinese as allies. Pressure from China had contributed to Khrushchev's stubborn negotiating position in the early 1960s. The development of nuclear weapons in China, by all accounts, was inevitable and concerned both Kennedy and Khrushchev. The Chinese and the Soviets had never been the best of friends. Despite their common embrace of communism, they interpreted and applied the ideology differently. Khrushchev had worked diligently since he had succeeded Stalin to bring the Chinese more in line with the Comintern. But, in the summer of 1963, only weeks after Kennedy's address at American University, the Chinese announced that they would replace the Soviets as the world leaders of communism. The break, between the Soviets and the Chinese often referred to as the "Sino-Soviet split," removed a major burden from the shoulders of the Soviet leadership with respect to arms control, and, by raising the prospect of a difficult if not antagonistic relationship with China, made détente with the United States all the more appealing. In fact, Lawrence Freedman argues, in the contest for international communist allies between the Soviets and the Chinese, a test ban treaty would reverse the pressure, highlighting the "recklessness" of the Chinese and the sound and cautious position of the Soviets. In July 1963, Americans and Soviets agreed to terms of a treaty limiting the testing of nuclear weapons in the atmosphere, underwater, or in space and limiting the proliferation of nuclear knowledge and materials. The language of the treaty also included a vague clause designed to allow withdrawal from the treaty in the case of "extraordinary events," namely in the case that the Chinese begin their own testing program.

With the treaty signed, Kennedy's efforts turned to ratification. Senator Wayne Morse (D-OR) was among those who raised relatively minor objections to the treaty by questioning the intentions of the U.S. government to abide by its nonproliferation clauses. Morse was particularly concerned about the sharing of information with America's ally France, which was in the process of developing a nuclear program of its own in the early 1960s. "If we share nuclear weapons information with [France]," Morse argued, "we shall be proliferating nuclear weapons. Worse still, we shall be inviting the Soviet Union to turn over nuclear weapons to various nations of her own choosing."[3] In a debate that continues into the twenty-first century, others argued that the treaty would prevent not only the testing of offensive nuclear missiles but defensive weapons as well. These critics, such as the Stanford scientist, Stefan T. Possony, argued that while the treaty proposed to govern testing and even the quantity of missiles produced by the two superpowers, American statements overlooked the sheer power of the weapons themselves. The treaty under consideration, Possony argued, did not sufficiently consider nuclear mega-tonnage (destructive power), and consequently, paved the way for the Soviets secretly to develop weapons systems, via underground testing, capable of destroying the United States, while preventing America from testing and developing adequate missile systems for its own defense. Naturally, certain military men opposed the treaty as well. Air Force Chairman Curtis LeMay was chief among them. Kennedy turned his attention to bringing the Joint Chiefs over to the side of the treaty. Fortunately, the chairman of the Joint Chiefs, General Maxwell Taylor, though more often than not hawkish on issues of armaments, was not, like LeMay, a "new look" man who believed that an awesome nuclear arsenal should be the cornerstone of U.S. defense policy. Moreover, General Taylor believed in a careful use of the military, as opposed to the more no-holds-barred philosophy held by others of the Joint Chiefs. Assurances to the Joints Chiefs that the treaty permitted the military to retain the ability to test nuclear weapons underground, revive atmospheric testing programs if international events warranted, and develop more sophisticated tools for detecting violations moved the military leaders to back the treaty. With the sanction of the military, the Senate voted overwhelmingly to ratify the treaty, 80–19.

NOTES

1. *Foreign Relations Series of the United States*, 1961–1963, Vol. VII, *Disarmament*, 524.

2. McGeorge Bundy, "Presidents and Arms Control: John F. Kennedy and Lyndon B. Johnson," presented in a Forum at the Miller Center of Public Affairs, University of Virginia, October 28, 1993.

3. *Congressional Record*, 88th Congress, 1st Session, 14934.

JOHN F. KENNEDY, COMMENCEMENT ADDRESS AT AMERICAN UNIVERSITY (JUNE 10, 1963)

I have . . . chosen this time and this place to discuss a topic on which ignorance too often abounds and the truth is too rarely perceived—yet it is the most important topic on earth: world peace.

What kind of peace do I mean? What kind of peace do we seek? Not a Pax Americana enforced on the world by American weapons of war. Not the peace of the grave or the security of the slave. I am talking about genuine peace, the kind of peace that makes life on earth worth living, the kind that enables men and nations to grow and to hope and to build a better life for their children—not merely peace for Americans but peace for all men and women—not merely peace in our time but peace for all time.

I speak of peace because of the new face of war. Total war makes no sense in an age when great powers can maintain large and relatively invulnerable nuclear forces and refuse to surrender without resort to those forces. It makes no sense in an age when a single nuclear weapon contains almost ten times the explosive force delivered by all the allied air forces in the Second World War. It makes no sense in an age when the deadly poisons produced by a nuclear exchange would be carried by wind and water and soil and seed to the far corners of the globe and to generations yet unborn. . . .

We have also been talking in Geneva about the other first-step measures of arms control designed to limit the intensity of the arms race and to reduce the risks of accidental war. Our primary long range interest in Geneva, however, is general and complete disarmament— designed to take place by stages, permitting parallel political developments to build the new institutions of peace which would take the place of arms. The pursuit of disarmament has been an effort of this Government since the 1920's. It has been urgently sought by the past three administrations. And however dim the prospects may be today, we intend to continue this effort—to continue it in order that all countries, including our own, can better grasp what the problems and possibilities of disarmament are.

The one major area of these negotiations where the end is in sight, yet where a fresh start is badly needed, is in a treaty to outlaw nuclear tests. The conclusion of such a treaty, so near and yet so far, would check the spiraling arms race in one of its most dangerous areas. It would place the nuclear powers in a position to deal more effectively with one of the greatest hazards which man faces in 1963, the further spread of nuclear arms. It would increase our security—it would decrease the prospects of war. Surely this goal is sufficiently important to require our steady pursuit, yielding neither to the temptation to give up the whole effort nor the temptation to give up our insistence on vital and responsible safeguards.

I am taking this opportunity, therefore, to announce two important decisions in this regard.

First: Chairman Khrushchev, Prime Minister Macmillan, and I have agreed that high-level discussions will shortly begin in Moscow looking toward early agreement on a comprehensive test ban treaty. Our hopes must be tempered with the caution of history—but with our hopes go the hopes of all mankind.

Second: To make clear our good faith and solemn convictions on the matter, I now declare that the United States does not propose to conduct nuclear tests in the atmosphere so long as other states do not do so. We will not be the first to resume. Such a declaration is no substitute for a formal binding treaty, but I hope it will help us achieve it.

Finally, my fellow Americans, let us examine our attitude toward peace and freedom here at home. The quality and spirit of our own society must justify and support our efforts abroad. We must show it in the dedication of our own lives—as many of you who are graduating today will have a unique opportunity to do, by serving without pay in the Peace Corps abroad or in the proposed National Service Corps here at home.

But wherever we are, we must all, in our daily lives, live up to the age-old faith that peace and freedom walk together. In too many of our cities today, the peace is not secure because the freedom is incomplete.

It is the responsibility of the executive branch at all levels of government —local, State, and National—to provide and protect that freedom for all of our citizens by all means within their authority. It is the responsibility of the legislative branch at all levels, wherever that authority is not now adequate, to make it adequate. And it is the responsibility of all citizens in all sections of this country to respect the rights of all others and to respect the law of the land.

All this is not unrelated to world peace. "When a man's ways please the Lord," the Scriptures tell us, "he maketh even his enemies to be at peace with him." And is not peace, in the last analysis, basically a matter of human rights—the right to live out our lives without fear of devastation—the right to breathe air as nature provided it—the right of future generations to a healthy existence?

While we proceed to safeguard our national interests, let us also safeguard human interests. And the elimination of war and arms is clearly in the interest of both. No treaty, however much it may be to the advantage of all, however tightly it may be worded, can provide absolute security against the risks of deception and evasion. But it can—if it is sufficiently effective in its enforcement and if it is sufficiently in the interests of its signers—offer far more security and far fewer risks than an unabated, uncontrolled, unpredictable arms race.

The United States, as the world knows, will never start a war. We do not want a war. We do not now expect a war. . . . We shall be prepared if others wish it. We shall be alert to try to stop it. But we shall also do our part to build a world of peace where the weak are safe and the strong are just. We are not helpless before that task or hopeless of its success. Confident and unafraid, we labor on—not toward a strategy of annihilation but toward a strategy of peace.

Source: John F. Kennedy Library, <http://www.cs.umb.edu/jfklibrary/j061063. htm>

JOHN F. KENNEDY, RADIO AND TELEVISION ADDRESS TO THE AMERICAN PEOPLE ON THE NUCLEAR TEST BAN TREATY (JULY 26, 1963)

Good evening my fellow citizens:
I speak to you tonight in a spirit of hope. . . .

Yesterday, a shaft of light cut into the darkness. Negotiations were concluded in Moscow on a treaty to ban all nuclear tests in the atmosphere, in outer space, and under water. For the first time an agreement has been reached on bringing the forces of nuclear destruction under international control....

The treaty initialed yesterday, therefore, is a limited treaty which permits continued underground testing and prohibits only those tests that we ourselves can police. It requires no control posts, no onsite inspection, no international body.

We should also understand that it has other limits as well. Any nation which signs the treaty will have an opportunity to withdraw if it finds that extraordinary events related to the subject matter of the treaty have jeopardized its supreme interests; and no nation's right of self-defense will in any way be impaired. Nor does this treaty mean an end to the threat of nuclear war. It will not reduce nuclear stockpiles; it will not halt the production of nuclear weapons; it will not restrict their use in time of war....

This treaty is in part the product of Western patience and vigilance. We have made clear—most recently in Berlin and Cuba—our deep resolve to protect our security and our freedom against any form of aggression. We have also made clear our steadfast determination to limit the arms race....

But the achievement of this goal is not a victory for one side—it is a victory for mankind. It reflects no concessions either to or by the Soviet Union. It reflects simply our common recognition of the dangers of further testing.

This treaty is not the millennium. It will not resolve all conflicts, or cause the Communists to forego their ambitions, or eliminate the danger of war. It will not reduce our need for arms or allies or programs of assistance to others. But it is an important first step—a step towards peace—a step towards reason—a step away from war....

But the difficulty of predicting the next step is no reason to be reluctant about this step. Nuclear test ban negotiations have long been a symbol of East-West disagreement. If this treaty can also be a symbol—if it can symbolize the end of one era and the beginning of another—if both sides by this treaty can gain confidence and experience in peaceful collaboration —then this short and simple treaty may well become an historic mark in man's age-old pursuit of peace....

A war today or tomorrow, if it led to nuclear war, would not be like any war in history. A full-scale nuclear exchange, lasting less than 60 minutes, with the weapons now in existence, could wipe out more than 300 million Americans, Europeans, and Russians, as well as untold numbers elsewhere. And the survivors, as Chairman Khrushchev warned the Communist Chinese "the survivors would envy the dead." For they would inherit a world so devastated by explosions and poison and fire that today we cannot even conceive of its horrors. So let us try to turn the world away from war. Let us make the most of this opportunity, and every opportunity, to reduce tension, to slow down the perilous nuclear arms race, and to check the world's slide toward final annihilation....

This treaty can be the opening wedge in that campaign. It provides that none of the parties will assist other nations to test in the forbidden environments. It opens the door for further agreements on the control of nuclear weapons, and it is open for all nations to sign, for its is in the interest of all nations, and already we have heard from a number of countries who wish to join with us promptly. . . .

If we are to open new doorways to peace, if we are to seize this rare opportunity for progress, if we are to be as bold and farsighted in our control of weapons as we have been in their invention, then let us now show all the world on this side of the wall and the other than a strong America also stands for peace. There is no cause for complacency. . . .

My fellow Americans, let us take that first step. Let us, if we can, step back from the shadows of war and seek out the way of peace. And if that journey is a thousand miles, or even more, let history record that we, in this land, at this time, took the first step.

Thank you and good night.

Source: John F. Kennedy Library, <http://www.cs.umb.edu/jfklibraryj072663. htm>

STEFAN T. POSSONY, CRITIQUE OF SECRETARY MCNAMARA'S TEST BAN TESTIMONY (AUGUST 13, 1963)

During his Senate testimony on August 13 supporting the partial test ban treaty, Secretary of Defense Robert S. McNamara talked about the increase in the number of nuclear warheads in the strategic alert force and the doubling of the megatonnage of that force, but passed over in silence the reduction of megatonnage due to the retirement of aircraft. If megatonnage is important, as his argument infers, the net changes in our overall capabilities must be considered.

Mr. McNamara also cast some doubt, though this doubt is now weaker than it was some time ago, on Soviet capability to deliver l00-megaton warheads. Yet in a recent article, Maj. Alexander P. de Seversky argued cogently that since the Soviets have advantages in missile boost, it is "dangerous naiveté for McNamara to speculate" that the Soviets "at this time" have no missile to deliver a l00-megaton warhead to ICBM range. Incidentally, Mr. McNamara's phrasing implies that the Soviets may now be able to deliver a 100-megaton warhead at closer range which, of course, has enormous implications with respect to such problems as Europe, Japan, and Cuba.

The presumed U.S. capability to develop relatively small warheads to assure penetration by saturation of "sophisticated and very elaborate ballistic missile defenses" would be meaningless or superfluous, if the Soviets as the President stated, cannot develop such defenses. On the other hand, if they are able to develop such defenses, then the question arises why we are delaying the U.S. antimissile and are depriving ourselves through the test ban treaty, of the particular type of firepower that is needed to render our missile defense truly effective? ... Indeed, if the Soviets were to strike by surprise, they could protect their population by prior evacuation against an anticipated less-than-5,000 megaton blast, while our population could not be effectively protected against 100,000 megatons delivered with the suddenness on which Soviet strategic planners place so much emphasis. ...

Mr. McNamara thinks that if we limit Soviet testing to underground, we can gain more experience more rapidly, because such testing is more difficult and more expensive. This is entirely fictional: the Soviets suffer from no scientific or economic constraints limiting underground tests. ...

With respect to the discovery of deep space tests ... of low kiloton shots in the atmosphere ... such tests could be conducted clandestinely. ... Secretary McNamara also admitted that the feasibility of testing in the South Pacific is rather good. He offered no reason for his assumption that underwater tests ... could be detected. ...

Mr. McNamara minimized the danger of surprise abrogation by saying that even if the Soviets suddenly resumed atmospheric testing, they would not be able to achieve a significant time advantage. However, if their atmospheric tests were preceded by extensive underground testing ... his assessment that the Soviets could not achieve a significant time advantage would be wrong: moreover, highly successful tests of unexpected weapons could demoralize US strategic leadership ...

[The] enormous military disadvantages [of the treaty] are allegedly overshadowed by the treaty's contribution toward the restraint on the further proliferation of nuclear weapons and the reduction of causes of world tension. ... Disregarding proliferation, how may international tension be reduced, international relations be stabilized, and a move toward a peaceful environment be achieved, if the USSR gains militarily, if the Soviet first strike becomes more potent, if the US second strike grows perceptibly weaker, if the MRBM threat is not neutralized, if the USSR gets a unilateral antimissile defense, and if they are overcoming their specific nuclear deficiencies, while we will be stuck with ours? ...

The greatest paradox is that, according to the administration's argument, this treaty is a first step to peace, but will not hinder the growth of our nuclear strength. We will build more bombs, warheads, nuclear artillery shells, and depth charges. Yet the allegation is that already we have tens of thousands of nuclear weapons, and hence nuclear superiority. The administration's argument makes not reference to the means of delivery without which these weapons cannot be used, and which we are not acquiring in the requisite type and numbers.

Mr. McNamara's arguments boils down to this: The United States can deter—and if necessary, win—a nuclear conflict by maintaining a strategic force which, in terms of missile firepower, will possess only 5 percent of the strength of the future Soviet strategic force. Against this superior force, we are told, the United States needs no particular defense. If this is the new strategy which the treaty inaugurates, only God can help us. What kind of defense miracle will have to come to pass if, as General Taylor expressed it: "militant communism remains committed to the destruction of our society?"

Source: *Congressional Record*, Vol. 109, Pt. 12, 16380–16382.

CIVIL RIGHTS

Despite campaign rhetoric promising to introduce a civil rights bill and to sign an order prohibiting segregation in federally funded housing, John Kennedy, like Eisenhower, did not wish to embark on an aggressive campaign to promote civil rights. Although he still had not mastered the game of politics in the Congress, by the time he was elected president, Kennedy had developed into a calculating politician who realized both the perils of taking on the issue of black civil rights in practice and the advantages of supporting the issue rhetorically. The closeness of the election of 1960 made Kennedy realize that he was not working with a strong mandate from Americans. Although civil rights legislation might help shore up the black faction of the New Deal constituency, such laws would surely turn another solid Democratic constituency, white South- erners, against him. Kennedy cautiously tried to balance his appeal to, and support from, these constituencies.

Kennedy did not have much empathy for the plight of African Americans. He illustrated his coolness on the issue when his response to the refusal of restaurants on the roads leading into Washington to serve black statesmen from Africa was to ask the ambassadors to fly into Washington, rather than drive.[1] Letters from black leaders to Kennedy, throughout his administration reveal a growing frustration with the President's lack of action on civil rights. When the Freedom Riders embarked on their journey to integrate the nation's highways in the summer of 1961, Kennedy tried to persuade the riders to quit their plan rather than be forced to lend them federal protection. As in the Eisenhower Administra- tion, the President only moved beyond rhetoric when events forced executive action.

As disciples of Kennan's containment policy[2] who were fully aware of the Cold War context in which foreigners perceived events in America, Kennedy and his aides began to worry that the disorder and violence of the civil rights movement were damaging the prestige of the United States abroad. These events, not personal convictions, forced Kennedy into action.

By 1963 Kennedy deployed federal troops to two Southern states. In the spring of 1961 the setting was Alabama: first, when white mobs beat Freedom Riders in Birmingham, and next in Montgomery, when white mobs held Martin Luther King, Jr. and 1,500 others hostage in the First Baptist Church. All the while, Alabama Governor John Patterson held state authorities out of the conflict, insisting that city police rather than state law enforcement had jurisdiction over such violence. By his inaction and de facto endorsement of the violence against the Freedom Riders, Patterson essentially provoked a reluctant Kennedy into using federal troops and marshals to protect and rescue the Freedom Riders. Utilizing a typical tactic of Southern leaders, Patterson could then claim that Kennedy's actions violated the principles of federalism and the rights of the states. Although Kennedy had wanted to remain uninvolved, focusing his attention on foreign policy, the President and his advisors began to see events in Alabama as an embarrassment to the United States. Kennedy believed that the United States could not possibly maintain its international credibility when Americans at home were engaged in racially motivated beatings and required federal troops to keep the peace between their own people.[3]

These problems were only compounded when the President and a state governor squared off yet again in September 1962, after Mississippi Governor Ross Barnett refused to allow James Meredith, a black student, to register for classes at the University of Mississippi. In the ensuring events, hundreds were injured and two people were killed. Kennedy was left with little choice but to send the U.S. Army, acting as "federal marshals," into Mississippi in order to enforce the Supreme Court's opinions ordering the desegregation of public educational institutions and a ruling by the Fifth Circuit of the United States Court of Appeals that the State of Mississippi had no authority to keep Meredith out of the public university. The "movement," now headed by Martin Luther King, Jr., was gaining momentum. All of this occurred during the beginning of the tensest situation of the Cold War, the Cuban Missile crisis; while Meredith was trying to integrate the University of Mississippi in the fall of 1962, administration officials were trying to determine the Soviet intent behind installing surface-to-air missiles in Cuba. Kennedy's address to the nation on the events at the University of Mississippi indicates at least the distraction that international events provided for the President and perhaps his disinterest in the civil rights movement. In his entire speech, he never used the term "civil rights," and only twice used the term "race." Instead, he peppered his address with the jargon of the Cold War, "law" and "freedom," and concluded by asking Americans to "close the books" on internal crises in favor of "greater" international crises.

The episode at the University of Mississippi did not "close the books" on the push for civil rights however. Events came to a head in April 1963 when King organized a protest against segregation in Birmingham, Alabama, a site he chose strategically. Birmingham had entrenched segregationist policies, and the city's head of public safety, Bull Connor, was infamous for his harsh treatment of blacks. King hoped and expected that a confrontation in Birmingham would serve as a wake-up call for politicians and the nation alike. King's prediction was on the mark. Connor's police used dogs and fire hoses to quell demonstrators, including women and children. Even King's protesters turned to violence, hurling stones and brandishing knives. Arrested and jailed, King crafted his now famous "Letter from Birmingham Jail" in which he described the urgency of the "movement." Perhaps more significantly, the events unfolded on national television for the entire nation and indeed many across the globe to see.

The increasing violence and national exposure again gave Kennedy little choice but to press ahead with a civil rights bill. Kennedy's hesitancy on the issue of civil rights jeopardized the Democratic Party's hold on the black vote. Civil rights leaders like Martin Luther King, Jr and James Farmer implored Kennedy to set aside politics and take action to support their efforts to achieve equal treatment for blacks, but his support from white Southerners, another traditional Democratic constituency, was at stake should he mobilize the federal government in favor of black civil rights. A Gallop Poll in the fall of 1963 showed that 70 percent of white Southerners opposed Kennedy's public views on civil rights, but the turmoil caused by the civil rights movement threatened his ability to conduct foreign policy. Kennedy appeared on national television in May 1963, and asked the nation "are we to say to the world that this is the land of the free, except for the Negroes, that we have no second-class citizens, except for Negroes . . . ?"[4]

Kennedy appears to have been driven chiefly by his concern for America's image in the world and by violence against civil rights protestors. The Kennedy brothers realized that they had no choice but to call for a massive civil rights bill when, in June, another Southern governor physically tried to block the process of integration. Alabama Governor George Wallace, one of the most determined political opponents of civil rights who had announced at his inauguration that he supported "segregation today . . . segregation tomorrow . . . [and] segregation forever," stood in the doorway of the University of Alabama to prevent two black students from entering. Wallace, who had articulated a strong states' rights position at his inauguration, told Robert Kennedy that he considered any attempt at integration by the federal government "illegal and unwarranted," and said that the "might of the central government offers a frightful example of the suppression of the rights, privileges, and sovereignty of" Alabama. In response, Kennedy federalized the Alabama National Guard, which forced Wallace to step aside and allow the integration of the University. Later that night, President Kennedy appeared on national television to announce his support for a civil rights bill. At the same time, an assassin's bullet killed NAACP activist Medgar Evers outside his home.

Like much of Kennedy's domestic program, the civil rights bill remained mired in Congress at the time of the President's death. Many credit the success of the civil rights bill to President Kennedy, but only the legislative mastery and courage of Kennedy's successor, Lyndon Johnson, overcame the resistance of Southern conservatives in Congress. The civil rights bill ultimately symbolized both Kennedy's promises, and his failure to move domestic legislation through Congress. Kennedy's introduction and support of the civil rights bill made the remainder of Kennedy's term in office difficult, as it alienated many of his supporters in Congress. "I'm sorry Mr. President," House Majority Leader Carl Albert (D-OR) informed Kennedy, "We lost some of the Southern boys that we would have otherwise had . . . . Civil rights, is overwhelming the whole program."[5] In the following months, Congress defeated Kennedy's bills on Appalachian development, farm subsidies, mass transit, and other issues, largely a result of the "no" votes of congressmen who had supported Kennedy initiatives before the civil rights legislation was introduced.

NOTES

1. Cited in James T. Patterson, *Grand Expectations: The United States, 1945–1974* (New York: Oxford University Press, 1996), 475.

2. The underlying ideology for U.S. policy during the Cold War, containment prescribed that the United States meet the challenge of communism when it tried to expand, and also project an image of stability and "spiritual vitality." On the other hand, evidence of "indecision, disunity, and internal disintegration," according to George Kennan, the author of containment policy, would "have an exhilarating effect on the whole Communist movement."

3. Richard Reeves, *President Kennedy: Profile of Power* (New York: Simon & Schuster, 1993), 125.

4. Cited in David Steigerwald, *The Sixties and the End of Modern America* (New York: St. Martin's Press, 1995), 54.

5. Reeves, *President Kennedy: Profile of Power*, 524.

JOHN F. KENNEDY, RADIO AND TELEVISION REPORT TO THE NATION ON THE SITUATION AT THE UNIVERSITY OF MISSISSIPPI (SEPTEMBER 30, 1963)

Good evening my fellow citizens:

The orders of the court in the case of Meredith versus Fair are beginning to be carried out. Mr. James Meredith is now in residence on the campus of the University of Mississippi. . . .

This is as it should be, for our Nation is founded on the principle that observance of the law is the eternal safeguard of liberty and defiance of the law is the surest road to tyranny. The law which we obey includes the final rulings of the courts, as well as the enactments of our legislative bodies. Even among law-abiding men few laws are universally loved, but they are uniformly respected and not resisted.

Americans are free, in short, to disagree with the law but not to disobey it. For in a government of laws and not of men, no man, however prominent or powerful, and no mob however unruly or boisterous, is entitled to defy a court of law. If this country should ever reach the point where any man or group of men by force or threat of force could long defy the commands of our court and our Constitution, then no law would stand free from doubt, no judge would be sure of his writ, and no citizen would be safe from his neighbors.

In this case in which the United States Government was not until recently involved, Mr. Meredith brought a private suit in Federal court against those who were excluding him from the University. A series of Federal courts all the way to the Supreme Court repeatedly ordered Mr. Meredith's admission to the University. When those orders were defied, and those who sought to implement them were threatened with arrest and violence, the United States Court of Appeals . . . made clear the fact that the enforcement of its order had become an obligation of the United States Government. Even though this Government had not originally been a party to the case, my responsibility as President was therefore inescapable. I accept it. My obligation under the Constitution and the statutes of the United States was and is to implement the orders of the court with whatever means are necessary, and with as little force and civil disorder as the circumstances permit.

It was for this reason that I federalized the Mississippi National Guard as the most appropriate instrument, should any be needed, to preserve law and order while United States marshals carried out the orders of the court and prepared to back them up with whatever other civil or military enforcement might have been required.

I deeply regret the fact that any action by the executive branch was necessary in this case, but all other avenues and alternatives, including persuasion and conciliation, had been tried and exhausted. Had the police powers of Mississippi been used to support the orders of the court, instead of deliberately and unlawfully blocking them, had the University of Mississippi fulfilled its standard of excellence by quietly admitting this applicant in conformity with what so many other southern State universities have done for so many years, a peaceable and sensible solution would have been possible without any Federal intervention. . . .

I recognize that the present period of transition and adjustment in our Nation's Southland is a hard one for many people. Neither Mississippi nor any other southern State deserves to be charged with all the accumulated wrongs of the last 100 years of race relations. To the extent that there has been failure, the responsibility for that failure must be shared by us all, by every State, by every citizen.…

You have a great tradition to uphold, a tradition of honor and courage won on the field of battle and on the gridiron as well as the University campus. You have a new opportunity to show that you are men of patriotism and integrity. For the most effective means of upholding the law is not the State policeman or the marshals or the National Guard. It is you. It lies in your courage to accept those laws with which you disagree as well as those with which you agree. The eyes of the Nation and of all the world are upon you and upon all of us, and the honor of your University and State are in the balance. I am certain that the great majority of the students will uphold that honor.

There is in short no reason why the books on this case cannot now be quickly and quietly closed in the manner directed by the court. Let us preserve both the law and the peace and then healing those wounds that are within we can turn to the greater crises that are without and stand united as one people in our pledge to man's freedom.

Thank you and good night.

Source: John F. Kennedy Library, <http://www.cs.umb.edu/jfklibrary/j093062.htm>

TELEGRAM, MARTIN LUTHER KING, JR.
TO JOHN F. KENNEDY
(SEPTEMBER 15, 1963)

Dear Mr. President,

I shudder to think what our nation has become when Sunday school children and their teachers are killed in church by racist bombs. The savage bombing of the 16th Street Baptist Church this morning is another clear indication of the moral degeneration of the state of Alabama and Governor George Wallace. Mr. President, you must call for legislation empowering the Attorney General to enter cases where any civil rights violation occurs. The lives of women and children are far more precious than the offense created by the elimination of outmoded customs and traditions.…I will plead with my people to remain nonviolent in the face of this terrible provocation. However I am convinced that unless some steps are taken by the federal government to restore a sense of confidence in the protection of life, limb, and property my pleas shall fall on deaf ears and we shall see the worst racial holocaust this nation has ever seen. After today's tragedy, investigation will not suffice. The nation and Birmingham needs your commitment to use everything within your constitutional power to enforce the deseg-regation orders of the courts.

Dr. Martin Luther King, Jr.

President, Southern Christian Leadership Conference

Source: John F. Kennedy Presidential Library, <http://www.cs.umb.edu/jfkli-brary/images/cr_doc36.1.jpg>

TELEGRAM, JAMES FARMER
TO JOHN F. KENNEDY
(MAY 8, 1963)

Tactics of Birmingham police appear to be aimed at intentionally provoking wide scale violence. There can be no truce with police brutality and police lawlessness such as we witness in Birmingham. Even if guns of Alabama succeed in quelling nonviolent struggle in Birmingham it will rise up again in place after place until such time as the president of the United States overcomes his fear of speaking out and decides to act forcefully to secure freedom of Negro Americans. Politics have too long ruled to acts of government on behalf of civil rights. No compromise with justice is possible. The demonstrations in Birmingham must continue until the rights of all Americans are secured. I urge you to do more than watch and wait while Americans struggle against armed might of tyranny in Alabama.

James Farmer

National Director, Congress on Racial Equality

Source: John F. Kennedy Presidential Library <http://www.cs.umb.edu/jfklibrary/images/cr_doc42.jpg>

INAUGURAL ADDRESS, GOVERNOR GEORGE C. WALLACE,
MONTGOMERY, ALABAMA (JANUARY 14, 1963)

... Today I have stood, where once Jefferson Davis stood, and took an oath to my people. It is very appropriate then that from this Cradle of the Confederacy, this very Heart of the Great Anglo-Saxon Southland, that today we sound the drum for freedom as have our generations of forebears before us done, time and time again through history. Let us rise to the call of freedom-loving blood that is in us and send our answer to the tyranny that clanks its chains upon the South. In the name of the greatest people that have ever trod this earth, I draw the line in the dust and toss the gauntlet before the feet of tyranny ... and I say ... segregation today ... segregation tomorrow ... segregation forever....

We are faced with an idea that if a centralized government assume enough authority, enough power over its people, that it can provide a utopian life ... that if given the power to dictate, to forbid, to require, to demand, to distribute, to edict and to judge what is best and enforce that will produce only "good" ... and it shall be our father ... and our God. It is an idea of government that encourages our fears and destroys our faith ... for where there is faith, there is no fear, and where there is fear, there is no faith. In encouraging our fears of economic insecurity it demands we place that economic management and control with government; in encouraging our fear of educational development it demands we place that education and the minds of our children under management and control of government, and even in feeding our fears of physical infirmities and declining years, it offers and demands to father us through it all and even into the grave. It is a government that claims to us that it is bountiful as it buys its power from us with the fruits of its rapaciousness of the wealth that free men before it have produced and builds on crumbling credit without responsibilities to the debtors ... our children. It is an ideology of government erected on the encouragement of fear and fails to recognize the basic law of our fathers that governments do not produce wealth ... people produce wealth ... free people; and those people become less free ... as they learn there is little reward for ambition ... that it requires faith to risk ... and they have none ... as the government must restrict and penalize and tax incentive and endeavor and must increase its expenditures of bounties ... then this government must assume more and more police powers and we find we are become government-fearing people ... not God-fearing people....

It is this theory of international power politic that led a group of men on the Supreme Court for the first time in American history to issue an edict, based not on legal precedent, but upon a volume, the editor of which said our Constitution is outdated and must be changed and the writers of which, some had admittedly belonged to as many as half a hundred communist-front organizations....

And so it was meant in our racial lives ... each race, within its own framework has the freedom to teach ... to instruct ... to develop ... to ask for and receive deserved help from others of separate racial stations.... This is the great freedom of our American founding fathers ... but if we amalgamate into the one unit as advocated by the communist philosophers ... then the enrichment of our lives ... the freedom for our development ... is gone forever. We become, therefore, a mongrel unit of one under a single all powerful government ... and we stand for everything ... and for nothing.

The true brotherhood of America, of respecting the separateness of others ... and uniting in effort ... has been so twisted and distorted from its original concept that there is a small wonder that communism is winning the world.

We invite the negro citizen of Alabama to work with us from his separate racial station...as we will work with him...to develop, to grow in individual freedom and enrichment. We want jobs and a good future for BOTH races...the tubercular and the infirm. That is the basic heritage of my religion, ... for we are all the handiwork of God.

But we warn those, of any group, who would follow the false doctrine of communistic amalgamation that we will not surrender our system of government...our freedom of race and religion...that freedom was won at a hard price and if it requires a hard price to retain it...we are able...and quite willing to pay it.

Source: Alabama Department of Archives & History, <http://www.archives.state. al.us/govs_list/inaugural speech.html>

RECOMMENDED READINGS

Beschloss, Michael. *The Crisis Years*. New York: Edward Burlingame Books, 1991.

Bissel, Richard M. *Reflections of a Cold Warrior: From Yalta to the Bay of Pigs*. New Haven: Yale University Press, 1996.

Blight, James G., Bruce J. Allyn, and David A Welch. *Cuba on the Brink: Castro, the Missile Crisis, and the Soviet Collapse*. New York: Pantheon Books, 1993.

Blight, James G., and Peter Kornbluh, eds. *Politics of Illusion: The Bay of Pigs Reexamined*. Boulder, CO: Lynne Reinner Publishers, 1998.

Brugioni, Dino. *Eyeball to Eyeball: The Inside Story of the Cuban Missile Crisis*. New York: Random House, 1993.

Garthoff, Raymond. "Berlin 1961: The Record Corrected." *Foreign Policy*, 84 (Fall 1991), 142–156.

Kennedy, Robert. *Thirteen Days: A Memoir of the Cuban Missile Crisis*. New York: W.W. Norton, 1999.

Kornbluh, Peter. *The Bay of Pigs Declassified*. New York: The New Press, 1998.

Lynch, Grayson L. *Decision for Disaster: Betrayal at the Bay of Pigs*. Washington, DC: Brassey's, 2000.

National Security Agency. NSA and the Cuban Missile Crisis, <http:// www.nsa.gov/docs/cuba/index.html>

National Security Archive. The Real Thirteen Days: The Hidden History of the Cuban Missile Crisis, <http://www.gwu.edu/~nsarchiv/nsa/ cuba_mis_cri/>

Rabe, Stephen. *The Most Dangerous Area in the Wood: John F. Kennedy Confronts Communists Revolution in Latin America* Chapel Hill: University of North Corolina Press, 1999.

Reeves, Richard. *President Kennedy: Profile of Power*. New York: Simon & Schuster, 1993.

Rogers, William D. *The Twilight Struggle: The Alliance for Progress and the Politics of Development in Latin America*. New York: Random House, 1967.

Scheman, Ronald, ed. *The Alliance for Progress: A Retrospective*. New York: Praeger, 1988.

Schlesinger, Arthur M., Jr. *A Thousand Days: John Kennedy in the White House*. Boston: Houghton Mifflin, 1965.

Walton, Richard J. *Cold War and Counterrevolution: The Foreign Policy of John F. Kennedy*. New York: Viking Press, 1972.

Wiersma, Kurt and Ben Larson. "Fourteen Days in October: The Cuban Missile Crisis", <http://library.thinkquest.org/11046/?tqskip=1>

Wyden, Peter. *Bay of Pigs: The Untold Story*. New York: Simon and Schuster, 1979.

Zubok, Valdimir. "Khrushchev and the Berlin Crisis (1958–62)." Cold War International History Project, Working Paper No. 6. Princeton: Woodrow Wilson International Center for Scholars.

3

LYNDON BAINES JOHNSON

(1963–1969)

INTRODUCTION

Had it not been for the war in Vietnam, Lyndon Baines Johnson would likely be remembered as one of America's greatest presidents. President Kennedy tapped Johnson, who had been a master legislator, as the Democratic vice presidential candidate in 1960. Johnson, who had his own presidential aspirations, reluctantly accepted the partnership with Kennedy, balancing Kennedy's elite New England appeal with his own rural southern background. Propelled into the office he had desired by an assassination after only three years as vice president, Johnson did not leave office five years later with the legacy he had coveted.

Johnson had been an ambitious legislator with an affinity for ideas and good intentions. He mastered the skill of getting legislation through the Congress by cutting deals, making promises, and using the power of persuasion. Capitalizing on his predecessor's death, Johnson appealed to Kennedy's "New Frontier" to promote his own far more ambitious package of domestic programs, which he called the "Great Society." Kennedy had begun the national dialogue on civil rights, equality for women, federal support for the arts, and education, among a plethora of other issues. Johnson dedicated himself to carrying out Kennedy's initiatives and argued that the nation owed it to the fallen president to fulfill his vision.

However, Johnson could not focus on domestic policy alone. In Cold War America, Johnson found that he had to direct manpower, physical and psychological resources, civilian commitment, and bureaucratic management that he could otherwise have focused on efforts to foster the "Great Society" to foreign aid programs, weapons building, covert and overt military operations, and, increasingly, to an "unofficial" war in Vietnam. Although Johnson accomplished much in health care, education, civil rights, environmental protection, transportation, and other areas, the specter of Vietnam overshadowed his presidency. Because America's experience in Vietnam and its domestic repercussions persuaded Johnson not to seek reelection in 1968, it is the first subject of this chapter.

VIETNAM

Scholars will never know what Kennedy would have done had he served for two full terms. Kennedy clearly intensified American involvement in Vietnam, both with respect to economic support and the presence of the U.S. military advisors. Similarly, Lyndon Johnson appealed to Kennedy's legacy as a guideline for his domestic agenda, at least as he served out the last year of Kennedy's term in office. Arms control provides a good example of how Johnson's foreign policy continued on the trajectory his predecessor established. Johnson's pattern of escalation in Vietnam also represented a continuation of Kennedy's policy. Although Johnson clearly called the shots on Vietnam policy, he was less interested than Kennedy in fighting the Cold War abroad than he was in fighting wars on poverty and civil rights at home. Despite his knowledge in this area, Johnson did not possess the confidence or resolve that characterized Kennedy or Eisenhower in foreign affairs. Moreover, although Kennedy sent him on a fact-finding mission to South Vietnam in 1961, Johnson had not been intimately involved in decision making on Vietnam, or on foreign policy in general, during his tenure as vice president.

Thus, Johnson's advisory team was all the more important to him, and on matters of defense, state, and diplomacy, Johnson drew most of his advisors from those who had worked with Kennedy. These confidants, Secretary of State Dean Rusk, State Department official Walt W. Rostow, CIA head John McCone, the president's special assistant for national security issues, McGeorge Bundy, and perhaps most important, Secretary of Defense Robert McNamara, all played key roles in helping Johnson shape and develop Vietnam policy. Moreover, Henry Cabot Lodge, Jr., served twice as ambassador to South Vietnam, under both Kennedy and Johnson while in the interregnum between Lodge's terms, Kennedy's Joint Chiefs Chairman, General Maxwell Taylor, filled the post. The two most notable objectors to escalation in the Kennedy White House, Attorney General Robert Kennedy and State Department official George Ball, had little impact during the Johnson years. The lone dissenter within the Johnson Administration on the question of America's role in Vietnam, Ball resigned in 1966 precisely because he was disenchanted with the Vietnam policy. As Attorney General, Robert Kennedy had been one of JFK's most important and trusted advisors on all matters, legal and otherwise, and had played an instrumental role in the resolution of the Cuban Missile crisis. But, RFK and LBJ failed to see eye to eye, and Johnson granted the Attorney General much less influence in his administration in affairs that did not concern the Justice Department.

Johnson faced the same dilemma, in Vietnam and elsewhere in the world, as the other Cold War presidents. How could he avert war and contain communism? Both concerns were deep seated in the American psyche in the 1950s and 1960s. Unconditional conduct of war, given the superiority of the American arsenal could assuredly win regional wars, but could provoke retaliation from the Soviet Union and/or China, leading to a global nuclear exchange that could bring massive destruction and yield no victors. At the same time, the failure to contain the expansion of communism threatened to ruin American credibility in the world and, should the domino theory prove accurate, even destroy the American way of life. For Johnson more than for Truman, Eisenhower, or Kennedy, Vietnam raised the stakes. Johnson inherited a situation to which Americans had already committed substantial economic and military resources, including the deployment of American troops. Foes might interpret a pullout or a reduction of the U.S. commitment as a sign of weakness, opening the door for communism to expand further.

America's ally in South Vietnam was in political chaos. An assassin's bullet killed South Vietnamese President Diem just weeks before President Kennedy suffered the same fate, and the United States had little chance of finding a South Vietnamese leader with either the popularity or the power to bring order to the country. Thus, the task of assisting the South Vietnamese in their own defense seemed almost impossible; if the North Vietnamese were to be kept out of South Vietnam, Americans would likely have to do it themselves. In addition, in South Vietnam, Johnson confronted a well-organized, well-armed, and well-entrenched Vietcong, rather than a rag-tag group of North Vietnamese agitators that had only been in its infancy during the Eisenhower and Kennedy years. "Strategic hamlets" no longer sufficed for insulating South Vietnamese peasants from contact with the Vietcong. Finally, Johnson inherited a demoralized and disenchanted South Vietnamese populace. Ineffective and in shambles, ARVN (the South Vietnamese army) neither resembled a competent fighting force, nor did ARVN soldiers evince a fighting spirit. The peasants in the South Vietnamese countryside, whose "hearts and minds" were the real battlefield in Vietnam, had endured years of rhetoric and repression with few improvements in their quality of life to show for their hardship. Thus, although Johnson did not face a simple choice, his range of options was limited.

Historian Michael Hunt has identified four major decisions that Johnson made with respect to Vietnam, two of which this chapter treats in greater detail: (1) the decision to continue American involvement in Vietnam using the same rationale as the Kennedy Administration; (2) the decision to conduct a bombing campaign, known as Operation Rolling Thunder, against North Vietnamese military installations and supply stations; (3) the decision to "Americanize" the war in Vietnam by introducing American ground troops into South Vietnam to fight the war rather than, as under Kennedy, simply acting as "advisors" to the South Vietnamese; and (4) the decision dramatically to expand the number of ground troops in South Vietnam, quadrupling the number from approximately 125,000 in 1966 to over 500,000 by 1968. Although Johnson escalated the war, it remained limited. Despite dropping massive tonnage and deploying numerous troops, Johnson did not use all of the military resources at his command. Along with his Secretary of Defense Robert McNamara, Johnson "managed" the conduct and progress of the war carefully and meticulously, often drawing the ire of military leaders in the process. Navy Chairman Admiral Ulysses S. Grant Sharp, Jr., for example, lamented the "reticence" of the President and the Secretary of State: "We could have flattened every war-making facility in North Vietnam. But, the most powerful country in the world did not have the willpower needed to meet the situation."[1]

McNamara, who had made a career as a business executive before entering the State Department, prided himself on efficiency and supervised the American effort in the war like he managed a business, attempting to get the most bang for the buck. Initially, McNamara sought to limit the deployment of troops and arms to Vietnam in order to avoid the kind of massive surplus of military supplies that remained in the fields and in the inventories after World War II. McNamara relied on casualty reports, body counts, and other such statistical measures to gauge the progress of the war, seemingly oblivious to the real conditions on the ground and the nature of the Viet Cong and North Vietnamese fighting forces. Moreover, American policymakers sought to conduct bombing campaigns they believed would be "clean," limiting risks to American troops while bringing the enemy into submission through the steady and relentless destruction of their resources, manpower, and will. Johnson and McNamara thought they could simply wear the North Vietnamese down with the superiority of American weaponry and economic resources. They intended to expand American firepower and manpower guardedly but incrementally until the enemy gave in. This strategy resulted in disastrous consequences, both at home and abroad.

When Johnson left the presidency, the American position in Vietnam was far worse than when he entered. Americans were no closer to ending the conflict or securing victory. Nearly 30,000 Americans had died, and the nation had spent billions on a war that the public no longer supported. Moreover, the war had derailed the implementation of an ambitious domestic program that had held great promise five years earlier. Although in 1964 most Americans supported the Gulf of Tonkin Resolution, the congressional act that effectively authorized Johnson to expand America's role in Vietnam, by 1968 many in the United States were ambivalent about the war. Others were taking drastic measures to express their disapproval of the President, both for his management of the war in Southeast Asia and for their feelings of disappointment and lack of fulfillment in their own lives. Although the Vietnam War is the ugliest blemish on the Johnson presidency, urban riots, student protests, and what some called moral collapse in America also tarnished the Johnson years. Frustration over the Vietnam conflict carried over, or overlapped with, violence and disillusionment at home. Americans' faith in their government and in themselves faded, despite unprecedented productivity and prosperity in the American economy. Although he tried, Johnson proved little better at managing the psyche of Americans concerned about life at home than he did at helping them cope with American actions abroad.

THE GREAT SOCIETY

Johnson's actions in Vietnam were tied to his domestic agenda. Johnson's deep-seated passion for his domestic agenda motivated him to end the conflict in Vietnam as quickly as possible. Although he considered foreign affairs to be important, Johnson's primary objective as president was the creation of a "Great Society" in America. Thus, from the outset, he hoped to end to the quagmire in Vietnam as efficiently and as hastily as he could, and with the least amount of divisiveness at home, so that his administration could devote its attention and resources to domestic reform. Tragically, the war in Vietnam continued throughout Johnson's presidency, and despite the important domestic legislation he signed during his five years in office, Johnson left the White House tired and maligned.

At the outset of his presidency, Johnson seemed poised for enormous popularity. His commitment to the Kennedy legacy, his plan for a "Great Society," and even his down-home style appealed to the great majority of Americans. He won the election of 1964 over Republican Senator Barry Goldwater of Arizona in dramatic fashion, becoming only the third president to win 60 percent or more of the popular vote. Moreover his party solidly controlled both houses of Congress, including a 2 to 1 advantage in the Senate, even though conservatives from both parties questioned the liberalism that had been gaining momentum since Kennedy's election four years earlier. Drawing inspiration and deriving conclusions about policy from his experience as a teacher in a poor Texas county in a school populated mostly by children of Mexican immigrants, Johnson envisioned a "great society" in which all Americans participated. Accordingly, in his first act as president, Johnson signed the Kennedy tax cut, which reduced personal income taxes and corporate taxes at all levels. Kennedy's chief advisor on the economy, Keynesian economist Walter Heller, had argued that a tax cut was the way to preserve prosperity by increasing both productivity and consumption, and both the Kennedy and Johnson teams agreed.

Historian John A. Andrew III emphasizes Johnson's desire for consensus. Johnson not only hoped that all Americans would participate in the "Great Society" for the benefits they would reap but also because he thought these programs required such widespread participation if they were to achieve their goals. Johnson predicated many of his "Great Society" programs, like the Model Cities initiative, on popular participation at the regional and local levels. Moreover, Johnson's faith in the capacity of the federal government to better the lives of its citizens was central to his plans for domestic programs. Johnson never joined those like Huey Long of Louisiana in the 1930s, or "new left" groups of the 1960s, such as Students for a Democratic Society (SDS), who advocated a complete structural overhaul of American society to redistribute wealth and power, but he did believe that wealth and power should be shared particularly in a time of prosperity such as the 1960s. His "Great Society" rested on idealism and optimism about America, and about Americans' relationship with each other and with their government. Unfortunately for Johnson and for America, local communities resisted Johnson's plans for a national community because they "did not want to be homogenized in some great national blender whose switch was controlled from the White House."[2]

The agenda for the "Great Society" was massive. By 1966, Johnson had introduced more than two hundred pieces of "Great Society" legislation in Congress; 181 of which had been passed and signed into law. The range and scope of this legislation was as great as the nation itself. Deeply concerned about equality and opportunity in America, Johnson created agencies within the federal government to promote job training. Johnson thought that opportunity began with education, and so building on the momentum of Eisenhower's commitment to federal support for education, Johnson's "Great Society" legislation included the National Elementary and Secondary Education Act expanding federal funding for education at all levels. Believing that federal support for education should begin earlier than elementary schools, Johnson created Head Start, a federally funded pre-school program designed to get students learning earlier and assisting parents with childcare.

Johnson favored extending these programs and other opportunities to all Americans equally. Accordingly, he was more committed to black civil rights than any postwar president. He demonstrated remarkable political courage by signing both the Civil Rights Bill of 1964 and Voting Rights Act of 1965, which not only alienated some Republicans but also many fellow Democrats. Black civil rights was not his only concern however. Johnson's domestic policy also offered new opportunities and legal protections to women, immigrants, and workers.

Johnson's "Great Society" also included a "War on Poverty." It began in Appalachia, historically one of America's most impoverished regions, and then extended into the nation's urban areas through community action programs and urban renewal efforts. The "War on Poverty" quickly became national in scope with the health care programs, Medicare and Medicaid, which provided federally funded health insurance for the aged and indigent, and the Housing Act of 1967, which not only represented the first major federal commitment to public housing but also included provisions to ensure that federal housing developments were "open," or nondiscriminatory. Accordingly, these health and housing programs, like the education bills, were important as well for what they did for civil rights. Combined with the force of the Supreme Court's decision in *Brown v. Board of Education* and the Civil Rights Act, federal involvement in health care and housing brought an end to "white" and "colored" facilities in hospitals and housing developments. Thus, Johnson tied the solutions to race relations, poverty, and education together to form an integrated package of programs to fulfill his domestic agenda.

In addition to targeting those who needed federal assistance to cope with historical disadvantages, those who were downtrodden, or those demanding "rights," Johnson also valued the environment. One of the first pieces of great society legislation, the Wilderness Act, which the president signed in 1964, protected federal lands, particularly in the Pacific Northwest, from development. Similarly, legislation governing the nation's rivers, "national trails," and land and water conservation efforts served to protect America's natural environment. At the behest of his wife, Ladybird Johnson, he also supported beautification efforts along the nation's highways and in other public places by signing into law the National Highway Beautification Bill in 1966. Laws restricting the placement of highway billboards and junkyards bordering interstate highways sought to beautify the "great society." In the same years Johnson signed legislation requiring urban road-building projects to protect historic landmarks in the path of projected roadways. Johnson included a myriad of other issues in the "Great Society": traffic and highway safety legislation, legislation to curb pollution, support for the arts, and consumer protections. Once referring to his presidency as "a consumer's administration," Johnson signed truth-in-packaging laws, protecting children from dangerous toys and consumers from flammable fabrics, linens, and furnishings. Building on weaker legislation from earlier eras, Congress under Johnson also passed new laws to curb the pollution of drinking water and improve air quality.

Historians remember Johnson for his ambitious agenda and the sincerity with which he worked to achieve it. Although conservatives, who complain about the size and power of the federal government have derided his legacy, Johnson's domestic programs were far from radical. To be sure, the federal government was bigger in size and spent more money in 1969 than in 1963, and it had a profoundly greater impact on the daily lives of Americans as a result of the "Great Society" legislation. However, Johnson also cut taxes and attacked waste in government, traditionally the preview of conservatives. More importantly, Johnson's idea of the "Great Society" took its inspiration in part from the New Deal of Franklin Roosevelt, Johnson's political hero, and the Progressive Era provided further precedents for aspects of Johnson's plan involving consumer protections, environmental protections, and workplace safety.

SUMMARY

Despite the goodwill, resources, and optimism that Johnson put into his domestic agenda, America did not look like a great society in 1969. Urban riots plagued U.S. cities from 1965 until the end of the decade. This violent and destructive expression of frustration revealed that the prosperity of the 1960s had not reached all Americans, and that, despite the "rights revolution" that the Warren Court had initiated, not all Americans were better off. In Watts, for example, where urban riots exploded in 1965, 75 percent of the adult male population, mostly black, was unemployed. In spite of all of the legal and legislative developments since 1954, de facto racial and gender discrimination persisted throughout America, especially in the South. Consequently, the efforts of civil rights advocates not only continued but developed more aggressive components. Others took up the banner of protest as well. Migrant workers and homosexuals demanded as "rights" legal protections that government had extended to others. Baby boomers coming of age also took their stand, rallying against authority by occupying campus administration buildings at Columbia, Cornell, Michigan, and Berkeley. Combining with these frustrations was a growing sense of concern about America's role in Vietnam, which sent protesters to sit-in on the Mall in Washington.

Johnson believed that all Americans would rally behind the idea of the "Great Society." Instead, anger, division, and disillusionment undermined this conception. By 1968, the public had turned against both Johnson's foreign and domestic programs. Mismanagement, naïveté, incompetence, and idealism led to competing interests, disconnection with the public, and endless criticism and debate. Commentator Nicholas Lemann's summary of the failing of the "War on Poverty" describes the sense of despair that came to characterize Johnson's programs and his administration as a whole: "the War on poverty was in trouble politically from the start. Its planners hoped to build public support for it by achieving quick, visible successes, but in setting up hundreds of separate anti-poverty organizations run largely by inexperienced people, they practically guaranteed that there would be quite a few highly publicized failures. These turned public opinion against the War on Poverty."[3] Like the patchwork of civil rights agencies and the inexperience of Robert McNamara in managing the War in Vietnam, the failings of the "War on Poverty" epitomized the difficulties Lyndon Johnson faced during his five years in the presidency.

NOTES

1. Cited in Larry Berman, *Lyndon Johnson's War: The Road to Stalemate in Vietnam* (New York: Norton), 12.

2. John A. Andrew, III, *Lyndon Johnson and the Great Society* (Chicago: Ivan R. Dee, 1998), 17.

3. Nicholas Lemann, "The Unfinished War," *The Atlantic* (December 1988).

THE WAR ON POVERTY

Civil rights and poverty topped Lyndon Johnson's agenda as president. His own background teaching the children of poor Mexican immigrants in Texas undoubtedly influenced his objectives as president, but Johnson was also committed to fulfilling Kennedy's legacy in these areas. Johnson deeply believed in the "Great Society" that he wished to create, and he was convinced that poverty in America was a fundamental roadblock to its creation. Believing that the federal government could and should play a role, Johnson was determined to use the power of the government to ameliorate substandard living conditions for everyone in the United States, particularly those who needed a helping hand. Thus, civil rights and what Johnson called the "War on Poverty" dominated the debate in Washington during Johnson's first year in office.

Academicians and politicians debated the causes of poverty during the 1950s. Some argued that poverty was primarily a cultural trait, inherent in the behaviors and lifestyles of certain groups. Others placed the burden of poverty on individuals, who they thought were lazy or lacked ambition. Still others advanced a structural definition of poverty, arguing that institutions (i.e., the tax structure, income distribution, differential education programs, and government policies on education, civil rights, and economic opportunity) created a class of poor people, who would only escape poverty if the structures of society changed. Johnson and others who directed the "War on Poverty" thought that job preparation was crucial. They believed that education and job training would stimulate individuals and provide them with opportunities to enter, and remain in, the world of work.

With this objective in mind, Johnson announced the "War on Poverty" in a message to Congress in March 1964. He said that a war on poverty was "right" and "wise" and that the profound expansion of the American economy in the 1960s made it possible "for the first time in history ... to conquer poverty." The Economic Opportunity Bill of 1964 was the root legislation of the "War on Poverty." The bill created the Office of Economic Opportunity to direct and coordinate the efforts of the war on poverty, along with several other federal agencies with more specific roles. More importantly, the Economic Opportunity Bill included provisions for job training, regional development, and community action programs. The two main programs the bill created, Community Action and the Job Corps, reflected the legislation's objectives to provide job training and create urban renewal through education and economic development. The first, based loosely on the Civilian Conservation Corps (CCC) of the New Deal, provided job training programs for unemployed youth. Young men between the ages of sixteen to twenty-one had an unemployment rate of 21 percent in 1963, the highest rate on record for that group. The Job Corps set up training centers, rural work camps, like those of the CCC, and urban boarding houses, where young men would learn new skills and the responsibilities of being employed. Community Action Programs (CAPs), which had been developed in theory during the Kennedy Administration, sought to involve the poor as participants in the effort to revitalize impoverished communities, rather than having them simply act as passive recipients of government policies. CAPs funded local activist groups, placed control of federal monies in local hands, and encouraged "maximum feasible participation" of the residents of the poverty areas. But, because no one ever defined "maximum feasible participation," this requirement turned out to have little impact on the composition of those who participated in CAPs. The Economic Opportunity Bill also included programs directed at fighting rural poverty and assisting migrants, efforts to help parents gain work experience to "break the pattern of poverty," and VISTA, or Volunteers in Service to America, a domestic version of the Peace Corps. The latter prefigured President Bill Clinton's AmeriCorps of the 1990s, which sent volunteers throughout America to fight poverty.

Despite the lack of consensus on poverty, the Economic Opportunity Bill easily cleared the Congress with voting largely along party lines. Johnson reassured conservative Southern Democrats, who might have opposed the "war on poverty," with his insistence that the "war on poverty" was not a handout program, but was instead based on creating opportunity. Not surprisingly, fiscal conservatives balked at the new programs. Some questioned the scope of poverty itself, suggesting that many of those considered poor in the 1960s would have been considered well off during the 1930s. Such critics argued that people who owned televisions and cars could not be categorized as "poor." Some resisted giving a "new look" to liberal policies that the government had tried in the past, like New Deal programs of job creation and economic development. Others, like Peter Frelinghuysen (R-NJ), criticized the program for its haphazard design, contending that it was a conglomeration of various initiatives to be run by various agencies. Some conservatives, like Republican Senate leader Everett Dirksen (R-IL) who called the "War on Poverty" a "boondoggle," criticized the massive expense associated with it.

Participants in the Republican National Convention of 1964 leveled the most significant opposition to Johnson's plans to solve poverty in America. More opposition to the "War on Poverty" arose as the program expanded. The Republican Governor of California, Ronald Reagan, and the Republican presidential candidate, Barry Goldwater of Arizona, harshly attacked Johnson's antipoverty programs for expanding the size and scope of the federal government, leading to increased taxes that made it more difficult for members of the middle class to raise their own standard of living, and creating a culture of dependency. Some viewed Community Action programs as simply another way to address civil rights issues, and some local leaders even restructured community action organizations so as to reduce minority participation. Likewise, others viewed the Economic Opportunity Act as a way of addressing the problems of the black urban poor; although race was not a qualification for participation, blacks in the cities were among the poorest in America. Johnson tried to expand the "War on Poverty" with Head Start and the Appalachia Aid Bill in 1965. Although these programs were more broad-based, and somewhat diffused the charges that the "War on Poverty" was simply an extension of the civil rights cause, they further fragmented the "War on Poverty" and created new disputes over control, race, and the origins of poverty.

An analysis of the success of the "War on Poverty" yields mixed results. The percentage of the American population that was "poor" fell from 18 percent to 9 percent by the end of the decade. Yet, many Americans still did not enjoy a standard of living that seemed appropriate for an affluent society like the United States. More importantly, many Americans were discontent with their standard of living, regardless of what it was. The "War on Poverty" failed to head off the waves of urban riots that struck American cities in the summers of 1965 through 1968. Johnson's interest in poverty also waned by the middle of his administration. Distracted by other components of the "Great Society" and by foreign affairs, Johnson devoted less attention to the workings of the Economic Opportunity Act. Never lavish, funding for "War on Poverty" programs declined as the decade progressed. Although some analysts argued that the "War on Poverty" would cost the government as much as $30 billion per year, Congress initially appropriated just over $800 million. This was not just a consequence of fiscal conservatives holding the line in Congress. Despite his passion for the "Great Society," Johnson did not believe in spending irresponsibly, and he never asked Congress for the massive funds that would have been needed to eliminate poverty completely in America. Nevertheless, the "War on Poverty" represents a landmark in American politics. Like other "Great Society" programs, the "War on Poverty" legislation constituted unprecedented action on the part of the federal government. The government had never before been so involved in job training, education, or regional development. Previous federal efforts, like those of the New Deal, had been only limited and temporary whereas the "War on Poverty" represented a more permanent federal role in social policy. By taking on poverty, along with health care, education, consumer protection, and the environment, the federal government assumed unprecedented responsibilities, which have for the most part, been enhanced in subsequent years.

LYNDON JOHNSON, STATE OF THE UNION ADDRESS (JANUARY 8, 1964)

... Unfortunately, many Americans live on the outskirts of hope—some because of their poverty, and some because of their color, and all too many because of both. Our task is to help replace their despair with opportunity.

This administration today, here and now, declares unconditional war on poverty in America. I urge this Congress and all Americans to join with me in that effort.

It will not be a short or easy struggle, no single weapon or strategy will suffice, but we shall not rest until that war is won. The richest Nation on earth can afford to win it. We cannot afford to lose it. One thousand dollars invested in salvaging an unemployable youth today can return $40,000 or more in his lifetime.

Poverty is a national problem, requiring improved national organization and support. But this attack, to be effective, must also be organized at the State and the local level and must be supported and directed by State and local efforts.

For the war against poverty will not be won here in Washington. It must be won in the field, in every private home, in every public office, from the courthouse to the White House.

The program I shall propose will emphasize this cooperative approach to help that one-fifth of all American families with incomes too small to even meet their basic needs.

Our chief weapons in a more pinpointed attack will be better schools, and better health, and better homes, and better training, and better job opportunities to help more Americans, especially young Americans, escape from squalor and misery and unemployment rolls where other citizens help to carry them.

Very often a lack of jobs and money is not the cause of poverty, but the symptom. The cause may lie deeper in our failure to give our fellow citizens a fair chance to develop their own capacities, in a lack of education and training, in a lack of medical care and housing, in a lack of decent communities in which to live and bring up their children.

But whatever the cause, our joint Federal-local effort must pursue poverty, pursue it wherever it exists—in city slums and small towns, in sharecropper shacks or in migrant worker camps, on Indian Reservations, among whites as well as Negroes, among the young as well as the aged, in the boom towns and in the depressed areas.

Our aim is not only to relieve the symptom of poverty, but to cure it and, above all, to prevent it. No single piece of legislation, however, is going to suffice.

We will launch a special effort in the chronically distressed areas of Appalachia.

We must expand our small but our successful area redevelopment program.

We must enact youth employment legislation to put jobless, aimless, hopeless youngsters to work on useful projects.

We must distribute more food to the needy through a broader food stamp program.

We must create a National Service Corps to help the economically handicapped of our own country as the Peace Corps now helps those abroad.

We must modernize our unemployment insurance and establish a high-level commission on automation. If we have the brain power to invent these machines, we have the brain power to make certain that they are a boon and not a bane to humanity.

We must extend the coverage of our minimum wage laws to more than 2 million workers now lacking this basic protection of purchasing power.

We must, by including special school aid funds as part of our education program, improve the quality of teaching, training, and counseling in our hardest hit areas.

We must build more libraries in every area and more hospitals and nursing homes under the Hill-Burton Act, and train more nurses to staff them.

We must provide hospital insurance for our older citizens financed by every worker and his employer under Social Security, contributing no more than $1 a month during the employee's working career to protect him in his old age in a dignified manner without cost to the Treasury, against the devastating hardship of prolonged or repeated illness.

We must, as a part of a revised housing and urban renewal program, give more help to those displaced by slum clearance, provide more housing for our poor and our elderly, and seek as our ultimate goal in our free enterprise system a decent home for every American family.

We must help obtain more modern mass transit within our communities as well as low-cost transportation between them.

Above all, we must release $11 billion of tax reduction into the private spending stream to create new jobs and new markets in every area of this land.

John Kennedy was a victim of hate, but he was also a great builder of faith—faith in our fellow Americans, whatever their creed or their color or their station in life; faith in the future of man, whatever his divisions and differences.

This faith was echoed in all parts of the world. On every continent and in every land to which Mrs. Johnson and I traveled, we found faith and hope and love toward this land of America and toward our people.

So I ask you now in the Congress and in the country to join with me in expressing and fulfilling that faith in working for a nation, a nation that is free from want and a world that is free from hate—a world of peace and justice, and freedom and abundance, for our time and for all time to come.

Source: *Public Papers of the Presidents of the United States: Lyndon B. Johnson, 1963–1964. Book I* (Washington, DC: Government Printing Office, 1965), 113–114.

SENATOR BARRY GOLDWATER (R-AZ), PRESIDENTIAL NOMINATION ACCEPTANCE SPEECH, SAN FRANCISCO (1964)

... During four, futile years the administration which we shall replace has distorted and lost that faith. It has talked and talked and talked and talked the words of freedom, but it has failed and failed and failed in the works of freedom. . . .

Rather than useful jobs in our country, people have been offered bureaucratic make-work; rather than more leadership, they have been given bread and circuses; they have been given spectacles, and yes, they've even been given scandals.

Tonight there is violence in our streets, corruption in our highest offices, aimlessness among our youth, anxiety among our elderly; and there's a virtual despair among the many who look beyond material success toward the inner meaning of their lives. And where examples of morality should be set, the opposite is seen. . . .

Fellow Republicans, it is the cause of Republicanism to resist concentrations of power, private or public, which enforce such community and inflict such despotism. . . .

We must assure a society here which while never abandoning the needy, or forsaking the helpless, nurtures incentives and opportunity for the creative and the productive. . . .

This nation, whose creative people have enhanced this entire span of history, should again thrive upon the greatness of all those things which we—we as individual citizens—can and should do.

During Republican years, this again will be a nation of men and women, of families proud of their role, jealous of their responsibilities, unlimited in their aspiration—a nation where all who can will be self-reliant. . . .

We see in private property and in economy based upon and fostering private property the one way to make government a durable ally of the whole man rather than his determined enemy. We see in the sanctity of private property the only durable foundation for constitutional government in a free society.

... We don't seek to live anyone's life for him. ...

We Republicans seek a government that attends to its inherent responsibilities of maintaining a stable monetary and fiscal climate, encouraging a free and a competitive economy, and enforcing law and order.

Thus do we seek inventiveness, diversity, and creative difference within a stable order, for we Republicans define government's role where needed at many, many levels—preferably, though, the one closest to the people involved: our towns and our cities, then our counties, then our states, then our regional contacts, and only then the national government. ...

Source: National Center for Public Policy Research, <http://www.nationalcenter. org/Goldwater.html>

RONALD REAGAN (R-CA), "A TIME FOR CHOOSING," DELIVERED AT THE REPUBLICAN NATIONAL CONVENTION (1964)

I am going to talk of controversial things. I make no apology for this.

It's time we asked ourselves if we still know the freedoms intended for us by the Founding Fathers. James Madison said, "We base all our experiments on the capacity of mankind for self government." ...

You and I are told we must choose between a left or right, but I suggest there is no such thing as a left or right. There is only an up or down. Up to man's age-old dream—the maximum of individual freedom consistent with order or down to the ant heap of totalitarianism. Regardless of their sincerity, their humanitarian motives, those who would sacrifice freedom for security have embarked on this downward path. Plutarch warned, "The real destroyer of the liberties of the people is he who spreads among them bounties, donations and benefits." ...

We need true tax reform that will at least make a start toward restoring for our children the American Dream that wealth is denied to no one, that each individual has the right to fly as high as his strength and ability will take him ...

Will you resist the temptation to get a government handout for your community? Realize that the doctor's fight against socialized medicine is your fight. We can't socialize the doctors without socializing the patients. ...

We are faced with the most evil enemy mankind has known in his long climb from the swamp to the stars. There can be no security anywhere in the free world if there is no fiscal and economic stability within the United States. Those who ask us to trade our freedom for the soup kitchen of the welfare state are architects of a policy of accommodation.

They say the world has become too complex for simple answers. They are wrong. There are no easy answers, but there are simple answers. We must have the courage to do what we know is morally right.

You and I have a rendezvous with destiny. We will preserve for our children this, the last best hope of man on earth, or we will sentence them to take the first step into a thousand years of darkness. If we fail, at least let our children and our children's children say of us we justified our brief moment here. We did all that could be done.

Source: The Ronald Reagan Home Page, <http://reagan.webteamone.com/speeches/the_speech.cfm>

THE WILDERNESS ACT AND CONSERVATION

Lyndon Johnson's "Great Society" included a variety of measures for improving the quality of life for Americans. Many of these addressed the needs of particular groups of individuals, like the poor and immigrants, or targeted very specific issues that plagued Americans, like poverty and low levels of education. But, in addition to helping groups looking for "rights" or seeking to overcome historic hardships, Johnson's "Great Society" package of legislation also included laws intended to improve the quality of life for all Americans. Thus, in addition to such issues as civil rights, poverty, and education, Johnson directed attention to beautification efforts; consumer protections; environmental concerns involving pollution, clean air, and clean water; and preserving America's natural landscapes. The last might have been the most comprehensive of these projects, and was, in fact, the first aspect of the "Great Society" that Congress considered in the form of the Wilderness Act of 1964. Johnson's efforts both to preserve American natural spaces and to encourage their use by the American public continued throughout his administration, as Johnson added the Land and Water Conservation Act and National Trails Act to the Wilderness Act in order to protect and promote America's "wilderness."

A national concern for the environment and its management in the United States dates back to the middle of the nineteenth century, when the United States created its first national parks. This interest continued through the Progressive Era, when Teddy Roosevelt promoted conservation and established national forests. However, these early attempts at environmental protection did not so much endeavor to keep natural spaces pristine as they intended to regulate and manage their use: The government allowed road building, cattle grazing, mining, and other activities on "protected" national lands, but regulated these activities. In the mid-1950s, Washington lawyer turned activist Howard Zahniser endeavored to change the way Americans and their government viewed wilderness areas and pressed for legislation to limit the use of land designed as "wilderness." Zahniser wanted to limit the use of these areas to recreational and scientific purposes, eliminating the economic activities that the government had previously allowed. Zahniser argued that the wilderness "meets fundamental human needs. These needs," he contended, "are profound. For the wilderness is essential to us, as human beings, for a true understanding of ourselves, our culture, our own natures, our place in all nature."[1] Zahniser's sentiments epitomized the aesthetic ideas that Johnson's concept of the "Great Society" envisioned.

Although Pennsylvania Republican John Saylor first introduced the "Wilderness Bill" in the House of Representatives in 1956, legislation on the wilderness was not a top national priority until Lyndon Johnson became president and incorporated the idea into his "Great Society." Moreover, as a letter from this early period by W. Howard Gray, chairman of the American Mining Congress indicates, the prospect of restricting the use of vast tracts of land across the United States did not sit well with cattle ranchers, miners, loggers, water developers, and others who relied on the resources of these lands for their economic livelihood and who believed that they contributed to regional and national economic progress. For Johnson though, protecting "beauty" in America was essential to "the good life," which he sought to enhance through "Great Society" programs. Just as opposition from local detractors or big business did not deter Johnson from pushing through civil rights legislation later in 1964, neither did microeconomic concerns prevent Johnson from forging ahead with a package of legislation on the environment. As president, Johnson was finally able to push the wilderness legislation through Congress and sign the act into law in order to "assure that an increasing population, accompanied by expanding settlement and growing mechanization, does not occupy and modify all areas within the United States . . . leaving no lands . . . in their natural condition."

The Wilderness Act of 1964 provided for the protection of lands with minimal effects from human action, in tracts of at least 5,000 acres, by creating the National Wilderness Protection System to encompass lands owned by the American people that remain "untrammeled by man." In such cases, the act gave Congress the authority to prevent further industrial or agricultural development. Wilderness areas are "devoted to public purposes of recreational, scenic, scientific, education, and historic uses" and mechanized vehicles and equipment, except for crisis management, were prohibited. The law also prohibited commercial activity, except for controlled touring. Initially, the Wilderness Act designated nine million acres of federally owned land as protected wilderness. Since 1964, Congress has added over 90 million acres to the federal wilderness areas.

Although the initial Wilderness Act of 1964 protected the largest land area, Johnson did not stop his efforts to create an aesthetically appealing "Great Society" there. In a special message to Congress in February 1965, Johnson celebrated the achievements of the Wilderness Act but proposed a much more ambitious national beautification effort. It included: water conservation; the preservation of nature in cities through the "Open Space Program;" the conversion of "surplus lands" owned by the government, particularly the military, to recreational uses; the appropriation of federal funds to "enhance beauty along the highway system"; pollution control and cleanup programs for the nation's river systems; and more general efforts to control air and water pollution. Johnson formalized many of these proposals through legislation during his tenure in office, and Americans have embraced others since the 1960s. State and local politicians and/or big businesses generally opposed to federal regulation, environmental or otherwise, have continued to express opposition. Disputes have continued into the administration of George W. Bush (who has favored extracting oil from governmentally owned preserves on the Alaskan North Shore over environmental concerns), especially in the face of the world's continuing dependence on resources from unstable areas of the world like the Middle East, Nigeria, and Venezuela.

NOTE

1. Quoted in Mark Harvey, "Howard Zahniser: Architect of the Wilderness Act." Southern Utah Wilderness Alliance Newsletter, Fall 1999: <http://www.suwa.org/newsletters/1999/fall/Lead%202.html>

LBJ, SPECIAL MESSAGE TO CONGRESS ON CONSERVATION AND RESTORATION OF NATURAL BEAUTY (FEBRUARY 8, 1965)

For centuries Americans have drawn strength and inspiration from the beauty of our country. It would be a neglectful generation indeed, indifferent alike to the judgment of history and the command of principle, which failed to preserve and extend such a heritage for its descendents....

A growing population is swallowing up areas of natural beauty with its demands for living space, and is placing increased demand on our overburdened areas of recreation and pleasure.

The increasing tempo of urbanization and growth is already depriving many Americans of the right to live in decent surroundings. More of our people are crowding into cities and being cut off from nature. Cities themselves reach out into the countryside, destroying streams and trees and meadows as they go. A modern highway may wipe out the equivalent of a fifty acre park with every mile. And people move out from the city to get closer to nature only to find that nature has moved farther from them. . . .

To deal with these new problems will require a new conservation. We must not only protect the countryside and save it from destruction, we must restore what has been destroyed and salvage the beauty and charm of our cities. Our conservation must be not just the classic conservation of protection and development, but a creative conservation of restoration and innovation. Its concern is not with nature alone, but with the total relation between man and the world around him. Its object is not just man's welfare but the dignity of man's spirit. . . .

Beauty is not an easy thing to measure. It does not show up in the gross national product, in a weekly paycheck, or in profit and loss statements. But these things are not ends in themselves. They are a road to satisfaction and pleasure and the good life. Beauty makes is own direct contribution to these final ends. Therefore it is one of the most important components of our true national income, not to be left out simply because statisticians cannot calculate its worth.

And some things we do know. Association with beauty can enlarge man's imagination and revive his spirit. Ugliness can demean the people who live among it. What a citizen sees every day is his America. If it is attractive, it adds to the quality of his life. If it is ugly, it can degrade his experience.

Beauty has other immediate values. It adds to safety whether removing direct dangers to health or making highways less monotonous and dangerous. We also know that those who live in blighted and squalid conditions are more susceptible to anxieties and mental disease. . . .

Certainly no one would hazard a national definition of beauty. But we do know that nature is nearly always beautiful. We do, for the most part, know what is ugly. And we can introduce, into all of our planning, our programs, our building and our growth, a conscious and active concern for the values of beauty. . . .

I am hoping that we can summon such a national effort. For we have not chosen to have an ugly America. We have been careless, and often neglectful. But now that the danger is clear and the hour is late, this people can place themselves in the path of a tide of blight which is often irreversible and always destructive.

Source: Lyndon Baines Johnson Library and Museum, <http://www.lbjliib.utexas. edu/johnson/archives.hom/speeches.hom/650208.asp>

LETTER BY W. HOWARD GRAY, CHAIR, THE AMERICAN MINING CONGRESS, TO SENATE INTERIOR AND INSULAR AFFAIRS COMMITTEE (JUNE 20, 1957)

GENTLEMEN: The American Mining Congress, a national organization composed of both large and small producers of all metals and minerals mined in the United States, wishes to register the opposition to pending measures which would establish a National Wilderness Preservation System on the public lands of the United States.

. . .

The pending measures . . . are contrary to the principles long espoused by the mining industry and are in contradiction of those principles, carried out by intrepid prospectors, which have furthered the development of our Western States. The great natural resources of the Western States formed the foundation for the development of the industrial and agricultural economies of those States and have made possible their rapid growth and progress over the years. Any measure which would deter further mineral development through the curbing of the ardor of the prospector would result in a great disservice not only to the Western States but to the Nation as a whole.

. . .

The broadest possible use of all of the resources of our public lands and forests for the benefit of the American people is a matter of great national import. The rapidly expanding population and economy of our Nation and of the Western States in particular, have been accompanied by an ever-growing need for more general and more intensive use of our natural resources. The high tempo of our housing industry has brought about heavy demands for timber: stock growers need more grazing area to meet the increasing consumption of meat, leather and wool; our mining industry is under the constant necessity of exploring for and developing additional sources of new and old minerals to meet the ever-increasing requirements of our national security and industrial economy; and our growing population requires expanded recreational areas.

. . .

We in the mining industry are unalterably opposed to the locking up of natural resources of any kind from development for the public good. We believe that the future of the Nation, and of the Western States in particular, lies in continued development of these resources.

. . .

Source: *Hearing before the Committee on Interior and Insular Affairs,* United States Senate, Eighty-fifth Congress First Session on S. 1176, June 19 and 20, 1957, pp. 327–329.

THE CIVIL RIGHTS ACT OF 1964

Unlike his two predecessors, Lyndon Johnson believed that the federal government had a responsibility to intervene in the affairs of states and locales in order to ensure the welfare of the people. This was particularly true in the case of civil rights. Johnson, however, was motivated by more than personal convictions. Kennedy's death profoundly impacted most Americans, including Johnson. Although he had only reluctantly accepted Kennedy's invitation to campaign as the vice presidential candidate, once Johnson became president, he used the Kennedy agenda as a foundation from which to propose his own package of programs and initiatives. Johnson capitalized on the sentiment of the American people, and he presented many of his ideas, including those on civil rights, in the context of fulfilling President Kennedy's dreams.

The Civil Rights Bill of 1964 is one of the best examples of Johnson's politicking and the deal-making skills he had mastered as Senate Majority Leader. Although Kennedy had ignored the issue for most of his presidency and the Civil Rights Bill he had half-heartedly supported was mired in Congress when he died in November 1963, Johnson told the nation that there could be no better way to honor the fallen leader than to pass legislation on civil rights "for which [Kennedy] fought so long and hard." Johnson thus utilized America's sympathy and feeling of loss after the Kennedy assassination to foster support for his own agenda and also to enhance and embellish the image and reputation of his predecessor.

By the beginning of the 1964 legislative year, many Americans were shocked, as Kennedy had been, by the tactics that Southern politicians and law enforcement officers employed in their attempts to put down black civil rights activists and maintain the discriminatory system of racial segregation referred to as "Jim Crow." Nationwide, television carried across the country horrific images from the Deep South of police-directed violence against peaceful protestors. In 1963 less than one-third of Americans believed that the drive for civil rights was moving too quickly. The time finally seemed right for civil rights legislation: The nation as a whole supported it; Johnson had pledged that the Senate would not debate any other legislation until it passed a civil rights law; and although divided by civil rights, the President's party controlled Congress.

Passage of the law was not, easy. Many in the business community opposed civil rights legislation. Representing the lobbying group, the Committee of 100 Businessmen, Bruce Butterfield argued that the law was too ambiguous, that it improperly attempted to use federal spending powers in an unconstitutionally coercive fashion, that it restricted the autonomy of business owners to manage their companies as they wished, and that it continued to allow blatant discrimination—against those who were atheists, for example—in areas unrelated to race. Southern Democrats in the Senate also feared the increased power of the federal government under the legislation, and did everything in their power to prevent the Civil Rights Bill of 1964 from passing. They argued that segregation did not equal discrimination. They contended that the federal government had no power to enforce such laws in the states. Some, such as Democratic Senator John Stennis of Mississippi, suggested, as Eisenhower had, that the issue was a question of human behavior, not lawmaking. Southern Democrats began a filibuster in the Senate that lasted over 500 hours (three months) and included Senator Robert Byrd's (D-WV) attempt to deliver an 800-page oration. The effort of Representative Howard Smith (D-VA) to derail the bill was the most novel. Believing that many in the Senate who supported black civil rights would not find equal rights for women palatable, Smith inserted a clause into Title VII of the bill forbidding discrimination in employment, not only based on race, national origin, and religion, but with respect to sex as well. Employers already feared that Title VII would rid them of their ability to hire and fire based on merit. Smith hoped that their fears would be further exacerbated if women were added to the "protected" classes.

The efforts of the Southern Democrats failed, and the Smith maneuver ultimately backfired, strengthening rather than destroying the bill. Johnson and his allies won the support of Republicans in Congress, including minority leader Everett Dirksen of Illinois. Dirksen was a longtime Republican leader and the quasi-representative of the Midwestern Republicans, who dominated the Republicans in Congress. Because Johnson did not have Southern Democrats behind him, Dirksen's endorsement of the bill was crucial. Dirksen did not oppose the notion of civil rights legislation, but he wanted the bill weakened, reducing the power the bill afforded to the federal government and minimizing the potential difficulties the bill might cause for business. Business leaders across the country protested the invasiveness of the proposed legislation and feared that the new law would impinge their ability to manage their companies effectively. Despite these myriad protests, Johnson and other sponsors of the bill (most notably future vice president, Minnesota's Democratic Senator Hubert Humphrey) did not back down. In the end, they gave in to only minor amendments, which limited the bringing of lawsuits based on employment discrimination to the Justice Department, rather than creating a new federal office to handle the complaints. Because the attorney general's department was relatively small, this restriction limited the number of cases against businesses and encouraged a greater degree of judiciousness when filing suits.

President Johnson signed the Civil Rights Act of 1964 into law on July 2, 1964. Major components of the law prohibited de jure and de facto segregation in public accommodations, such as parks, beaches, motels, restaurants, barber shops, etc. (Title I and II), and discrimination in employment (Title VII). The impact of the Civil Rights Act 1964 was profound and immediate, ending Jim Crow in public accommodations and encouraging further efforts to desegregate other aspects of Southern life. The bill dealt a severe blow to the entrenched opposition to civil rights. Opponents of civil rights were never able to mount the kind of racist platform they had put forth against the Civil Rights Act again. Moreover, the passage of the Civil Rights Act of 1964 cleared the way for the Voting Rights Act of 1965, which further advanced the black struggle for equality by eradicating practices and procedures that had denied blacks the ability to vote.

LBJ ON CIVIL RIGHTS ACT OF 1964 (JUNE 19, 1964)

Senate passage of the civil rights bill is a major step toward equal opportunities for all Americans. I congratulate Senators of both parties who worked to make passage possible....

No single act of Congress can, by itself, eliminate discrimination and prejudice, hatred and injustice. But this bill goes further to invest the rights of man with the protection of law than any legislation in this century.

First it will provide a carefully designed code to test and enforce the right of every American to go to school, get a job, to vote, and to pursue his life unhampered by the barriers of racial discrimination.

Second, it will, in itself, help educate all Americans to their responsibility to give equal treatment to their fellow citizens.

Third, it will enlist one of the most powerful moral forces of American society on the side of civil rights—the moral obligation to respect and obey the law of the land.

Fourth, and perhaps the most important, this bill is a renewal and a reinforcement, a symbol and a strengthening of that abiding commitment to human dignity and the equality of man which has been the guiding purpose of the American Nation for almost 200 years.

It is the product, not of any man or group of men, but of a broad national consensus that every person is entitled to justice, to equality, and to an even chance to enjoy the blessings of liberty. It is in the highest tradition of a civilization which, from the Magna Carta on, has used the fabric of law for the fulfillment of liberty.

Lastly, this bill is a challenge. It is a challenge to men of good will in every part of the country, to transform the commands of our law into the customs of our land. It is a challenge to all of us, to go to work in our States and communities, in our homes, and in the depths of our hearts to eliminate the final strongholds of intolerance and hatred. It is a challenge to reach beyond the content of the bill to conquer the barriers of poor education, poverty, and squalid housing which are an inheritance of past injustice and an impediment to future advance....

I do not underestimate the depth of the passions involved in the struggle for racial equality. But I also know that throughout this country, in every section of this land there is a large reservoir of good will and compassion, of decency and fair play which seeks a vision of justice without violence in the streets. If these forces do not desert the field, if they can be brought to the battle, then the years of trial will be a prelude to the final triumph of a land "with liberty and justice for all"

Source: *Public Papers of the Presidents, Lyndon B. Johnson, 1963–1964, Book I—November 22, 1963 to June 30, 1964*, 787–788.

LETTER TO SENATOR EVERETT DIRKSEN FROM COMMITTEE OF 100 BUSINESSMEN (FEBRUARY 24, 1964)

Dear Senator Dirksen,

After reading some of the now available material on the fine points of the bill . . . I feel that some searching questions need to be asked and answered.

One of the most obvious flaws in the bill is its ambiguity. It lacks a satisfactory definition of "discrimination" and of "civil rights." Can so-called civil rights really be defined? I feel that they can be in a limited way, and it is in the limited areas where the federal government has most of its proper authority. It is the right of everyone to have access to school, parks, and other facilities supported by public funds and to the voting booth.

The attempt to extend federal jurisdiction by arguing that anything touched by federal monies comes under federal control is fraudulent, unconstitutional, and dangerous. You are on record as opposing Title II of the bill for these reasons. I maintain that the entire bill should be opposed for the same reasons. Every section of the bill indicates to me motives more political than social. It calls for the establishment of a commission here, a study group there, and the showering of great quantities of funds on almost any community, group, or individual who can claim even a remote concern with so-called civil rights.

The really shocking thing about the bill, however, is that in opposing "discrimination" it discriminates. Under the title covering discrimination in employment, the bill states that an employer may not deny someone a job on the bases of race, color, creed, national origin, religion, etc. It goes on to state, however, that employment may be denied an atheist, a Communist, or a person listed by the Attorney General as subversive. I can understand the latter two, but to deny someone protection because he does not have a religion and to do it under the law is appalling. Freedom of religion must include freedom from religion.

There is no doubt that much needs to be done in the area of civil rights. But this bill succeeds only in extending federal powers in the most brazenly unconstitutional way. True, minorities are guaranteed protection from the majority, but the majority deserves protection from minority legislation such as this which, in the long run, will be detrimental to both.

Sincerely,
Bruce Butterfield

Source: Congresslink, <http://www.congresslink.org/civil/cr9.html>

THE ORIGINS OF MEDICARE AND MEDICAID

With the "War on Poverty" underway, and civil rights legislation on the books, Johnson's first priority in 1965 was health care. Again drawing on his experience in south Texas, Johnson believed that government-funded health care needed to be an integral aspect of the "War on Poverty." Advocates of government-sponsored health care who had introduced proposals since the New Deal had little to show for their efforts by 1965. Congress had discussed the issue at length beginning in 1956, but Eisenhower did not support a major role for the federal government in health care, even one limited to senior citizens. Some congressional leaders, including Lyndon Johnson, had worked hard during the late 1950s to pass health care legislation, but their efforts yielded only a modest plan. This program under the Kerr-Mills Act provided federal funding to the states for those of their aged populations that could not afford private insurance but did not qualify for welfare. The program was poorly administered, few states participated, and its coverage was very limited. But, by the mid-1960s, the population of the United States over age 65 had increased from just over 12 million in 1950 to more than 17 million, and health care costs were increasing. Although these Americans received Social Security, their benefits were inadequate to cover the rising costs of health care. Given these demographic changes, the momentum behind reform, rights, and access, and Johnson's own occupancy of the presidency, by 1965 the time was right for the passage of major health care legislation.

In his first speech to Congress in 1964, Johnson mentioned Medicare as one of his top priorities. Both houses of Congress passed health care legislation in 1964, but conference committee negotiations broke down, and Congress sent no bill to the President. On the first day of the 1965 congressional session, Johnson presented a report to Congress detailing the limited access to high-quality health care in the United States, and noted "I expect you to do something about it." Half of all Americans in 1965 had no health insurance. It was clear though that Congress should first address the plight of those most adversely affected by the high costs of health care, the elderly and the poor. Liberal Democrats, such as Senator Jacob Javits (D-NY) and Johnson himself, were the key proponents of a federally funded insurance policy for old and poor people. They had been laboring since the mid-fifties to solve the crisis in the cost of health care for the elderly.

Conservative Democrats, mostly from the South, and Republicans, who had consistently resisted any legislation increasing the power of the federal government, both opposed the plan. In contrast to education, where most leading professional organizations supported "Great Society" legislation, the members of health care's most important and powerful body, the American Medical Association (AMA), firmly opposed any expanded role for the federal government in health care, fearing that government insurance would threaten their autonomy, and possibly their incomes, as physicians.

Johnson's preferred initiatives (initially designated, as the King-Anderson bill, after its House sponsors, but ultimately entitled Medicare) was a compulsory program for those over 65 years old. Under the plan the federal government would assume the costs of hospital stays, some tests, home health care, and some doctor visits. Patients would pay a small portion of their bills, but monies from government coffers supplied by an increase in the Social Security tax would cover most of their costs. Congress added Medicaid to assist the poor with their health care costs. Although private insurance companies would administer the Medicaid program, government funds would cover the medical costs of those like single mothers with dependent children and the physically and mentally disabled who qualified for other forms of categorical assistance.

Medicare/Medicaid, Johnson's preferred program of legislation, faced several alternative proposals in the Congress. The AMA sponsored the Herlong-Curtis bill, the most important challenge to Johnson's plan. The AMA and the insurance industry argued that the Medicare plan would destroy private enterprise in health care by providing government entitlements to everyone, regardless of their economic standing. They feared price-fixing and predicted the arrival of socialized medicine if the Medicare bill became law. The doctors proposed "Eldercare," a voluntary program that private insurance companies would run, in which the aged would enroll at their option, pay regular premiums, and have the states and the federal government share the costs of their health care once patients incurred those costs. The "Eldercare" program, as it was proposed, would also be optional for the states. The AMA proposals received wide publicity but won minimal congressional support. Instead, most ridiculed the proposal, calling it "Don't Care" and "Elder scare." Republican Representative John Byrnes of Wisconsin proposed another voluntary plan for the elderly, which the federal government and the states would fund but which would require the insured to pay scaled premiums for the health care services they received. In the end, instead of providing alternative plans, these ideas were incorporated into the final Medicare legislation. The AMA's claim that its Eldercare plan was more comprehensive than Medicare led congressmen to expand the benefits and scope of Medicare in the final discussions before voting on the bill. Policymakers incorporated

Byrnes's proposal into the final Medicare legislation, as Medicare B. Under Medicare Part A, a compulsory program, beneficiaries received nearly comprehensive coverage for hospital stays and services. Under Medicare Part B, an optional program, the insured would pay a small premium and receive coverage for the majority of the costs they incurred for doctor visits, nursing home stays, lab work, and other services.

Despite opposition, Medicare/Medicaid passed both houses of Congress without difficulty. Some fears about the increasing power of the federal government were assuaged by the fact that beneficiaries would still be insured by private insurances companies through Medicare—the federal government would only fund the program, not provide the insurance. Johnson signed the legislation into law on July 30, 1965 at a ceremony in Independence, Missouri, the birthplace of President Harry Truman, who received the first Medicare beneficiary card at the ceremony. Almost 19 million Americans enrolled in Medicare or Medicaid in the first year of the programs. Both programs succeeded in extending the benefits of health care insurance to many Americans who would otherwise carry no health insurance. They also led to a dramatic expansion in the involvement of the federal government in the health care system, which has continued to expand the scope of its coverage. In 1972 the law extended eligibility to disabled persons under the age of 65 and those with chronic renal failure.

With the American population constantly aging, this aspect of the budget and the bureaucracy grows continuously. Today's policymakers find it especially difficult to manage the system, as the issues are not only economic and demographic, but political hot-buttons as well. The program had become so expensive by the 1980s that the price-fixing fears of the AMA finally came to pass, as the government instituted the "prospective payment" system, whereby it paid consistent, previously set fees to regardless of the health care provider's customary charges for that service. This provoked a new round of debates over the proper place of the federal government in the personal life of Americans.

PRESIDENT LYNDON JOHNSON, SIGNING
THE MEDICARE BILL (JULY 30, 1965)

... Because the need for this action is plain; and it is so clear indeed that we marvel not simply at the passage of this bill, but what we marvel at is that it took so many years to pass it....

There are more than 18 million Americans over the age of 65. Most of them have low incomes Most of them are threatened by illness and medical expenses that they cannot afford. And through this new law, ... every citizen will be able, in his productive years when he is earning, to insure himself against the ravages of illness in his old age....

During your working years, the people of America—you—will contribute through the social security program a small amount each payday ... the employer will contribute a similar amount ...

No longer will older Americans be denied the healing miracle of modern medicine. No longer will illness crush and destroy the savings that they have so carefully put away over a lifetime so that they might enjoy dignity in their later years. No longer will young families see their own incomes, and their own hopes, eaten away simply because they are carrying out their deep moral obligations to their parents, and to their uncles, and their aunts.

And no longer will this nation refuse the hand of justice to those who have given a lifetime of service and wisdom and labor to the progress of this progressive country.

DONOVAN F. WARD, M.D., PRESIDENT OF THE AMERICAN MEDICAL ASSOCIATION, DELIVERED AT THE SPECIAL CONVENTION OF THE AMERICAN MEDICAL ASSOCIATION HOUSE OF DELEGATES (FEBRUARY 6, 1965)

Are 200,000 doctors wrong?

I put the question, first, to the members of this house: Is it possible for an entire profession of dedicated men and women—engaged in all the arts, the sciences and the practices of merciful healing—to be so nearly of one mind about a matter affecting human health—and, at the same time, be wrong?

My answer—and do not be shocked—is "Yes," we have been wrong.

Oh, no—not wrong in our assessment on the King-Anderson bill which has so shamefully been misnamed "medicare"—not at all wrong in our steadfast opposition to this measure, nor in our exposing of it, page by page, for the cruel hoax that it is. No, in our opposition to this political creation called medicare—which has no medical care in it—we doctors have been professionally justified and morally right. Therefore, we will continue—and, in the time that remains for truth to take hold—we will intensify our efforts to advise the American people, yet again, that medicare is a lure—not a cure—for the problems of the aged, and that a genuine medical program is available.

But I did say we doctors have been wrong about something. In one important aspect of this crucial struggle which now approaches a climax in Congress, we made an erroneous assumption. We assumed, wrongly it appears, that the truth—spoken to the people—would overcome the lie in short order. ...

Year after year we have seen a piece of political quackery called medicare die in Congress, its promoters defeated by the sound judgment of the majority of the House and Ways Committee and by lack of support in our

National Legislature. After each of those beatings, we thought medicare would not dare show its false face again. We were wrong—it came back during the next election. . . .

In the meantime, we doctors—on those occasions and through those channels which have grudgingly been made available to us—have gone before our patients, the American people, and tried to tell them the truth about medicare. We have called it a deception, and publicly proved it, itemizing these as the reasons: Medicare would cover only a miserly fraction of the total medical costs of someone who is really sick. It would provide only limited hospital benefits and some nursing home care in some nursing homes. . . . That is all there is to medicare. The patient pays the entire cost of everything else. Doctors and surgical care would not be provided by medicare.

We doctors have charged—not only that medicare is a deception, but it is also a danger—and we have itemized our reasons: It would impose Federal controls upon our hospitals, adding to their costs and burdens of administration, determining admissions and discharges of patients; and setting budgetary standards that have nothing to do with sickness. We know who suffers when a budget replaces medical judgment—our patients. Medicare would endanger the relationship between the patient and his doctor his full range of choices in treatment and also by institutionalizing that which is private. And another danger—to the social security system itself. . . . Raising social security taxes to cover the enormous and unpredictable costs of hospitalization for millions must certainly endanger the entire system. . . .

All these things we have cited to the American people to support our contention that the King-Anderson medicare scheme is a deception and a danger. . . .

If the drums can be stilled long enough to make this comparison, it will be found that the Herlong-Curtis eldercare bill can cover not only the cost of hospital care and nursing homes for the aged, but also payment of physicians and surgical and drug costs which medicare would not do. . . . Are 200,000 doctors wrong in asking that careful study be given to the Herlong-Curtis eldercare bill, the only medical aid for the aged measure now before Congress that was drawn up in consultation with the medical profession? . . .

Are 200,000 doctors wrong in pointing out that our senior citizens should have a health program that does not turn its back upon the views of private medicine? Can the objections of the doctors be considered an asset in drawing up a national health care program?

Are 200,000 doctors wrong when they insist that the American people do not have clamped down upon them, and upon their children, an irrevocable Government health care program that is not understood or it misunderstood by three-quarters of the people themselves?

I will ask you who sit in this highest house of medicine. I will ask those who sit in our Houses of Congress. I will ask our patients, the American people—are 200,000 doctors wrong?

Source: *Congressional Record*, Vol. III, Pt. 2, 2420–2421.

ELEMENTARY AND SECONDARY EDUCATION ACT

As a former teacher from a poor immigrant region of Texas, Johnson regarded education as a key pillar in his war against poverty. As in the case of his proposed "War on Poverty" and legislation on health care programs, he sought to increase access, especially in poor and immigrant communities. Although presidents since Truman had federal aid to education on their agendas, historian James T. Patterson has documented three important changes that had occurred by the mid-1960s that allowed Congress to pass legislation which for the first time substantially committed the resources of the federal government to education. First, the Civil Rights Act of 1964, which prevented federal aid to segregated schools, ensured that aid would not be restricted to white schools. This potential had held up education acts before, as liberals opposed laws that would have benefited only such schools. Second, Johnson, a Protestant, was able to structure and present his education bill in a way that mollified those who feared that students at parochial, predominately Catholic, schools would come out on the short end of the stick. Third, and most importantly, Johnson introduced poverty into the debate on education. Johnson knew that education was essential for individuals and communities to escape poverty. He emphasized the idea of compensatory education and promised that even though the majority of schools in the nation would receive federal funding, this would not diminish the autonomy of local school districts—laws would give local educators ample freedom to determine how to spend the money.

Given the building momentum of the "Great Society," the new set of circumstances after the passage of the Civil Rights Act of 1964, and Johnson's personal emphasis on the bill, the Elementary and Secondary Education Act (ESEA) passed the Congress rather easily in April 1965. In the spirit of the "Great Society," proponents of the education bill argued that access to quality education was lacking. Their solution was money to purchase better materials, pay for the improvement of facilities, and fund the development of more innovative teaching programs. Opponents were primarily conservative Democrats and Republicans, motivated by concerns for states' rights. Traditionally, states and localities had assumed almost complete responsibility for elementary and secondary education. Republican Representatives, such as John Anderson of Illinois and Clarence Brown of Ohio, thus couched the debate in terms of those who believed education was a "federal function" and those who did not. Democrats were divided. While some, like Montana Senator Mike Mansfield (D-MT) called the law "a milestone in its comprehensive and enlightened approach to providing full educational opportunity for every American," Southern Democrats, notably Senator Strom Thurmond of South Carolina, vigorously attacked the bill, arguing that the ESEA signaled the end of local control of education. The congressional debate, which Democratic leaders highly controlled, was brief, and neither house added many amendments. Most policymakers tied poverty to the lack of education and agreed that the major problem facing schools in America was that of money. Although some, like Senator Edward Kennedy (D-MA), claimed that even more needed to be done, ultimately the primary concern of the Elementary and Secondary Education Act was that of increasing federal spending on education and dispersing that money to schools. The Act passed both Houses of Congress, and the president signed it into law April 1965.

Most of the debate over the ESEA occurred in the aftermath of its passage. Historian John A. Andrew has linked the ESEA to the Civil Rights Act of 1964. The latter required withholding federal funds from segregated schools, and, even before the bill was passed, detractors identified this as an example of the federal control which the legislation embodied. The ESEA, of course, represented the allocation of massive amounts of federal money (federal aid tripled from 1965 to 1966), which Congress would deny to schools that did not comply with the Civil Rights Act. Although they failed to implement many of them, Southerners formulated a variety of plans for desegregation. Race also became an important factor in the North. Andrew points out that in Chicago, where de facto segregation prevailed, a major confrontation ensued between Mayor Richard Daley and the head of the U.S. Office of Education, who withheld $34 million from Chicago schools claiming that they could not receive ESEA monies because they did not comply with the Civil Rights Act of 1964.[1]

The debate extended beyond race. Many argued that the money was not, in fact, reaching the poor. Some argued that the formula by which funds were collected and allocated sent money to affluent school districts that did not need federal assistance while short-changing more needy schools. Lawmakers and educators argued over who would determine how the money would be spent, foreshadowing the 1990s debate over block grants. Most congressional attempts to convert allocations into block grants failed. A contentious debate also followed the publication of the Coleman Report in 1966. The report claimed that family life and cultural influences (including pervasive segregation in some areas), rather than factors at schools, explained why people became trapped in cycles of poverty and/or why the educational system at times seemed to be ineffective. Moreover, the ESEA set the precedent for federal involvement in education on a large scale. Thus, debates over the federal role in, and control of, education, broadened to include civil rights and busing, bilingual education, higher education, and, by the late 1970s, questions of gender and athletics. These remain among the most hotly discussed issues in the funding of education. Recently the question of federal content standards for education content have been important as well.

NOTE

1. John A. Andrew, *Lyndon Johnson and the Great Society*, (Chicago: Ivan R. Dee, 1998) 122–123.

PRESIDENT LYNDON JOHNSON, "FULL EDUCATIONAL OPPORTUNITY," MESSAGE TO CONGRESS (JANUARY 12, 1965)

In the United States today—

One-quarter of all Americans are in the Nation's classrooms.
High school attendance has grown eighteen fold since the turn of the century—six times as fast as the population.
College enrollment has advanced eighty fold. Americans today support a fourth of the world's institutions of higher learning and a third of its professors and college students.

In the life of the individual, education is always an unfinished task. And in the life of this Nation, the advancement of education is a continuing challenge.
There is a darker side to education in America:

One student out of every three now in the fifth grade will drop out before finishing high school—if the present rate continues.
Almost a million young people will continue to quit school each year—if your schools fail to stimulate their desire to learn.
Over 100,000 of our brightest high school graduates each year will not go to college—and many others will leave college—if the opportunity for higher education is not expanded.

The cost of this neglect runs high.... Every child must be encouraged to get as much education as he has the ability to take. We want this not only for his sake, but for the nation's sake. Nothing matters more to the future of our country: not our military preparedness—for armed might is worthless if we lack the brainpower to build a world of peace; not our productive economy—for we cannot sustain growth without trained manpower; not our democratic system of government—for freedom is fragile if citizens are ignorant.

We must demand that our schools increase not only the quantity but the quality of America's education. For we recognize that nuclear age problems cannot be solved with horse-and-buggy learning. The three R's of our school system must be supported by the three T's—teachers who are superior, techniques of instruction that are modern, and thinking about education which places it first in all our plans and hopes.

Specifically, four major tasks confront us:

To bring better education to millions of disadvantaged youth who need it most.
To put the best educational equipment and ideas and innovations within reach of all students.
To advance the technology of teaching and the training of teachers.
To provide incentives for those who wish to learn at every stage along the road to learning.

Our program must match the magnitude of these tasks. . . . In all that we do, we mean to strengthen our State and community education systems. Federal assistance does not mean Federal control—as past programs have proven. . . . In this spirit, I urge that we not push ahead with the No. 1 business of the American people—the education of our youth in preschools, elementary and secondary schools, and in the colleges and universities. . . .

When the country has been most astir with creative activity, when it most keenly senses the sturdiness of the old reaching out for the vigor of the new, it has given special attention to its educational system. . . . We are now embarked on another venture to put the American dream to work in meeting the new demands of a new day. Once again we must start where men who would improve their society have always known they must begin —with an educational system restudied, reinforced, and revitalized.

Source: *Congressional Record*, Vol. 111, Pt. 1, 508–511.

SENATOR STROM THURMOND (R-SC), "EDUCATION AND TAX SOURCES" (JANUARY 15, 1965)

For the fiscal year beginning July 1, 1965, the President has requested authority to spend approximately one-third as much as is now being spent for education by all the States. This money will go to public, private, and church-supported schools at all levels, beginning with kindergarten and extending through college postgraduate work. Each year federal spending will go higher until total control and responsibility rests in Washington with Federal bureaucrats spelling out the contents of textbooks and curriculums and controlling teacher pay and standards.

The recent order enforcing the fund withholding provisions of title VI of the Civil Rights Act of 1964 provide all the proof necessary on the element of control which lurks behind all Federal aid dollars.

There is a good alternative for all Federal aid to public education, and I have introduced legislation to make this alternative possible. The President is suggesting the elimination of some Federal excise taxes. I have thus proposed that the Federal Government withdraw its excise taxes on alcoholic beverages and tobacco products so the States can have the full benefit of these tax sources. . . . All states now tax alcohol and tobacco, but they are limited in their revenues here as elsewhere by the intrusion of the Federal Government.

In fact, preemption of tax source by the Federal Government is one of the primary reasons for the gradual erosion of State and local powers of government and the shift of more and more authority to Washington.

If the President truly is concerned about promoting more progress in education and States responsibilities—as well as preserving States rights and our Federal system of divided powers—then he should support this proposal to keep tax dollars at home so progress for the people can be promoted at the appropriate level of government. He could also back a proposal I am cosponsoring to provide a tax credit for taxpayers who spend money to pay for education expenses of students.

The only feature lacking in these two proposals is the element of control—which, in his education message, the President professes not to desire.

Source: *Congressional Record*, Vol. 111, Pt. 1, 936.

REPRESENTATIVE CLARENCE J. BROWN (R-OH)
(MARCH 24, 1965)

I have read and studied this legislation. This bill is one of the most dangerous measures that has come before us in my time. As one reads the provisions of this bill, as one applies what knowledge one may have gained from experience with other programs of a Federal nature, with other embarkations that we have made upon new activities in the field of Federal-State-local relations, one becomes convinced that sooner or later Federal bureaucracy under this legislation, unless it is greatly amended . . . we shall have bureaucratic control from Washington that will take away from present school officials, boards of education, State and local, and educators, State and local, the power and authority, the rights and duties which they now have to direct, regulate, and administer education at the State and local level. This legislation will make one man [Commissioner of Education] at the head of the great bureaucracy all powerful, able to have his own way, to say, "You must do it this way or I will move in and do something else." ...

Source: *Congressional Record*, Vol. 111, Pt. 5, 5728.

MARINES IN THE DOMINICAN REPUBLIC

Although Johnson's major foreign policy engagement was in Vietnam, military management also confronted Johnson closer to home. While he busily sent troops across the world to maintain the American commitment in Vietnam, Johnson ordered American intervention in a civil conflict in the Dominican Republic, the Caribbean state that shares the island of Hispañola with Haiti. For thirty years the government of the Dominican Republic remained stable under the dictatorship of General Rafael Trujillo, but after his assassination in 1961, Dominicans had difficulty establishing political calm. For four years, political power changed hands between leftist presidents and military backed regimes, until in April 1965, soldiers loyal to Juan Bosch, who had been elected democratically in 1962 but quickly fled into exile amid a military coup on the island, led a coup d'etat to return Bosch to power. Rebels supporting Bosch's constitutional right to the presidency of the Dominican Republic arrayed against military loyalists defending the military government and the right of the military to intervene in political affairs.

The rebels fighting to return Bosch to power had to contend with more than just the Dominican military in their attempt to return the Dominican government to constitutionalism. In the United States, President Johnson, already frustrated by the manner in which Vietnam was distracting attention from his "Great Society," was determined to prevent the turmoil in the Dominican Republic from further derailing his domestic agenda. Initially Johnson kept his political concerns about the Dominican Republic between his advisors and himself, vowing that the United States would not allow the Dominican Republic to become a "second Cuba." However, reports from the Dominican Republic to the State Department indicated that the rebel groups supporting Bosch were advancing a communist agenda. This concerned U.S. policymakers, especially conservatives in the State Department and in Congress. Thus, Johnson decided to deploy the American military to put down the insurrection as quickly as possible and redirect attention again toward his domestic program. Publicly, the President defended U.S. intervention in the Dominican Republic as an effort to protect foreign nationals there. After deploying an initial 400 Marines to the Dominican Republic, supplemented the following day by 1,400 more, Johnson found some of the circumstances in the Dominican Republic to be eerily similar to those in Vietnam. One parallel was particularly troubling: government troops in the Dominican Republic, like ARVN in South Vietnam, were willing to let American troops do their fighting for them.

Another parallel to the episode in Vietnam was the pressure for more troops that U.S. military personnel on the ground placed on Johnson. Although the scale of the two crises differed profoundly, Johnson deployed troops in similar ways in both cases. Within three days, he had supplemented the initial landing of 400 Marines by more than 16,000 American troops. Feeling pressure from Embassy officials and military advisors, and recognizing the reluctance of the government troops in the Dominican Republic, Johnson thought that he had no choice but to expand the U.S. presence on the island. As in Vietnam, Johnson attempted to project an air of neutrality. Throughout May, despite coordinated efforts with loyalist troops, and negotiations to conclude a peace agreement allowing the internment and even deportation of Communist and leftist leaders, publicly the Johnson Administration continued to define the U.S. role in the Dominican Republic as one of protecting Americans, and preventing the deterioration of the situation such that the country would become vulnerable to foreign agitators. With great care, U.S. spokesmen avoided the suggestion of U.S. sympathy for one side or another in the Dominican Republic. In his television address to the American people on May 2, Johnson insisted that he had deployed U.S. troops to defend American lives and interests, and that the United States had no particular interest in the nature of the political outcome of the event, as long as a communist-controlled government did not result. This was problematic, because while U.S. officials promulgated a policy of neutrality in the affair, the media in the United States and in the Dominican Republic reported actions of American troops that clearly indicated American preference for the loyalists. As in Vietnam, the Administration began quickly to lose credibility both with the parties in the Dominican Republic and with some Americans. Although many Americans supported American actions against communism during the majority of the time American troops were deployed in the Dominican Republic, others criticized the management of the U.S. role in those affairs. As on Vietnam, Senator J. William Fulbright (D-AR), Chairman of the Senate Foreign Relations Committee, was the leading critic. Fulbright conducted televised hearings of the progress of the war in Vietnam in 1966 and 1967 and lashed out against Johnson's handling of the Dominican crisis. On both occasions, the Senator was particularly critical of the way the Johnson Administration disseminated information to the public.

By the end of the summer, the situation in the Dominican Republic had quieted. Johnson seemed to lose interest in events there, preferring to focus on Vietnam and the "Great Society", and a stalemate prevailed on the island. Johnson appointed a new negotiator to try to mediate between the loyalists and rebels, and a plan at the negotiating table quickly gathered support from all sides. Developed and promoted by former Dominican president Joaquin Balaguer, the plan called for a twelve-month provisional government to be followed by national elections, which Balaguer believed he would win. Compromises appeased the concerns of both loyalists and rebels on control of the military, for whoever controlled the military controlled the country. When the plan was put before Johnson, his only concern was how the provisional government would deal with communists. Once he became convinced that the provisional President Godoy Garcia would not allow communists to gain power in the interim period, Johnson agreed to the peace plan. The elections the peace plan called for took place on June 1, 1966, giving Balaguer the presidency, and beginning "Operation Well Done," as the United States dubbed its evacuation of troops. The United States continued to support the Dominican government with financial assistance and preferential trade deals for decades, during which Balaguer won the presidency nine times. The increasingly conservative, corrupt, and repressive nature of the Balaguer governments caused little concern in the United States. For American officials, the instability and underdevelopment of the Dominican Republic, combined with its proximity to other trouble spots like Cuba made it particularly vulnerable to communist infiltration. Thus, despite the Dominican Republic's lack of democratic procedures, Washington continued to count that country as a stable, non communist an ally throughout the twentieth century.

JOHNSON TELEVISION ADDRESS ON DOMINICAN REPUBLIC INTERVENTION (MAY 2, 1965)

Good evening ladies and gentlemen:

There are times in the affairs of nations when great principles are tested in an ordeal of conflict and danger. This is such a time for the American nations.

At stake are the lives of thousands, the liberty of a nation, and the principles and the values of all the American Republics. That is why the hopes and the concern of this entire hemisphere are, on the Sabbath—Sunday, focused on the Dominican Republic.

In the dark mist of conflict and violence, revolution and confusion, it is not easy to find clear and unclouded truths.

But certain things are clear. And they require equally clear action. . . .

In this situation hesitation and vacillation could mean death for many of our people, as well as many of the citizens of other lands.

I thought that we could not and we did not hesitate. Our forces, American forces, were ordered in immediately to protect American lives. They have done that, they have attacked no one, and although some of our servicemen gave their lives, not a single American civilian and the civilian of any other nation, as a result of this protection, lost their lives. . . .

I want you to know that it is not a light matter to send our American boys to another country, but I do not think that the American People expect their President to hesitate or to vacillate in the face of danger because the decision is hard when life is in peril.

... the revolutionary movement took a tragic turn. Communist leaders, many of them trained in Cuba, seeing a chance to increase disorder, to gain a foothold, joined the revolution. They took increasing control. And what began as a popular democratic revolution, committed to democracy and social justice, very shortly moved and was taken over and really seized and placed into the hands of a band of Communist conspirators.... The revolution was now in other and dangerous hands.

When these new and ominous developments emerged, the OAS met again and it met at the request of the United States. I am glad to say that they responded wisely and decisively. A five-nation OAS team is now in the Dominican Republic acting to achieve a cease-fire to ensure the safety of innocent people, to restore normal conditions, and to open a path to democratic process....

The American nations cannot, must not, and will not permit the establishment of another Communist government in the Western Hemisphere. This was the unanimous view of all the American nations when, in January 1962, they declared, and I quote, "the principles of communism are incompatible with the principles of the inter-American system."

This is what our beloved President John F. Kennedy meant when, less than a week before his death, he told us, "We in this hemisphere must also use every resource at our command to prevent the establishment of another Cuba in this hemisphere."

This is and this will be the common action and the common purpose of the democratic forces of the hemisphere. For the danger is also a common danger, and the principles are common principles....

Our goal is a simple one. We are there to save the lives of our citizens and to save the lives of all people. Our goal, in keeping with the great principles of the inter-American system is to help prevent another Communist state in this hemisphere. And we would like to do this without bloodshed or without large scale fighting.

The form and nature of a free Dominican Republic government I assure you, is solely a matter for the Dominican people, but we do not know what kind of government we hope to see in the Dominican Republic. For that is carefully spelled out in the treaties and agreements which make up the fabric of the entire inter-American system. It is expressed, time and time again, in the words of our statesmen and in the values and hopes which bind us all together....

And before I leave you, my fellow Americans, I want to say this personal word: I know that no American serviceman wants to kill anyone. I know that no American President wants to give an order which brings shooting and casualties and death. I want you to know and I want the world to know that as long as I am President of this country, we are going to defend ourselves. We will defend our soldiers against attackers. We will honor treaties. We will keep out commitments. We will defend our Nation against all those who seek to destroy not only the United States but every free country of this hemisphere. We do not want to bury anyone as I have said so many times before. But we do not intend to be buried.

Thank you. God bless you. Good night.

SENATOR WILLIAM J. FULBRIGHT (D-AK), SPEECH IN U.S. SENATE (SEPTEMBER 15, 1965)

The United States intervened in the Dominican Republic for the purpose of preventing the victory of a revolutionary force which was judged to be Communist dominated. On the basis of Ambassador Bennett's messages to Washington, there is no doubt that the threat of communism rather than danger to American lives was his primary reason for recommending military intervention. . . .

The evidence does not establish that the Communists at any time actually had control of the revolution. There is little doubt that they had influence within the revolutionary movement, but the degree of that influence remains a matter of speculation.

The administration, however, assumed almost from the beginning that the revolution was Communist-dominated, or would certainly become so, and that nothing short of forcible opposition could prevent a Communist takeover. In their apprehension lest the Dominican Republic become another Cuba, some of our officials seem to have forgotten that virtually all reform movements attract some Communist support, that there is an important difference between Communist support and Communist control of a political movement, that it is quite possible to compete with the Communists for influence in a reform movement rather than abandon it to them, and, most important of all, that economic development and social justice are themselves the primary and most reliable security against Communist subversion. . . .

Communists are present in all Latin American countries, and they are going to inject themselves into almost any Latin American revolution and try to seize control of it. If any group or any movement with which the Communists associate themselves is going to be automatically condemned in the eyes of the United States, then we have indeed given up all hope of guiding or influencing even to a marginal degree the revolutionary movements and the demands for social change which are sweeping Latin America. Worse, if that is our view, then we have made ourselves the prisoners of the Latin American oligarchs who are engaged in a vain attempt to preserve the status quo-reactionaries who habitually use the term "Communist" very loosely, in part out of emotional predilection and in part in a calculated effort to scare the United States into supporting their selfish and discredited aims....

In the eyes of educated, energetic and patriotic young Latin Americans— which is to say the generation that will make or break the Alliance for Progress—the United States committed a worse offense in the Dominican Republic than just intervention; it intervened against social revolution and in support, at least temporarily, of a corrupt, reactionary military oligarchy.

By our intervention on the side of a corrupt military oligarchy in the Dominican Republic, we have embarrassed before their own people the democratic reformers who have counseled trust and partnership with the United States. We have lent credence to the idea that the United States is the enemy of social revolution in Latin America and that the only choice Latin Americans have is between communism and reaction.

Source: *Congressional Record: Proceedings and Debates of the 89th Congress, 1st Session,* Volume III, No. 170, Daily Edition (September 15, 1965), 22998–23005.

THE VOTING RIGHTS ACT OF 1965

Throughout his presidency, Johnson was forced to balance foreign policy and domestic affairs. The year 1965 might have required the best balancing act. Johnson was determined that foreign U.S. military engagements would not deter work toward creating the "Great Society" at home. To many in America, the Civil Rights Act of 1964 was not enough. Civil rights activists associated with groups like the Student Non-Violent Coordinating Committee (SNCC), the Congress on Racial Equality (CORE), and the Southern Christian Leadership Conference (SCLC) saw it as only the beginning of a comprehensive effort to deal with issues of discrimination, segregation, and equality that would involve not simply where one could eat but access to political and economic power. President Johnson believed this too. He criticized those in power in the South for evading the spirit of the Fifteenth Amendment, prohibiting discrimination in voting on the basis of race, and argued that all citizens were entitled to voting rights. Johnson felt compelled to use the power of the federal government to deal with Southerners who sought to elude, or simply ignore, the Constitution. Although Johnson was deeply committed to equality before the law, he also realized that black voters were an important political constituency for the liberal wing of the Democratic Party, especially after the passage of the Civil Rights Act of 1964, which had alienated many conservative Southern Democrats. Johnson had lost the South to Republican Barry Goldwater in the election of 1964, and in the few places he won in the South, he had done so due to black voters. But, in 1965, only about half of the eligible black voters in the South were registered, and in some places that percentage was much lower. Johnson then decided that voting rights legislation was in order.

Martin Luther King, Jr., and SCLC protesters also motivated the Voting Rights Act of 1965. They resumed nonviolent demonstrations and provoked violent responses from law enforcement. This time, King and his supporters chose Selma, Alabama, as their stage, and the infamously violent county sheriff, James Clark, as their foil. Not only did Dallas County (Selma was the county seat) have a volatile and brutal sheriff, but it was also in the state of the arch-nemesis of the civil rights movement, Governor George Wallace, who could be counted on for a short temper and violent response if Clark proved unsuccessful in putting down the protest with local sources. Selma also had some of the most obviously suspect voter registration statistics: while the county population was almost 58 percent black, blacks comprised only 2.1 percent of registered voters. King led the protesters into Selma and then across Alabama in February and March. As anticipated, Clark resorted to violence, distributing electric cattle prods to his officers to assault the protesters, and Wallace deployed armies of state troopers against them. Just as Little Rock and Birmingham had effectively mobilized the nation during the previous two administrations, so Selma provided a catalyst for Americans and Johnson in 1965.

The threat in the Voting Rights Act to impose the power of the federal government in the states did not resonate well with many Southerners. The act's primary intent was to prevent the use of discriminatory procedures to prevent blacks or others from registering to vote. The Fifteenth Amendment and the Civil Rights Act of 1964, which outlawed the literacy test as a criterion for voter registration, already had established legal obstacles for these tactics. Yet there had been little enforcement, and no law granted the federal government the authority to impose punitive measures on Southern locales that violated the laws. Legal challenges had been the only recourse. The Voting Rights Act sought to change that. That Act gave the federal government the power to invalidate tests or qualifications used to deny persons the right to vote and to deploy federal officials to conduct voter registration in those areas where less than 50 percent of the voting-age population was registered or voting. Finally, the act required that those areas falling under the "50 percent formula" would be required to get approval from the Justice Department any time they intended to change qualifications or procedures used in voter registration.

The Voting Rights Act outraged Southern conservatives. They argued that the "50 percent formula" of the bill made the law unconstitutional because the federal government was required only to intervene in those areas whose violation was deemed particularly egregious and not in any area employing discriminatory registration tactics. Clauses in the bill exempted any area whose non-white voting-age population was less than 20 percent, thus exempting almost all areas in the North and West from the potential for federal intervention. Southern Democrats, like Herman Talmadge (D-GA) and Harry Byrd (D-VA), attacked all these provisions of the voting rights bill, alleging that the bill itself was discriminatory, and designed simply to penalize past practices in a handful of Southern states. Not surprisingly, they also called the bill unconstitutional, contending that it violated traditional states' rights to determine the eligibility of their voters and to conduct their own elections and was merely a malicious attempt by the federal government to expand its power and punish the South. They argued that Congress had been "blackmailed" by "threats of violence," and democracy was yielding to "mobocracy" and "hysteria." These conservative opponents of the Voting Rights Act were outnumbered. This time, Southern Democrats, like Senate Judiciary Committee Chairman James Eastland (D-MS), were unable to mount a filibuster. The House voted for passage of the act on August 3, by a vote of 328–74, and the Senate followed suite the next day with a vote of 79–18. Johnson signed the bill into law on August 6.

The Voting Rights Act had an immediate impact. Federal registrars flooded the South, and thousands of voters registered within weeks. Nongovernmental organizations like SNCC and the NAACP also worked hard to get Southern blacks registered. Not wanting blacks to overwhelm their voices at the polls, whites also joined the drive to register. The impact also extended further, as an increasing number of white Democrats turned against their party, a shift that became more evident in future elections. Strom Thurmond, the old Dixiecrat from South Carolina, abandoned his party altogether, shifting his affiliation to the Republicans. Still, the Civil Rights Act and Voting Rights Act did little for blacks outside the South, primarily those living in the urban centers of the West and North. They had neither faced the hatred of Jim Crow, nor had they encountered serious obstacles when voting. They were, however, largely poor. Black unemployment in certain parts of Los Angles reached 75 percent in 1965. Feeling left out, these blacks resorted to their own form of protest and violence only five days after Johnson signed the Voting Rights Act into law. The riots in Watts in the summer of 1965 began three years of sporadic looting, rioting, violence, and killing in cities across the United States. The midterm elections of 1966 weakened Johnson's hold on the Congress, dooming Johnson's attempt to extend the Civil Rights Act in 1966 into housing and employment.

LYNDON JOHNSON'S SPECIAL MESSAGE TO CONGRESS ON THE RIGHT TO VOTE (MARCH 15, 1965)

... I must regretfully report to the Congress the following facts:

1. That the Fifteenth Amendment of our Constitution is today being systematically and willfully circumvented in certain State and local jurisdictions of our Nation.

2. That representatives of such State and local governments acting "under the color of law" are denying American citizens the right to vote on the sole basis of race or color.

3. That, as a result of these practices, in some areas of our country today no significant number of American citizens of the Negro race can be registered to vote except upon the intervention and order of a Federal Court.

4. That the remedies available under law to citizens thus denied their Constitutional rights—and the authority presently available to the Federal Government to act in their behalf—are clearly inadequate.

5. That the denial of these rights and the frustration of efforts to obtain meaningful relief from such denial without undue delay is contributing to the creation of conditions which are both inimical to our domestic order and tranquility and incompatible with the standards of equal justice and individual dignity on which out society stands.

I am therefore calling on the Congress to discharge the duty authorized in Section 2 of the Fifteenth Amendment "to enforce this Article by appropriate legislation."

It could never be a welcome duty for any President to place before Congress such a report of the willful failure and refusal of public officials to honor, respect and abide by any provision of the Constitution of the United States. It is especially repugnant to report such disregard directed against the Fifteenth Amendment by officials at the State and local levels....

The challenge now presented is more than a challenge to our Constitution —it is a blatant affront to the conscience of this generation of Americas. Discrimination based on race or color is reprehensible and intolerable to the great American majority. In every national forum, where they have chosen to test popular sentiment, defenders of discrimination have met resounding rejection. Americans now are not willing that the acid of the few shall be allowed to corrode the souls of the many....

Unless the right to vote be secure and undenied, all other rights are insecure and subject to denial for all our citizens. The challenge to this right is a challenge to American itself. We must meet this challenge as decisively as we would meet a challenge mounted against our land from enemies abroad....

The issue presented by the present challenge to our Constitution and our conscience transcends legalism, although it does not transcend the law itself. We are challenged to demonstrate that there are no sanctuaries without our law for those who flaunt it. We are challenged, also, to demonstrate by our prompt, fitting, and adequate response now that the hope of our system is not force, not arms, not the might of militia or marshals—but the law itself....

The national will is being denied. The integrity of our Federal system is in contest. Unless we act anew, with dispatch and resolution, we shall sanction a sad and sorrowful course for the future. For if the Fifteenth Amendment is successfully flouted today, tomorrow the First Amendment, the Fourth Amendment, the Fifth Amendment—the Sixth, the Eighth, indeed all the provisions of the Constitution on which our system stands—will be subject to disregard and erosion. Our essential strength as a society governed by the rule of law will be crippled and corrupted and the unity of our system hollowed out and left meaningless. . . .

Our purpose is not—and shall not be—either the quest for power or the desire to punish. We seek to increase the power of the people over all their governments, not to enhance the power of the Federal Government over any of the people. . . .

I am determined that these years shall be devoted to perfecting our unity so that we may pursue more successfully the fulfillment of our high purposes at home and in the world. While I have proposed to you other measures to serve the strengthening of our free society and the happiness of our free people, I regard action on the measures proposed in this Message to be first in priority. We cannot have government for all the people until we first make certain it is government of and by all the people.

Source: *Public Papers of the Presidents, Lyndon Baines Johnson, Book I—January 1 to May 31, 1965* (Washington: GPO, 1966), 287–291.

SENATOR HERMAN TALMADGE (D-GA), "THE FEDERAL GOVERNMENT HAS NO CONSTITUTIONAL AUTHORITY TO TAKE OVER CONTROL OF CITY, COUNTY, AND STATE ELECTIONS" (MARCH 16, 1965)

No patriotic law-abiding citizen condones discrimination against other citizens in the exercise of the constitutional right to vote. Under the laws of our land, every citizen must be accorded this right.

This right is enforceable in the courts, both State and Federal. . . . The administration's voting rights bill is unnecessary and unwise. While attempting to remedy one evil, it creates a far greater one. It ignores constitutional provisions concerning the State's authority to determine the qualification of voters, and bypasses numerous court decisions upholding this authority.

The Federal Government has no more authority to take over the control of city, county, or state election that it has to supplant mayors, country officials, State legislators, and Governors with appointed Federal officials.

History teaches us that republic forms of government have often died in the name of worthy causes. I hope that an emotional issue will not stampede the American people and the Congress into passing legislation that is so patently and obviously unconstitutional.

Source: *Congressional Record*, Vol. 111, Pt. 4, 5158.

SENATOR JAMES EASTLAND (D-MS) (MARCH 25, 1965)

I deny that either Congress or the Attorney General has any constitutional power to make a judicial determination that the State of Mississippi has violated the 15th Amendment to the Constitution of the United States and that Congress has both the power and right to put the Attorney General in the place of the legislature and constitution of the State of Mississippi and let him arbitrarily fix the voter qualifications of all the people of Mississippi, both black and white.

This is an insult not only to the white people of the State of Mississippi, but also to those numerous members of our Negro population who, as responsible citizens, have qualified to vote and have voted over a long period of time. Even if there have been in the past some indications or evidence of a denial or abridgement of the right to vote on the part of any individual in Mississippi by reason of his race or color, there is no justification or logic in taking a position that two wrongs make a right, and rather than have a uniform application of a reasonable literacy test against both white and Negro applicants, all literacy tests will be nullified and both literates and illiterates of each race will be registered just as fast as they can run to a Federal examiner appointed under the direction of the Attorney General....

Source: *Congressional Record*, Vol. 111, Pt. 5, 5871.

SENATOR HARRY F. BYRD (D-VA), "THE ADMINISTRATION'S SO-CALLED VOTING RIGHTS ACT OF 1965" (APRIL 5, 1965)

This is a statement about the administration's so-called Voting Rights Act of 1965. I am making it as a Member of the US Senate representing Virginia under oath to uphold the Federal Constitution....

Now the Federal administration is allowing itself to be influenced beyond reason by the emotion of domestic hysteria; and by its own actions it is inflaming so-called civil rights issues....

It is a vicious bill. It clearly bears the unreasonable stamp of hysteria....

I have analyzed all provisions of the bill. They are iniquitous in effect and contemptible in design. The administration has been advised of the odium in which I hold its proposal....

A written Constitution protects us from despotic rule. For this protection against oppressive government we rely on check and balances of division of power and separation of powers....

The Federal Attorney General, speaking for the administration, is demanding that the legislative branch...empower him—a political appointee in the executive branch—to preempt the judicial branch in areas he has chosen to punish. That is not all. He is demanding power under by Federal legislation to usurp the constitutional power of the States he has already chosen to be his victims....

The Federal Attorney General—by asserting that the voting requirements in a target area are racially discriminatory—may indict a whole State or any subdivision as violating the Constitution of the United States and Federal law....

When a state or locality is convicted by this kangeroo procedure, the Federal Attorney General order invasion of the State or subdivision by an unspecified number of Federal registrars. Occupation of the State or subdivision by the Federal registrars will continue for an unspecified time. The purpose of the Federal registrars is to enforce the will of the Federal Attorney General with respect to voting laws....

The Federal administration and its Attorney General propose by a single Federal statue to take away the constitutional rights of State and substitute Federal Executive decree. If this can be done for this administration, for the purposes of this bill, to punish the states it has chosen, it can be done at other times for other purposes to destroy the constitutional rights of others, the Constitution not withstanding.

Source: *Congressional Record*, Vol. 111, Pt. 5, 6928–6929.

HART-CELLAR IMMIGRATION ACT OF 1965

Johnson's "Great Society" was an inclusive society, and his efforts to create that society included a myriad of legislative initiatives on civil rights, voting, education, and the like, which aimed to make the United States a more inclusive place to live. As America entered the decade of the 1960s, however, immigration policy may have been the most exclusive area of American society. Prevailing immigration policy, created in 1924 in the National Origins Act and then modified to suit the conditions of the Cold War in 1952's McCarran-Walter Act, established quotas for the number of immigrants from foreign countries. Although the McCarran-Walter Act eliminated the outright exclusion of immigrants from Asia, which had been a part of the earlier immigration policy, it retained the quota system limiting the number of immigrants from any given country. This system discriminated against Asians and Eastern Europeans by giving them low quotas while favoring Western European immigrants with higher quotas. This legislation allocated almost three quarters of the slots to Great Britain, Ireland, and Germany. By the 1960s, however, times and leaders had changed. Despite the idealism of Camelot, immigration reform had not been one of Kennedy's top priorities. Neither was immigration one of Johnson's front burner issues, although his background in Texas had certainly sensitized him to the plight of immigrants, and his efforts to create a "Great Society" could hardly ignore the prejudiced immigration policy that existed. Many in the mid-1960s, including President Johnson, saw immigration reform as a logical extension of the civil rights agenda. Thus immigration legislation became one of the landmark pieces of legislation that Congress passed in 1965.

The 1965 Hart-Cellar Immigration Bill eliminated the quota system put in place by the 1924 and 1952 acts, and liberalized not only the numbers of immigrants that the United States would receive, but the methods by which they could qualify for residency in the United States. The 1965 law limited annual immigration into the United States to 290,000, which was the typical annual number for the years before 1965. For the first time, immigration legislation addressed immigration from Western Hemisphere nations. It limited the number of immigrants from that region to 120,000 per annum, even though not nearly that many were immigrating from Western Hemisphere countries at the time. The law eliminated all other national quotas. In their place, the law limited immigration from any one country to 20,000, except for the countries of the Western Hemisphere, for which the law set no maximum limits.

The new law did give some preferences though. First and foremost, the law preferred immigrants with "special skills" deemed to be "advantageous" to the United States. This included scientists and other professionals with "exceptional abilities" and workers in occupations for which labor was in short supply in the United States. The law did not require such immigrants, like others, to demonstrate proof of employment, and it exempted them from the maximum quotas placed on the Eastern and Western Hemispheres, and the total maximum number of immigrants. This provision helped mollify labor groups that had historically opposed any legislation liberalizing immigration laws. Because the legislation gave the U.S. Department of Labor the discretionary authority to determine which occupations were underemployed in the United States, the department could deny admission to immigrants in fields of employment that threatened to compete with U.S. workers. The new law also preferred relatives of American citizens and others living in the United States. The government could exempt these people from the hemispheric and total annual quotas established by the law as well. The law's third preference was to immigrants from the Western Hemisphere. In the mid-1960s, not many were emigrating from Latin America, and thus immigrants from the Western Hemisphere were exempted from any numerical limits.

Immigration preferences for employment and family reunification are still fundamental to immigration policy today.

Few opposed the bill. Most Americans did not view immigration as a major concern, and they devoted little attention to it. Some opponents argued against the "radical departure" from the historic immigration policy that favored certain national origins. Defenders of the bill responded by insisting that the U.S. image was at stake. They argued that racial preferences in immigration policy did not project the same image of the United States as other "Great Society" initiatives, like civil rights legislation. They insisted that a more tolerant immigration policy was an essential component of a foreign policy which had as at least one of its goals winning allies in the Third World. Others worried that the bill would lead to greater levels of unemployment in the United States as new immigrants flooded into American cities. Myra C. Hacker, the vice president of the New Jersey Coalition, suggested that liberal immigration policy would increase unemployment, change the racial composition of the United States, raise tensions inherent in cultural pluralism, and the like. In the same vein, Republicans proposed an alternative immigration bill, which would curtail the total numbers of immigrants at a lower number than Johnson's bill and emphasize family reunification and the protection of American workers.

However, most proponents of the bill predicted little change in the numbers and composition of immigrants. Supporters of the new legislation rebuffed the charges of the critics. They failed to foresee the dramatic consequences of the new immigration policy that its opponents accurately predicted. Few thought that the annual number of immigrants would increase, and even fewer expected a substantial increase in the number of people arriving from Latin America. However, thanks to the family reunification preferences, while the Hart-Cellar bill placed a limit of 290,000 total immigrants per year, in 1968, the first year that maximum was to apply, almost 400,000 immigrants came to the United States. By 1978, the average number of immigrants entering the United States was 547,000. Moreover, although many predicted little change in the national origins of immigrants, in the years after the bill took effect, the number of immigrants from Europe decreased, while the number of immigrants from Latin America and Asia rose dramatically. Many Latin Americans had entered the United States before 1965, when there had been no national origins quota for that region, and many of those residing in the United States sent for their relatives who qualified for exemptions under Hart-Cellar. By the 1970s, 42 percent of immigrants were coming from Latin America.

PRESIDENT LYNDON JOHNSON, SPECIAL MESSAGE
TO THE CONGRESS ON IMMIGRATION
(JANUARY 13, 1965)

To the Congress of the United States:

A change is needed in our laws dealing with immigration. Four Presidents have called attention to serious defects in this legislation. Action is long overdue.

I am therefore submitting, at the outset of this Congress, a bill designed to correct the deficiencies. I urge that it be accorded priority consideration.

The principal reform called for is the elimination of the national origins quota system. That system is incompatible with our basic American tradition.

Over the years the ancestors of all of us—some 42 million human beings—have migrated to these shores. The fundamental, longtime American attitude has been to ask not where a person comes from but what are his personal qualities. On this basis men and women migrated from every quarter of the globe. By their hard work and their enormously varied talents they hewed a great nation out of a wilderness. By their dedication to liberty and equality, they created a society reflecting man's most cherished ideals.

Long ago the poet Walt Whitman spoke our pride: "These States are the amplest poem." We are not merely a nation but a "Nation of Nations."

Violation of this tradition by the national origins quota system does incalculable harm.

The procedures imply that men and women from some countries are, just because of where they come from, more desirable citizens than others. We have no right to disparage the ancestors of millions of our fellow Americans in this way. Relationships with a number of countries, and hence the success of our foreign policy, is needlessly impeded by this proposition.

The quota system has other grave defects. Too often it arbitrarily denies us immigrants who have outstanding and sorely needed talents and skills. I do not believe this is either good government or good sense.

Thousands of our citizens are needlessly separated from their parents or other close relatives. To replace the quota system, the proposed bill relies on a technique of preferential admissions based upon the advantage of our nation of the skills of the immigrant, and the existence of a close family relationship between the immigrant and people who are already citizens or permanent residents of the United States. Within this system of preferences, and within the numerical and other limitations prescribed by law, the issuance of visas to prospective immigrants would be based on the order of their application.

First preference under the bill would be given to those with the kind of skills or attainments which make the admission especially advantageous to our society. Other preferences would favor close relatives of citizens and permanent residents, and thus serve to promote the reuniting of families— long a primary goal of American immigration policy. Parents of United States citizens could obtain admission without waiting for a quota number.

Transition to the new system would be gradual, over a five-year period. Thus the possibility of abrupt changes in the pattern of immigration from any nation is eliminated. In addition, the bill would provide that as a general rule no country could be allocated more than ten percent of the quota numbers available in any one year.

In order to insure that the new system would not impose undue hardship on any of our close allies by suddenly curtailing their emigration, the bill authorizes the President, after consultation with an Immigration Board established by the legislation, to utilize up to thirty percent of the quota numbers available in any year for the purpose of restoring cuts made by the new system in the quotas established by existing law.

Similar authority, permitting the reservation of up to ten percent of the numbers available in any year, would enable us to meet the needs of refugees fleeing from catastrophe or oppression. . . .

This bill would not alter in any way the many limitations in existing law which prevent an influx of undesirables and safeguard our people . . . [nor] relieves any immigrant of the necessity of satisfying all of the security requirements we now have, or the requirements designed to exclude persons likely to become public charges. No immigrants admitted under this bill could contribute to unemployment in the United States.

The total number of immigrants would not be substantially changed. . . . I urge the Congress to return the United States to an immigration policy which both serves the national interest and continues our traditional ideals. No move could more effectively reaffirm our fundamental belief that a man is to be judged—and judged exclusively—on his worth as a human being.

Source: *Public Papers of the Presidents, Lyndon B. Johnson*, 1965, Vol. 1, 13–15.

STATEMENT OF HOUSE REPUBLICAN POLICY COMMITTEE ON H.R. 2580

The Republican policy committee recommends that the nationals of all countries be treated equally. We endorse H.R. 2580, which amends the Immigration and Nationality Act and adopts a new system for the admission of aliens, but we believe it essential that an amendment be adopted which places the Western Hemisphere also under a reasonable numerical limitation.

For many years, the Republican Party has advocated an Immigration policy based upon the individual merit of each applicant rather than upon the individual's race, place of birth, or ancestry. On several occasions, President Eisenhower sent messages to Congress recommending Immigration reform and noting that experience in the postwar world had demonstrated that the present national origins system of admitting aliens needed reexamination.

This Republican-sponsored legislation will:

1. Abolish the national origins system;
2. Adopt a new Immigration system which emphasizes the reuniting of families and the individual merit of each applicant;
3. Set a limitation of 170,000 (Including 10,200 refugees) on the number to be admitted each year (exclusive of the Western Hemisphere);
4. Eliminate discrimination based upon race;
5. Safeguard the American workingman from Unfair competition and a lowering of wages and working standards.

We congratulate the Republican members of the Committee on the Judiciary on their contribution to this historic legislation. Due to their efforts, the provisions which surrendered to the executive wide discretionary powers over Immigration policy were deleted from the administration proposal. They successfully insisted that reuniting of families be given first priority, that the American workingman be protected. And they initiated the provisions of the bill which will give immediate relief to the heavily oversubscribed countries such as Italy, Greece, Poland, Spain, and China.

The proposed bill with respect to Western Hemisphere immigration is stronger than the present Walter-McCarran Act. In three different instances Republican amendments were adopted that provide a qualitative control over Immigration from this area. We are concerned, however, by the fact that this broad reform of our immigration system and policy continues a form of discrimination by not including the Western Hemisphere countries under a numerical ceiling concept.

Despite our close and continuing ties with our friends in the Western Hemisphere, we do not believe that the citizens of the 24 independent countries of the Western Hemisphere should remain in a highly preferred position to that of the citizens of the more than 100 countries in the rest of the world.

Source: *Congressional Record*, Vol. 111, Pt. 16, 21789.

LYNDON B. JOHNSON, REMARKS AT THE SIGNING
OF THE IMMIGRATION BILL, LIBERTY ISLAND, NEW YORK
(OCTOBER 3, 1965)

This bill that we will sign today is not a revolutionary bill. It does not affect the lives of millions. It will not reshape the structure of our daily lives, or really add importantly to either our wealth or our power.

Yet it is still one of the most important acts of this Congress and of this administration.

For it does repair a very deep and painful flaw in the fabric of American justice. It corrects a cruel and enduring wrong in the conduct of the American Nation. . . .

This bill says simply that from this day forth those wishing to immigrate to America shall be admitted on the basis of their skills and their close relationship to those already here.

This is a simple test, and it is a fair test. Those who can contribute most to this country—to its growth, to its strength, to its spirit—will be the first that are admitted to this land.

The fairness of this standard is so self-evident that we may well wonder that it has not always been applied. Yet the fact is that for over four decades the immigration policy of the United States has been twisted and has been distorted by the harsh injustice of the national origins quota system. . . .

This system violated the basic principle of American democracy—the principle that values and rewards each man on the basis of his merit as a man.

It has been un-American in the highest sense, because it has been untrue to the faith that brought thousands to these shores even before we were a country.

Today, with my signature, this system is abolished.

We can now believe that it will never again shadow the gate to the American Nation with the twin barriers of prejudice and privilege.

Our beautiful America was built by a nation of strangers. From a hundred different places or more they have poured forth into an empty land, joining and blending in one mighty and irresistible tide.

The land flourished because it was fed from so many sources—because it was nourished by so many cultures and traditions and peoples.

And from this experience, almost unique in the history of nations, has come America's attitude toward the rest of the world. We, because of what we are, feel safer and stronger in a world as varied as the people who make it up—a world where no country rules another and all countries can deal with the basic problems of human dignity and deal with those problems in their own way.

Now, under the monument which has welcomed so many to our shores, the American Nation returns to the finest of its traditions today.

The days of unlimited immigration are past.

But those who do come will come because of what they are, and not because of the land from which they sprung.

When the earliest settlers poured into a wild continent there was no one to ask them where they came from. The only question was: Were they sturdy enough to make the journey, were they strong enough to clear the land, were they enduring enough to make a home for freedom, and were they brave enough to die for liberty if it became necessary to do so?

And so it has been through all the great and testing moments of American history. Our history this year we see in Viet-Nam. Men there are dying— men named Fernandez and Zajac and Zelinko and Mariano and McCormick.

Neither the enemy who killed them nor the people whose independence they have fought to save ever asked them where they or their parents came from. They were all Americans. It was for free men and for America that they gave their all, they gave their lives and selves.

By eliminating that same question as a test for immigration the Congress proves ourselves worthy of those men and worthy of our own traditions as a Nation. . . .

Over my shoulders here you can see Ellis Island, whose vacant corridors echo today the joyous sound of long ago voices.

And today we can all believe that the lamp of this grand old lady is brighter today—and the golden door that she guards gleams more brilliantly in the light of an increased liberty for the people from all the countries of the globe.

Thank you very much.

Source: *Public Papers of the Presidents of the United States: Lyndon B. Johnson, 1965, Book II* (Washington, DC: Government Printing Office, 1966), 1037–1040.

THE AIR WAR IN VIETNAM

Some historians have suggested that Johnson wanted to win in Vietnam more than Kennedy and that he consequently was willing to use more extreme measures, including massive firepower and significant deployments of American troops, to do so. Evidence clearly suggests both that Johnson badly wanted to win the war in Vietnam and that he was highly conflicted about the tactics he should employ. By the end of 1963, when Johnson came into the presidency, over 16,000 American troops were on the ground in South Vietnam acting as "advisors" to the South Vietnamese military, the political situation in South Vietnam was nothing less than chaotic, and the Viet Cong were gaining strength in South Vietnam each day. Moreover, the overwhelming majority of Americans supported U.S. objectives in Vietnam in 1964; in fact, not until 1967 did any serious faction of the American populace question the purpose of American activities in Vietnam. Nonetheless, the optimism about a quick resolution to the conflict in Vietnam was beginning to wane. Even though State Department and military officials still believed victory was possible, by 1964 they were no longer making the kind of quick and easy prescriptions they had been providing earlier in the decade. In December 1964, only a month after Johnson assumed the presidency, Secretary of Defense Robert McNamara and CIA Director John McCone advised him that the situation in South Vietnam was in fact worsening, and that without more aggressive U.S. intervention, South Vietnam would likely succumb to communist control within several months. Unlike Kennedy, Johnson did not have to display will and resolve in order to redeem an international reputation marred by events like the Bay of Pigs and Berlin, but at the same time, as a Cold War president he could not abandon America's commitment to containment and the defense of "freedom" without wrecking his credibility both with domestic constituencies and with allies abroad. A "loss" in Vietnam was simply unacceptable. Thus, the conditions that prevailed when Johnson inherited command of the Vietnam conflict seemed to leave him little maneuvering room.

Johnson made two fateful full decisions about American activity in Vietnam that left him even fewer options for conducting the war. The first was to commence a massive bombing campaign, initially confined to targets in North Vietnam but later extended into enemy strongholds in the South. The second was the initiation of "Americanization" of the war with the introduction of American ground troops.

Johnson's made his mark on the war quickly. In the first months of his Administration, Johnson had hoped that public warnings and a final burst of military and financial aid to ARVN might obviate the need for an air campaign, especially leading to the 1964 presidential election. Accordingly, he funneled more money and "advice" to South Vietnam. In August 1964, Johnson reported to the American public that North Vietnamese gunboats had fired on two U.S. destroyers (now known to have been engaged in covert operations) in the Gulf of Tonkin, off the coast of South Vietnam. Analysts still dispute claims of an attack, but the incident provided all the ammunition Johnson needed to mobilize Congress and the nation behind a more aggressive American posture in the region. Proclaiming "aggression unchallenged is aggression unleashed," Johnson asked Congress for approval to respond to the hostile actions of the North Vietnamese. In perhaps one of the most famous congressional authorizations on foreign policy in American history, the Senate, with only two dissenting votes, gave Johnson the authority "to take all necessary measures" to halt aggression and protect U.S. forces in Southeast Asia. Interpreted by the Johnson administration as a "blank check," the now infamous Gulf of Tonkin

Resolution cleared the way for a dramatic and unrestrained escalation of American involvement in Vietnam.

Johnson initially avoided using the authority that the Gulf of Tonkin Resolution had provided him to expand American activity in Vietnam. However, after the North Vietnamese attacked an American base in Pleiku, northeast of the South Vietnamese capital of Saigon, in February 1965, Johnson responded to recommendations by McNamara and the Joint Chiefs of Staff by employing air power directly against North Vietnam in retaliation. Even before Pleiku, Johnson's advisors were pushing for escalation. "Bob [McNamara] and I believe," National Security Advisor McGeorge Bundy wrote Johnson, "that the worst course of action is this essentially passive role which can only lead to eventual defeat and an invitation to get out in humiliating circumstances."[1] Air strikes, under the code name Operation Rolling Thunder, began almost immediately, targeting naval stations and supply depots along the North Vietnamese coast. The air strikes appeared to succeed: they evoked no immediate response from the North Vietnamese, or from the Soviets or the Chinese who had both formalized agreements with North Vietnam to assist militarily and enter the war if the United States initiated an invasion of North Vietnam. Johnson was elated with the successful sorties of these first bombing efforts. This first air campaign succeeded at home as well; Americans, who had reelected Johnson in a landslide, seemed to like his show of strength. With the encouragement of McNamara and McGeorge Bundy, Johnson continued Operation Rolling Thunder, extending both the range of targets in North Vietnam and conducting bombing sorties to root out guerrillas in South Vietnam as well. The objectives of the bombing changed. Initially a retaliatory measure against the North Vietnamese, administration officials now hoped that relentless bombing would break the will of Ho Chi Minh and bring him to the negotiating table. Johnson carefully controlled and monitored Rolling Thunder, selecting bombing targets on a daily basis while McNamara attempted to calculate the efficacy of the campaigns by gathering data detailing the death and destruction wrought by U.S. firepower.

It soon became clear, however, that U.S. bombing efforts would not persuade the North Vietnamese to give up their fight. George Ball, who never advocated expansion of the war, tried as early as May 1965 to persuade Johnson to scale back U.S. involvement in Vietnam. He warned: "continuance of the war on the assumption that—by military pressure— we can force Hanoi to say 'uncle' may lead to a gradual escalation of the conflict. . . . "[2] After a 37 day respite in the bombing—the Christmas pause of 1965—failed to result in any concessions from the North Vietnamese, nearly everyone in the Johnson Administration knew that bombing alone would not force the North Vietnamese into submission. With ARVN demoralized and disorganized, the United States would have to make a substantial commitment of American ground forces as well. Johnson appeased military leaders on the ground in Vietnam, increasing the number of American troops there consistently between 1965 and 1968. All the while, the bombing campaign continued, intensifying after the bombing hiatus in late 1965. This pattern continued throughout Johnson's presidency. General Westmoreland asked for more troops; he got them. At the same time, bombing campaigns intensified without any signs of softening on the part of the North Vietnamese. The weight of bombs America dropped in North Vietnam grew from 63,000 tons in 1965 to 226,000 tons in 1966, while by 1967 the United States had dropped over 1,000,000 tons of bombs on various enemy-controlled areas in South Vietnam.

After two years of bombing, and an intensified effort by American ground forces, the North Vietnamese showed no sign of capitulating. Instead, dissention and disagreement began to appear in the American public, in Congress, and within the Johnson Administration itself. Administration officials and military men squabbled over tactics, as well as the accuracy of information that the United States had gathered about the enemy. Perhaps one of the greatest divisions among Johnson officials, and one of Johnson's most difficult decisions during the war, was the question of whether to extend the scope of the bombing campaign to Haiphong harbor in North Vietnam, and then ultimately to the cities of Haiphong and to Hanoi, the North Vietnamese capital. Seeing few signs of U.S. progress in the war, in May 1967 the chairman of the Joint Chiefs of Staff, General Earl Wheeler, reversed his previous position on the issue. He recommended the bombing of Haiphong harbor, calling it the "single most important lines of communication" in North Vietnam and insisting that China and the Soviets were supplying war materials to North Vietnam through the harbor. With the port at Haiphong operable, Wheeler maintained, the North Vietnamese would continue to be able to support their war efforts in both North and South Vietnam.

Many close to Johnson, however, viewed expanding the scope of the bombing as risky. The North Vietnamese could retaliate by attacking the Gulf of Tonkin, thereby cutting off the major sea route into South Vietnam. Targeting Haiphong could provoke the Chinese or the Soviets, particularly if bombs hit their ships in the harbor. McNamara further argued that the American objective in Vietnam was to stabilize the South Vietnamese government, not to pummel North Vietnam. Moving the bombing from strictly military targets to a major city would bring civilian casualties, another downside to widening the bombing campaign. Johnson weighed the question of bombing the harbor carefully, and sought advice from all sides. In addition to McNamara's opposition, McGeorge Bundy and other intelligence officials also doubted that bombing Haiphong or Hanoi would have any discernable effect on the war. After more than two years of enduring American bombs, they did not believe that more bombing would break the will of the North Vietnamese or that destruction of the harbors would foil North Vietnamese efforts to supply their forces in the South. Despite the opposition, the arguments of those who favored expanding U.S. efforts and positive assessments of U.S. progress coming from South Vietnam swayed Johnson. The Joint Chiefs of Staff told Johnson that the use of American force in Vietnam "incrementally and with restraint" had prolonged the war and urged more firepower. On July 26, the U.S. Ambassador in South Vietnam wrote to Johnson saying that the Embassy was confident that "we are moving steadily ahead" and "in the right direction." In September Johnson gave the go-ahead for expanding Operation Rolling Thunder to the ports of North Vietnam. By 1968, the United States had dropped almost 3,000,000 tons, nearly 50 percent more firepower from bombs than the U.S. Air Force dropped in all of World War II.

Within the Administration, few dissented from Johnson's escalation of the war. By 1967 pessimism pervaded the Johnson foreign policy team, but, by and large, Johnson's advisors stood behind him. Initially, congressional leaders also supported the president, as evidenced by the Gulf of Tonkin Resolution and congressional appropriations for the deployment of additional troops throughout 1965. But enthusiasm for Johnson's tactics began to dissipate. In the Senate, Democrats Wayne Morse (OR), George McGovern (SD), Richard Russell (GA), and Senate Foreign Relations Committee Chairman, J. William Fulbright (AR), all expressed concern over the intensification of the war. They pressed for alternative solutions, the most popular of which was a negotiated agreement producing a neutral government in Vietnam, similar to that fashioned to settle the civil strife in Laos earlier in the decade. Senate Majority Leader Mike Mansfield (D-MT) was the most outspoken critic of Johnson's Vietnam policy. Mansfield protested the massive drain on financial resources that the American commitment in Vietnam required and feared a more lengthy engagement in Vietnam than the Johnson team predicted. Popular voices began to rise against Johnson's Vietnam policy as well, ranging from students to actors and including boxer, Muhammad Ali, and diplomat turned commentator, George Kennan.

NOTES

1. Memo, McNamara and Bundy to Johnson, "The Fork in the Y," January 27, 1965, cited at <http://www2.centenary.edu/vietnam/lairnson/simulation/mac.html>

2. *Foreign Relations of the United States, Vietnam, January 1965–June 1965* (Washington, DC: Government Printing Office), 300.

PRESIDENT LYNDON JOHNSON, NEWS CONFERENCE (JULY 5, 1966)

I cannot understand the thinking of any country or any people, or any person, that says we should sit by with our hands tied behind us while these men bring their mortars, their hand grenades and their bombs into our barracks and kill our Marines, attack our camps, murder the village chief, and that we should not do anything about it. Now we have tried to make this difficult for them to continue at their present rate. We do not say it will stop the infiltration. We do not say that it will even reduce it.

But we do think it will make it more difficult for them, and we do think it will require them to assign additional people. We do think it will give them problems.

We have had a policy of measured response and gradually increased our strength from time to time. We plan to continue that.

Source: *Public Papers of the Presidents*, Lyndon B. Johnson, 1966, 711.

PRESIDENT LYNDON JOHNSON, LETTER TO SENATOR HENRY JACKSON CONCERNING THE BOMBING OF VIETNAM (MARCH 1, 1967)

... By February 1965 it was unmistakably clear there was armed attack in the most literal sense: South Vietnam was almost lost to that armed attack. And in that month, on the recommendation of the National Security Council, I decided that we had to "meet the common danger" by bringing our air power to bear against the source of aggression.

We never believed aerial attack on Viet Nam would, alone, end the war. We did, however, have three objectives.

The first was to back our fighting men and our fighting allies by demonstrating that the aggressor could not illegally bring hostile arms and men to bear against them from the security of a sanctuary.

Second, we sought to impose on North Viet Nam a cost for violating its international agreements [respecting the border between North and South as determined by the Geneva Accords of 1954].

Third, we sought to limit or raise the cost of bringing men and supplies to bear against the South.

All three of these important objectives have been achieved.

First you should note that the military leaders now responsible for the safety and morale of our men in the field, without exception, back our bombing of the North. ... Second, we are, with remarkably limited cost in civilian lives, imposing a major cost on North Viet Nam. ... At the cost of about 500 gallant American airmen killed, captured, or missing, we are bringing to bear on North Viet Nam a burden roughly equivalent to that which the Communists are imposing through guerilla warfare on the South —and we are doing it with far fewer civilian casualties in the North. Finally, the bombing of North Viet Nam has raised the cost of bringing an armed man or a ton of supplies across the border from the North to the South. Substantial casualties are inflicted on infiltrators and substantial tonnages of supplies are destroyed en route. . . .

The bombing in the North is an action undertaken by your Government only after the most careful reflection. . . . It is an integral part of our total policy which aims not to destroy North Viet Nam but to force Hanoi to end its aggression so that the people of South Viet Nam can determine their own future without coercion.

Both the reasons for—and the results of—the bombing of North Viet Nam make it imperative that we continue to use this instrument of support for our men and our allies. It will end when the other side is willing to take equivalent action as part of a serious effort to end this war and bring peace to the people of Southeast Asia. . . .

Source: *Public Papers of the Presidents*, Lyndon B. Johnson, 1967, 267–269.

SENATOR J. WILLIAM FULBRIGHT, *ARROGANCE OF POWER* (1966)

We are now engaged in a war to "defend freedom" in South Vietnam. Unlike the Republic of Korea, South Vietnam has an army which [is] without notable success and a weak, dictatorial government which does not command the loyalty of the South Vietnamese people. The official war aims of the United States Government, as I understand them, are to defeat what is regarded as North Vietnamese aggression, to demonstrate the futility of what the communists call "wars of national liberation," and to create conditions under which the South Vietnamese people will be able freely to determine their own future. I have not the slightest doubt of the sincerity of the President and the Vice President and the Secretaries of State and Defense in propounding these aims. What I do doubt—and doubt very much—is the ability of the United States to achieve these aims by the means being used. . . . Our handicap is well expressed in the pungent Chinese proverb: "In shallow waters dragons become the sport of shrimps." . . .

The cause of our difficulties in southeast Asia is not a deficiency of power but an excess of the wrong kind of power which results in a feeling of impotence when it fails to achieve its desired ends. We are still acting like boy scouts dragging reluctant old ladies across the streets they do not want to cross. We are trying to remake Vietnamese society, a task which certainly cannot be accomplished by force and which probably cannot be accomplished by any means available to outsiders. The objective may be desirable, but it is not feasible. . . .

If America has a service to perform in the world—and I believe it has—it is in large part the service of its own example. In our excessive involvement in the affairs of other countries, we are not only living off our assets and denying our own people the proper enjoyment of their resources; we are also denying the world the example of a free society enjoying its freedom to the fullest. . . .

If we can bring ourselves so to act, we will have overcome the dangers of the arrogance of power. It will involve, no doubt, the loss of certain glories, but that seems a price worth paying for the probable rewards, which are the happiness of America and the peace of the world.

Source: J. William Fulbright, *The Arrogance of Power*, 1966.

THE GROUND WAR IN VIETNAM

While decisions about bombing campaigns in Vietnam consumed a great deal of President Johnson's attention, airpower was only one major aspect of the war. When Johnson assumed the presidency, American planes were not dropping bombs in Vietnam, but American soldiers were on the ground in South Vietnam. Sent merely to counsel and train the South Vietnamese army (ARVN), American military personnel in South Vietnam under Eisenhower and Kennedy were not on the front lines. Before 1964 Americans neither assumed, nor wanted to assume, a primary role in repelling the guerilla attacks of the Vietcong. That all changed quickly in 1965.

President Kennedy had left 16,000 "advisors" in South Vietnam; by 1965, 75,000 U.S. servicemen were on the ground in South Vietnam, still acting in an advisory role. Johnson did little in the way of expanding America's role in the war during the election contest of 1964, but after Congress adopted the Gulf of Tonkin Resolution in November of that year, Johnson used the authority that Congress provided him by that act to dramatically increase American involvement in South Vietnam. Despite Johnson's record in Vietnam, he always wanted to follow what he called "a middle way." With Republican war hawks and military leaders constantly clamoring for more firepower—a decisive display of American might and determination in the battle against international communism—the President could hardly afford to minimize American fortitude or the importance of its effort in Vietnam. By the same token, because Johnson had promised to build Americans a "Great Society," he could not afford to spend American resources in Vietnam that would otherwise be used on social programs at home. Maintaining a proper balance prove to be impossible.

In spite of Johnson's determination to stick to a middle way, two fateful decisions made a moderate course nearly impossible. Johnson followed his decision to initiate the bombing campaign Operation Rolling Thunder, in

February 1965, by deciding to increase American ground troops in South Vietnam by 50,000 men. This brought the total to 125,000 and temporarily satisfied the commander of American troops in Vietnam, General William Westmoreland. At this time though, Johnson resisted the advice of the Joint Chiefs of Staff (JCS), who warned Johnson about the potential for a protracted war, to call up reservists, fearing that such an action would lead to public panic about the war. Not unlike the question of American bombing in Vietnam, the commitment of American ground troops was a consistent and trying issue for the President throughout his second term in office. The story of American ground troops in Vietnam was even more dramatic than the bombing campaigns. Throughout the war, the military increasingly pressured Johnson to send more troops to Vietnam. Initially, most of Johnson's advisors supported increasing the number of American soldiers in Vietnam. Buoyed by optimistic reports from Vietnam, Johnson and his Secretary of Defense Robert McNamara acquiesced to the pleas of Westmoreland and the JCS. After the battle of the Ia Drang Valley in November 1965, in which 1,200 Vietcong were killed with the loss of only 200 American soldiers, feelings were high that the United States would ultimately prevail in a war of attrition even though McNamara warned Johnson that the army had been "too optimistic" about a quick victory. Accordingly, in February 1966 Johnson fulfilled Westmoreland's request for still more troops, pledging to increase American ground forces to a total of 429,000 by the end of 1966. Johnson, his military, and most of his close advisors believed in late 1965 and early 1966 that, with a strong show of American force on the ground and in the air, Ho Chi Minh and the North Vietnamese would not and could not sustain their effort. Americans were sure that their firepower would intimidate even the most formidable and determined foes. To be sure that Americans, allies, and foes understood Johnson's resolve and commitment to the contest in Vietnam, he told reporters at a news conference on February 26, that "as far as I am concerned . . . as he [Westmoreland] makes his requests, they will be considered and they will be met."

By late 1966, however, some of Johnson's closest foreign policy advisors began to express doubt about the ability of the United States ever to deal a fatal blow to the resolve of the North Vietnamese. Secretary of Defense Robert McNamara and National Security advisor McGeorge Bundy began to question the potential for success in Vietnam. McNamara, doubting reports from the field about American successes in establishing control of villages and towns in South Vietnam, began recommending in October 1966 a strategy by which the United States would stabilize its forces in South Vietnam, at a number of 470,000, to establish a position such that the North Vietnamese would find the option of "waiting out" the United States "less attractive." But McNamara already had concluded that even more than 470,000 troops would not "break their morale." Thus the U.S. effort should be refocused, McNamara argued, from an attempt to root out Vietcong from South Vietnam to trying to prevent the infiltration of Vietcong and supplies from the North to the South. He proposed building a complex "infiltration barrier" of fences and other obstacles along the border. This proposal was flatly rejected. At the same time as McNamara was suggesting capping the numbers of American troops in Vietnam, General Westmoreland was asking for more men and more bombs. Meeting with the President at a conference in Manila in October 1966, Westmoreland told Johnson that while he could "see the light at the end of the tunnel," he could "certainly use more troops." Westmoreland also objected to any proposals that called for stabilizing the American effort, either on the ground or in the air. The JCS, who were simultaneously calling for escalating the bombing campaign, supported Westmoreland's position.

Estimates of enemy strength continued to bedevil assessments of the effectiveness of American ground troops. Vietnam commanders consistently sent optimistic reports to Washington. Even when statistical evidence did not suggest progress in weakening the enemy, reports usually included positive narratives about the prospects for the future or put a spin on the numbers minimizing the impact of a setback in American efforts. However, by the end of 1966, policymakers in Washington were expressing doubts about the numbers the military was generating in Vietnam. In June 1967, the CIA released its own estimates of enemy strength, which deviated sharply from the military's estimates. While the latter estimated enemy strength at between 270,000 and 299,000, the CIA's calculations put the number at 456,000 to 561,000, with a bias toward the higher number. Tragically, the discrepancy between the numbers that the military and the nonmilitary agencies developed throughout the remainder of the war, making personnel and strategic decisions even more difficult and fracturing public support for American efforts in Vietnam. Some began to use the term "stalemate" to characterize the war in Vietnam. After more than two years of fighting and bombing, this was not something that Johnson wanted to hear. His attempts to bring the war to an end by expanding the war thus far had failed.

Despite his own reservations about American progress in Vietnam, McNamara returned from a visit to Vietnam and told the President that there was "no evidence of a stalemate." For his part, Westmoreland called reports of a stalemate "complete fiction." On July 12 1967, Johnson agreed to provide Westmoreland with more troops, increasing the commitment by 45,000 to 50,000 men, bringing the total in South Vietnam to 515,000. In the fall of 1967 the Administration embarked on an intense public relations campaign to convince the American public of progress in Vietnam, but the Administration could point to little tangible evidence that anything good was happening in South Vietnam. Although the public did not yet know it, the CIA and military estimates of enemy strength continued to exhibit wide disparities—in June of 1967 Westmoreland estimated enemy strength at 298,000 men while the CIA's estimate put enemy strength between 460,000 and 570,000.

What the public did know, however, was that American casualties were mounting. Dan Rather, Walter Cronkite, and other newsmen reported as much on location from Vietnam on the evening news. By the end of 1967 the number of Americans killed or wounded totaled 80,000, an increase of 47,000 in 1967. Draft calls were increasing as well; the United States drafted more than 300,000 men into service in 1966 alone. Although students and intellectuals had opposed Johnson's escalation of the war from the beginning, by late 1967 more serious opposition was beginning to surface—by October 1967 only 58 percent of the public supported the America's involvement in Vietnam, down from 72 percent in July. Only 28 percent of Americans agreed with Johnson's handling of the war. In that same month, 20,000 protesters gathered on the grounds of the Pentagon to express their dismay over the war. Increasingly, men were attempting to avoid being drafted, and some were publicly protesting conscription by burning their draft cards. African American leaders were intensifying their criticism of the war, while members of Congress publicly and privately expressed reservations about American involvement in Vietnam to Johnson and his staff. Criticism was coming from both sides. While Senate Foreign Relations Committee Chairman J. William Fulbright (D-AR) and other Democratic leaders like Senators Mike Mansfield (D-MT) and Wayne Morse (D-OR) were encouraging Johnson to reduce American engagement in Vietnam, Republicans like Senator Strom Thurmond (R-SC) and former President Dwight Eisenhower were calling for further expansion of America's role in Vietnam, the latter suggesting an invasion of North Vietnam. As the public became increasingly uneasy about war, Johnson's advisory team was beginning to fracture as well. While CIA Director Richard Helms told Johnson in November 1967 that the "war is going in our favor," Secretary of Defense Robert McNamara, troubled by the direction of the American war effort, announced his resignation.

January 1968 marked a turning point in the war in Vietnam, and in Johnson's handling of the war. The now infamous Tet Offensive, though not a military victory for the North Vietnamese, proved to be a fatal blow for the American cause in Vietnam. A surprise raid on 34 major cities in South Vietnam, including an attempt to sack the U.S. Embassy, and hundreds of smaller villages and towns, the Tet Offensive evidenced that the United States was in fact making no progress in Vietnam. Even though the North Vietnamese failed to wrestle control of any cities from the South Vietnamese, Tet was a victory nonetheless, for it further soured the American public on the war, and discouraged policymakers. Experts estimate that 40,000 North Vietnamese died in the Tet Offensive, compared to 2,300 South Vietnamese and 1,100 Americans, but Tet proved that American efforts to that point had not seriously weakened the North Vietnamese. Tet showed that they had manpower, the ability to infiltrate South Vietnam, and, perhaps most importantly, still very much the will to fight. Not surprisingly, after Tet the JCS again called for increased bombing campaigns in North Vietnam and again recommended that Johnson call up reservists. On February 12, General Westmoreland asked Johnson for 35,000 more troops. The JCS wanted to deploy 206,000 thousand more men. JCS Chairman Earl Wheeler and General Westmoreland even discussed the possibility of using tactical nuclear weapons in Vietnam. Arguing that history had shown that incremental increases in American troops in South Vietnam were ineffective, Clark Clifford, McNamara's replacement at the Department of Defense, called for increasing the American ground commitment by 500,000 to 1,000,000 men. Clifford suggested that only a substantial show of American determination could persuade the North Vietnamese to negotiate an end to the war. Despite public proclamations to the contrary, Johnson had decided that the United States could not achieve its objectives through the tactics it was employing in Vietnam. Concern about public opinion convinced him not to expand American efforts there.

By March, even the hawkish Clifford had reassessed his position on Vietnam. He used the analogy of a sinkhole in a conversation with Johnson to describe the futility of sending more troops to the war. On March 25 Johnson convened a meeting of his closest foreign policy advisors, who had also changed their tune. In November of 1967 they had urged Johnson to press forward with the war effort in Vietnam, but they now concluded that the prospects for success were poor. Resisting the pleas of his military advisors, in an emotional address to the nation on March 31 Johnson announced that he would not send more ground troops to Vietnam, and that he would halt American bombing of North Vietnam in a goodwill gesture to get Ho Chi Minh to negotiate a peace. The most dramatic moment of Johnson's speech however, came when he announced that he would not run for reelection. Johnson told the American people that he did not want electoral politics to compromise his position in negotiating an end to war. Johnson was tired, beleaguered, and maligned by a public that no longer trusted him or his administration. Americans had indicated their displeasure with Johnson in the New Jersey Democratic primary on March 13, in which dovish Senator Eugene McCarthy won 42 percent of the vote to Johnson's 48 percent. This inspired Robert Kennedy, one of Johnson's greatest rivals within the Democratic Party, to declare his own candidacy three days later. Johnson had tried, and failed, to contain communism in Vietnam. His obsession with the war combined with his self-described "love affair" with the "Great Society" proved incompatible; he could not devote the resources of America to both and produce both "guns" and "butter." His "middle way" had failed. Tragically, when he left office, Johnson and the

American people were frustrated. There had been no "light at the end of the tunnel" in Vietnam, and at home the "Great Society" remained elusive.

PRESIDENT LYNDON B. JOHNSON, "PEACE WITHOUT CONQUEST," JOHNS HOPKINS UNIVERSITY (APRIL 7, 1965)

Tonight Americans and Asians are dying for a world where each people may choose its own path to change.

This is the principle for which our ancestors fought in the valleys of Pennsylvania. It is the principle for which our sons fight tonight in the jungles of Viet-Nam.

Viet-Nam is far away from this quiet campus. We have no territory there, nor do we seek any. The war is dirty and brutal and difficult. And some 400 young men, born into an America that is bursting with opportunity and promise, have ended their lives on Viet-Nam's steaming soil.

Why must we take this painful road?

Why must this Nation hazard its ease, and its interest, and its power for the sake of a people so far away?

We fight because we must fight if we are to live in a world where every country can shape its own destiny. And only in such a world will our own freedom be finally secure. . . .

The Nature of the Conflict

. . . The first reality is that North Viet-Nam has attacked the independent nation of South Viet-Nam. Its object is total conquest.

Of course, some of the people of South Viet-Nam are participating in attack on their own government. But trained men and supplies, orders and arms, flow in a constant stream from north to south.

This support is the heartbeat of the war.

And it is a war of unparalleled brutality. . . .

Over this war—and all Asia—is another reality: the deepening shadow of Communist China. The rulers in Hanoi are urged on by Peking. This is a regime which has destroyed freedom in Tibet, which has attacked India, and has been condemned by the United Nations for aggression in Korea. It is a nation which is helping the forces of violence in almost every continent. The contest in Viet-Nam is part of a wider pattern of aggressive purposes.

Why are we in Viet-Nam?

Why are these realities our concern? Why are we in South Viet-Nam?

We are . . . there to strengthen world order. Around the globe, from Berlin to Thailand, are people whose well-being rests, in part, on the belief that they can count on us if they are attacked. To leave Viet-Nam to its fate would shake the confidence of all these people in the value of an American commitment and in the value of America's word. The result would be increased unrest and instability, and even wider war.

We are also there because there are great stakes in the balance. Let no one think for a moment that retreat from Viet-Nam would bring an end to conflict. The battle would be renewed in one country and then another. The central lesson of our time is that the appetite of aggression is never satisfied. To withdraw from one battlefield means only to prepare for the next. We must say in southeast Asia—as we did in Europe—in the words of the Bible: "Hitherto shalt thou come, but no further." . . .

Our Objective in Viet-Nam

Our objective is the independence of South Viet-Nam, and its freedom from attack. We want nothing for ourselves--only that the people of South Viet-Nam be allowed to guide their own country in their own way.

We will do everything necessary to reach that objective. And we will do only what is absolutely necessary.

In recent months attacks on South Viet-Nam were stepped up. Thus, it became necessary for us to increase our response and to make attacks by air. This is not a change of purpose. It is a change in what we believe that purpose requires.

We do this in order to slow down aggression. . . .

We know that air attacks alone will not accomplish all of these purposes. But it is our best and prayerful judgment that they are a necessary part of the surest road to peace. . . .

Such peace demands an independent South Viet-Nam—securely guaranteed and able to shape its own relationships to all others—free from outside interference—tied to no alliance—a military base for no other country.

These are the essentials of any final settlement.

We will never be second in the search for such a peaceful settlement in Viet-Nam.

There may be many ways to this kind of peace: in discussion or negotiation with the governments concerned; in large groups or in small ones; in the reaffirmation of old agreements or their strengthening with new ones.

We have stated this position over and over again, fifty times and more, to friend and foe alike. And we remain ready, with this purpose, for unconditional discussions. . . .

Conclusion

We often say how impressive power is. But I do not find it impressive at all. The guns and the bombs, the rockets and the warships, are all symbols of human failure. They are necessary symbols. They protect what we cherish. But they are witness to human folly. . . .

Every night before I turn out the lights to sleep I ask myself this question: Have I done everything that I can do to unite this country? Have I done everything I can to help unite the world, to try to bring peace and hope to all the peoples of the world? Have I done enough?

Ask yourselves that question in your homes—and in this hall tonight. Have we, each of us, all done all we could? Have we done enough?

We may well be living in the time foretold many years ago when it was said: "I call heaven and earth to record this day against you, that I have set before you life and death, blessing and cursing: therefore choose life, that both thou and thy seed may live."

This generation of the world must choose: destroy or build, kill or aid, hate or understand.

We can do all these things on a scale never dreamed of before.

Well, we will choose life. In so doing we will prevail over the enemies within man, and over the natural enemies of all mankind.

Source: *Public Papers of the Presidents, Lyndon B. Johnson, 1965,* 394–399.

UNDERSECRETARY OF STATE, GEORGE BALL TO LBJ, "A COMPROMISE SOLUTION IN SOUTH VIETNAM" (FEBRUARY 1965)

1. A Losing War: . . . No one can assure you that we can beat the Viet Cong or even force them to the conference table on our terms, no matter how many hundred thousand white, foreign (U.S.) troops we deploy.

No one has demonstrated that a white ground force of whatever size can win a guerrilla war. . . .

2. The Question to Decide: Should we limit our liabilities in South Vietnam and try to find a way out with minimal long-term costs?

The alternative—no matter what we may wish it to be—is almost certainly a protracted war involving an open-ended commitment of U.S. forces, mounting U.S. casualties, no assurance of a satisfactory solution, and a serious danger of escalation at the end of the road.

3. Need for a Decision Now: So long as our forces are restricted to advising and assisting the South Vietnamese, the struggle will remain a civil war between Asian peoples. Once we deploy substantial numbers of troops in combat it will become a war between the U.S. and a large part of the population of South Vietnam, organized and directed from North Vietnam and backed by the resources of both Moscow and Peiping. The decision you face now, therefore, is crucial. Once large numbers of U.S. troops are committed to direct combat, they will begin to take heavy casualties in a

226 FROM EISENHOWER THROUGH JOHNSON

war they are ill-equipped to fight in a non-cooperative if not downright hostile countryside.

Once we suffer large casualties, we will have started a well-nigh irreversible process. Our involvement will be so great that we cannot-without national humiliation—stop short of achieving our complete objectives. Of the two possibilities I think humiliation would be more likely than the achievement of our objectives—even after we have paid terrible costs....

Source: Neil Sheehan, et al., *The Pentagon Papers*, Vol. 2, 615–617.

SENATOR J. WILLIAM FULBRIGHT (D-AK), FROM
ARROGANCE OF POWER (1966)

Our search for a solution to the Vietnamese war must begin with the general fact that nationalism is the strongest single political force in the world today and the specific fact,... that in Vietnam the most effective nationalist movement is communist-controlled. We are compelled, therefore, once again to choose between opposition to communism and support of nationalism. I strongly recommend that for once we give priority to the latter. The dilemma is a cruel one, and one which we must hope to avoid in the future by timely and unstinting support of non-communist nationalist movements, but it is too late for that in Vietnam. I strongly recommend, therefore, that we seek to come to terms with both Hanoi and the Viet Cong, not, to be sure, by "turning tail and running," as the saying goes, but by conceding the Viet Cong a part in the government of South Vietnam....

Despite brave talk about having both "guns and butter," the Vietnamese war has already had a destructive effect on the Great Society....

My own view is that there is a kind of madness in the facile assumption that we can raise the many billions of dollars necessary to rebuild our schools and cities and public transport and eliminate the pollution of air and water while also spending tens of billions to finance an "open-ended" war in Asia. But even if the material resources can somehow be drawn from an expanding economy, I do not think that the spiritual resources will long be forthcoming from an angry and disappointed people.

Source: Richard Hofstadter, *Great Issues in American History*, 562–563.

MARTIN LUTHER KING, JR., "DECLARATION OF
INDEPENDENCE FROM THE WAR IN VIETNAM" (APRIL 1967)

There is something seductively tempting about... sending us all off on what in some circles has become a popular crusade against the war in

Vietnam. I say we must enter that struggle, but I wish to go on now to say something even more disturbing. The war in Vietnam is but a symptom of a far deeper malady within the American spirit, . . .

I am convinced that if we are to get on the right side of the world revolution, we as a nation must undergo a radical revolution of values. When machines and computers, profit and property rights are considered more important than people, the giant triplets of racism, materialism, and militarism are incapable of being conquered.

A true revolution of values will soon cause us to question the fairness and justice of many of our past and present policies. . . . A nation that continues year after year to spend more money on military defense than on programs of social uplift is approaching spiritual death. . . .

There is nothing, except a tragic death wish, to prevent us from re-ordering our priorities, so that the pursuit of peace will take precedence over the pursuit of war. . . .

This kind of positive revolution of values is our best defense against communism. . . .

Source: *Ramparts* (May 1967), 33–37 cited at American Civil Rights Review, Document Archive, <http://webusers.anet-stl.com/~civil/docs-mlkvietnamwar speech1967.htm>

URBAN RENEWAL AND THE MODEL CITIES PROGRAM

Despite the distraction of Vietnam, Johnson did not abandon the "Great Society" program at home. In his last years in office, he signed legislation on fair and open housing, consumer protections, and highway safety. The Model Cities Project illustrated the ideas behind both Johnson's "War on Poverty" and "Great Society." Previously, government efforts at urban renewal had focused almost exclusively on housing issues. While housing was still an important aspect of federal efforts to deal with the problems of urban decay under Johnson, the President believed that urban problems were more complex than housing alone. For Johnson, a sincere urban renewal program entailed not only questions of housing, but also of schools, hospitals, crime, and recreational facilities. Johnson displayed his vision of cities in the "Great Society" in his conservation programs, which called for the creation of public "open spaces" and land in the cities for recreational use. Although the legislation creating the Model Cities Project moved through Congress with the title "Demonstration Cities," Johnson renamed the program when he signed the bill. He described "Model Cities" in which cooperative projects between the federal government and local governments to revitalize urban areas across the nation would focus on housing, crime, transportation, and other development projects in order to demonstrate the potential of Americans working together to create a "Great Society."

Johnson had attempted to address the issues of the slums and ghettos of America's cities as soon as he took office, by initiating the Community Action Programs (CAPs), proposed by his predecessor. Community Action Programs placed antipoverty lawyers, social workers, and others on the federal payrolls in order to make a national push for the expansion of welfare. The CAPs also attempted to turn over control of federal programs to local agencies and involve local residents in the refurbishing of their own communities. But, by 1965, it appeared that the CAPs had not led to great improvements in the nation's cities. Despite their intent, they had often only further contributed to de facto segregation. Tensions were high, and in the summer of that year, several of America's cities, most notably Watts, in Los Angles, California erupted in violence. Reflecting the frustration of high unemployment rates (75 percent of men living in Watts in 1965 were unemployed), the cycle of poverty, and urban blight, these uprisings clearly indicated that the CAPs and other antipoverty, job, and housing programs aimed at urban renewal were not working.

The Ford Foundation, through its Grey Areas programs, had tried to jump-start urban renewal in five U.S. cities. After this model showed some hope for success in New Haven, Connecticut, Johnson and others promoted the "Model Cities" initiative for cities all across America. The program designated the newly created Department of Housing and Urban Development, along with the Department of Health, Education, and Welfare and the Labor Department, to coordinate housing and the myriad of other "Great Society" programs, in order to tackle the problems facing urban areas. Johnson aimed to combine "Great Society" housing and job-training programs with integration efforts to create great cities. The Model Cities program would involve cooperation between federal and local governments and require the participation of local residents. Unlike many previous federally funded urban renewal efforts, which simply moved poor residents out of the inner cities, the Model Cities program insisted both on local participation and the retention of local residents, hopefully in refurbished housing. Johnson hoped to run the program through the Department of Housing and Urban Development, which was already active in the inner cities, managing federally funded housing programs. He envisioned a more holistic approach to urban development that included not only housing programs, but a litany of programs aimed at repairing the physical and social infrastructures of cities as well. In a speech on "The Crisis of the Cities" in February of 1968, Johnson outlined proposals for housing, insurance, transportation, long-range planning, lending, technology, and "future cities," all aimed at improving the quality of life for urban dwellers in America.

Like other "Great Society" programs, the Model Cities program faced a tough fight in the Congress. Some liberals like Senator Abraham Ribicoff (D-CT), formerly Kennedy's Secretary of Health, Education, and Welfare, supported the Model Cities program while others like Senator Robert Kennedy (D-NY), criticized Johnson's proposals as being too meager to solve America's urban problems. Ribicoff held hearings on the Model Cities legislation, which focused national attention on urban decay, while conservatives, particularly those in the House, fought the legislation. Some, led by Representative Paul Fino (R-NY), opposed the legislation as simply another way for the Johnson Administration to allow localities to develop their own local versions of the civil rights bill passed by the federal government in 1964. Others, such as Representative Joe Waggoner (R-LA), argued that the bill would only increase the power and authority of the federal government, and do little to help cities, many of which were beyond hope. Southern conservatives also opposed Johnson's program, as bringing the federal government into localities even more than Johnson's other "Great Society" programs had already done. These Southerners argued that the Model Cities plan would only throw money at the problems of the cities rather than address individual attitudes of dependency that were the real causes of urban crises. Addressing the urban crisis, Senator Robert Byrd (D-WV), opined that he was "afraid that most of what the poor people's campaign seeks is simply greater handouts." Others still, like Senator Mark Hatfield (R-OR), argued that massive government welfare programs had failed in the past because they targeted "sociological groups" rather than "individuals with individual problems." "The economically deprived," Hatfield contended, "are people first and poor second." Moreover, Hatfield called for the restoration of "a greater sense of personal responsibility for the well-being of others." In a theme that portends modern discussions of faith-based and other community initiatives, Hatfield argued that charitable organizations, middle-class philanthropy, and student movements were integral elements in the alleviation of the problems that American urban dwellers faced. "Government can furnish financial resources and act as a stimulus to private action," he said, "but it cannot provide the personal interaction and compassion that is vital to the solution of social problems."[1]

One of the staunchest opponents of Johnson's methods of aiding the cities was former vice president, and, by 1968, Republican presidential candidate, Richard Nixon. He echoed Byrd's and Hatfield's concerns about the federal government's expansive role in the lives of individuals. Arguing that "the first need is to replace dependence with independence," Nixon did not exude the pessimism of many of the opponents of the Model Cities plan. Instead, in two radio addresses in May of 1968, entitled "Bridges to Human Dignity," Nixon proposed his own remedy for the "urban crisis." His plan focused on private investment in urban areas. Among the "bridges" Nixon proposed were tax incentives for businesses locating operations in poverty-stricken areas—urban or rural; the promotion of black-owned and black-run businesses through loan, insurance, and tax programs; tax incentives to corporations that employed and trained unskilled workers; the creation of a national "computer job bank;" a national tutoring program for inner-city children; the reassimilation of black veterans into communities as teachers; and the promotion of individual home ownership.

The Model Cities legislation underwent dramatic changes before it was finally approved and signed into law. Congress cut its life span from six to two years, reduced appropriations from $2.3 billion to $900 million, and doubled the number of cities enumerated to participate in the program from 66 to over 120, thus diluting the already watered-down budget request for the program. It took HUD until December of 1968 to approve Seattle's development plan, the first allocation of funds under the Model Cities legislation, more than two years after the president signed it into law. Moreover, critics of the program who feared that it was just another liberal attempt to address race, stripped the legislation of its integration requirements. This change—combined with requirements for local participation, and restrictions on certain federal mandates, like busing—actually contributed to new forms of segregation in some cities. Efforts to reform the education system in New York, for example, though not a direct component of the Model Cities program, led to sharp divisions between blacks and whites, pitting the American Federation of Teachers against the African-American Federation of Teachers as both struggled to control reform efforts. In Atlanta, the city proposal submitted to the federal government for funding included two white neighborhoods and four black neighborhoods. Although the federal government funded the proposal, those who thought that the Model Cities program was intended primarily for black cities, and that white areas did not require such federal assistance, criticized the program. Urban uprisings broke out in Detroit in the summer of 1967, illustrating the degree of tension in cities, and the nature of the obstacles associated with race. Despite the desperation evident in the urban riots each summer after 1965, Congress refused to increase appropriations for the Model Cities programs. Partly as a consequence of congressional disinclination to expand the Model Cities program, and partly because of a growing personal concern that inflation would derail the Great Society, Johnson turned his primary attention from pressing Congress for more money for urban development toward getting congressional cooperation on open housing legislation, preventing racial discrimination in the sale and rental of housing.

NOTE

1. *Congressional Record*, Vol. 114, Pt 19, 24484–24485.

PRESIDENT LYNDON JOHNSON, "THE CRISIS OF THE CITIES," MESSAGE TO CONGRESS (FEBRUARY 26, 1968)

Today America's cities are in crisis. This clear and urgency warning rises from the decay of decades—and is amplified by the harsh realities of the present. . . .

We see the results dramatically in the great urban centers where millions live amid decaying buildings—with streets clogged with traffic; with air and water polluted by the soot and waste of industry . . . ; with crime rates rising so rapidly each year that more and more miles of city streets become unsafe after dark; with increasingly inadequate public services and a smaller and smaller tax base from which to raise the funds to improve them. . . .

The city will not be transformed until the lives of the least among its dwellers are changed as well. Until men whose days are empty and despairing can see better days ahead, until they can stand proud and know their children's lives will be better than their own—until that day comes, the city will not truly be rebuilt. That is the momentous and inescapable truth we face in this hour of America's history. . . .

The last several years have witnessed a remarkable record of legislative achievement—and most of it has borne on the problems of the cities. . . .

But almost 29 million citizens still remain in poverty. . . .

Today . . . I want to speak of programs designed especially for our cities— of shelter for its citizens and plans for its revitalization. This message, too, is for men and their families. For our lives are profoundly affected by the environment in which we live, the city in which we work and reside, the home in which we relax and renew our strength. . . .

I propose the Housing and Urban Development Act of 1968—a character of renewed hope for the American city. With this Act, the nation will set a far reaching goal to meet a massive national need: the construction of 26 million new homes and apartments. . . . Six million of these will finally replace the shameful substandard units of misery where more than 20 million Americans still live. . . .

The slum is not solely a wasteland of brick and mortar. It is also a place where hope dies quickly, and human failure starts early and lingers long. Just as the problem of the slum is many-faced, so must the effort to remove it be many-sided.

The Model Cities . . . program is simply an outline—to encourage the city to develop and carry out a total strategy to meet the human and physical problems left in the rubble of a neighborhood's decay. That strategy, which Model Cities spurs through special grants, is to bring to a dying area health care services, as well as houses; better schools and education, as well as repaved streets and improved mass transit; opportunities for work, as well as open space for recreation. . . .

Last year I requested full funding of the amount authorized for the Model Cities. . . . But Congress approved less than half that amount. To the cities of this land, that cut came as a bitter disappointment. In the cities struggle for survival, we dare not disappoint them again. We must demonstrate that they can rely on continued Federal support. . . .

Urban renewal is the weapon that deals primarily with the physical side of removing blight. An essential component of the Model Cities program, it is a major instrument of reform in its own right. . . . To apply our resources more quickly, I recommend that Congress authorize a new Neighborhood Development Program under Urban Renewal. . . . With this program, cities can start work quickly on the most pressing problems that are to be renewed, with the emphasis on construction of new and rehabilitated housing. . . .

The federal role . . . is designed to assure that every citizen will be decently housed. The Government's concern is to stimulate private energy and local action—to provide capital where needed, to guarantee financing, to offer assistance that encourages planning and construction.

The real job belongs to local government and the private sector—the home builder, the mortgage banker, the contractor, the non-profit sponsor, the industrialist who now sees in the challenge of the cities a new opportunity for American business. . . .

. . . the city's tides have been ebbing for several decades. We are the inheritors of those tragic results of the city's decline. But we are the ones who must act. For us that obligation is inescapable.

Our concern must be as broad as the problems of men—work and health, education for children and care for the sick. These are the problems of men who live in cities. And the very base of man's condition is his home: he must find promise and peace there. The cry of the city, reduced to its essentials, is the cry of a man for his sense of place and purpose. Violence will not bring this. But neither should fear forestall it. . . .

To us, in our day, falls the last clear chance to assure that America's cities will once again "gleam, undimmed by human tears."

No one can doubt that the hour is late.

No one can underestimate the magnitude of the work that should be done.

No one can doubt the costs of talk and little action.

As we respond to the cities' problems . . . let us recall and reaffirm the reason for our national strength: unity, growth and individual opportunity. And recalling these truths, let us go forward, as one nation in common purpose joined, to change the face of our cities and to end the fear of those— rich and poor alike—who call them home.

Source: *Congressional Record*, Vol. 114, Pt. 3, 3956–3961.

REPUBLICAN PRESIDENTIAL CANDIDATE
RICHARD NIXON, RADIO ADDRESS, "BRIDGES
ACROSS AMERICA" (APRIL 25, 1968)

Every age has its special set of problems, and every problem has its special catch-phrases. Today, we commonly speak of "the urban crisis." And yet the problems wrenching America today are only secondarily problems of the cities. Primarily, they are problems of the human mind and spirit.

Over and over again, we ask ourselves whether our cities can survive, whether they can remain livable, whether the races can co-exist within them, whether poverty and squalor must inevitably consume the inner city. In asking these questions, we are asking, in effect: how long can Americans ignore the race condition? . . .

For too long, white America has sought to buy off the Negro—and to buy off its own sense of guilt—with ever more programs of welfare, of public housing, of payments *to* the poor, but not *for* anything except for keeping out of sight: payments that perpetuated poverty, and that kept the endless, dismal cycle of dependency spinning from generation to generation. . . .

The reality of the national economic condition is such that to talk of massively increasing the budget in order to pour additional billions into the cities this year is a cruel delusion. . . .

We won't get at the real problems unless and until we rescue the people in the ghetto from despair and dependency.

There's no pride at the receiving end of the dole, and unless and until there is pride in the ghetto—personal pride and racial pride—we're not going to get anywhere in tackling the real problems of a real world. . . .

If the ghettos are to be renewed, their people must be moved by hope. But hope is a fragile thing, easily destroyed and even more easily weakened—and nowhere is it more fragile than among those whose hopes over the years have been repeatedly raised only to be cruelly dashed.

What we do not need now is another round of unachievable promises of unavailable Federal funds.

What we do need is imaginative enlistment of private funds, private energies, and private talents, in order to develop the opportunities that lie untapped in our own underdeveloped urban heartland.

It costs little or no government money to set in motion many of the programs that would in fact do the most, in a practical sense, to start building a firm structure of Negro economic opportunity.

We need new bridges between the developed and underdeveloped segments of our own society—human bridges, economic bridges, bridges of understanding and of help.

We need incentives to private industry to make acceptable the added risks of ghetto development and of training the unemployed for jobs.

Helping provide these incentives is the proper role of government; actually doing the job is not—because industry can do it better....

Bridges of understanding can be built by revising the welfare rules, so that instead of providing incentives for families to break apart, they provide incentives for families to stay together ... We must make welfare payments a temporary expedient, not a permanent way of life, something to be escaped from. Our aim should be to restore dignity to life, not to destroy dignity....

The ghettos of our cities will be remade—lastingly remade—when the people in them have the will, the power, the resources and the skills to remake then. They won't be remade by government billions; the sad history of urban renewal, for example, has shown how often this results in an actual decrease in the number of housing units available for the poor, with one slum torn down and another created—because the basic conditions of slum life haven't been changed. These conditions are what we have to get at—the human and social conditions, the conditions of the spirit—and these in turn rest in large part on our laying in place the economic structure that can support a rebirth of pride and individualism and independence.

Source: *Congressional Record*, Vol. 114, Pt. 9, 11409–11410.

RECOMMENDED READING

Andrew, John A., III. *Lyndon Johnson and the Great Society*. Chicago: Ivan R. Dee, 1998.

Center for Immigration Studies. "Three Decades of Mass Immigration: The Legacy of the 1965 Immigration Act," No 3, Sept. 1995, <http://www.cis.org/articles/1995/30thAnniversary.html>

Chester, Eric Thomas. *Rag-tags, Scum, Riff-raff, and Commies : The U.S. Intervention in the Dominican Republic, 1965–1966*. New York: Monthly Review Press, 2001.

Corning, Peter. *The Evolution of Medicare ... from Idea to Law*. Washington: Government Printing Office, 1969.

Dudziak, Mary. *Cold War Civil Rights: Race and the Image of American Democracy*. Princeton: Princeton University Press, 2002.

Gleijeses, Piero. *The Dominican Crisis: The 1965 Constitutionalist Revolt and the American Intervention*. Baltimore: The Johns Hopkins University Press, 1978.

Graham, Hugh Davis. *The Civil Rights Era: Origins and Development of National Policy 1960–1972*. New York: Oxford University Press, 1990.

———. *The Uncertain Triumph: Federal Education Policy in the Kennedy and Johnson Years*. Chapel Hill: University of North Carolina Press, 1984.

Haar, Charles M. *Between the Idea and the Reality: A Study in the Origin, Fate, and Legacy of the Model Cities Program*, Boston: Little, Brown, 1975.

Halperin, Robert. *Rebuilding the Inner City: A History of Neighborhood Initiatives to Address Poverty in the United States.* New York: Columbia University Press, 1994.

Hayward, Steven. "Broken Cities: Liberalism's Urban Legacy." *Policy Review*, 88 (March–April) 1998 at <http://www.policyreview.org/mar98/cities.html>

Howe, Harold, III. "LBJ as the Education President." Charlottesville: Miller Center of Public Affairs, 1998.

Hunt, Michael H. *Lyndon Johnson's War: America's Cold War Crusade in Vietnam, 1945–1965: A Critical Issue.* New York: Hill and Wang, 1996.

Husock, Howard. "The Inherent Flaws of HUD." Cato Policy Analysis No. 292 (December) 1997 at <http://www.cato.org/pubs/pas/pa-292.html>

Jeffery, Julie Roy. *Education for Children of the Poor: A Study of the Origins and Implementation of the Elementary and Secondary Education Act of 1965.* Columbus: Ohio State University Press, 1978.

Marmor, Theodore. *The Politics of Medicare* 2nd ed. New York: A de Gruyter, 2000.

Martz, John D. *United States Policy in Latin America: A Quarter Century of Crisis and Challenge, 1961–1986.* Lincoln: University of Nebraska Press, 1988.

O'Connor, Alice. "Evaluating Comprehensive Community Initiatives: A View From History." In *New Approaches to Evaluating Community Initiatives*, James P. Connell, Anne C. Kubisch, Lisbeth B. Schorr, and Carol H. Weiss. eds. The Aspen Institute, 1999 at <http://www.aspeninstitute.org/vol1/oconnor.htm>

BIBLIOGRAPHY

Ambrose, Stephen. *Eisenhower: Soldier and President*. New York: Touchstone, 1990.

Andrew, John A., III. *Lyndon Johnson and the Great Society*. Chicago: Ivan R. Dee, 1998.

Ben-Ziv, Abraham. *Decade of Transition: Eisenhower, Kennedy, and the Origins of the American-Israeli Alliance*. New York: Columbia University Press, 1998.

Berman, Larry. *Lyndon Johnson's War: The Road to Stalemate in Vietnam*. New York: Norton, 1993.

Beschloss, Michael. *The Crisis Year*. New York: Edward Burlingame Books, 1991.

Bissel, Richard M. *Reflections of a Cold Warrior: From Yalta to the Bay of Pigs*. New Haven: Yale University Press, 1996.

Blight, James G., Bruce J. Allyn, and David A. Welch. *Cuba on the Brink: Castro, the Missile Crisis, and the Soviet Collapse*. New York: Pantheon Books, 1993.

Blight, James G., and Peter Kornbluh, eds. *Politics of Illusion: The Bay of Pigs Reexamined*. Boulder, CO: Lynne Reinner Publishers, 1998.

Brugioni, Dino. *Eyeball to Eyeball: The Inside Story of the Cuban Missile Crisis*. New York: Random House, 1993.

Bundy, McGeorge. "Presidents and Arms Control: John F. Kennedy and Lyndon B. Johnson." Presented in a Forum at the Miller Center of Public Affairs, University of Virginia, October 28, 1993.

Center for Immigration Studies. September, 1995. "Three Decades of Mass Immigration: The Legacy of the 1965 Immigration Act." No. 3, <http://www.cis.org/articles/1995/30thAnniversary.html>

Chester, Eric Thomas. *Rag-tags, Scum, Riff-raff, and Commies: The U.S. Intervention in the Dominican Republic, 1965–1966*. New York: Monthly Review Press, 2001.

Cohen, Warren I. *America in the Age of Soviet Power, 1945–1992*. Vol. 4 of the *Cambridge History of American Foreign Relations*. Cambridge: Cambridge University Press, 1993.

Connell, James P., Anne C. Kubisch, Lisbeth B. Schorr, and Carol H. Weiss, eds. *Approaches to Evaluating Community Initiatives*. The Aspen Institute, 1999. <http://www.aspeninstitute.org/vol1/oconnor.thm>

Corning, Peter. *The Evolution of Medicare . . . from Idea to Law*. Washington: Government Printing Office, 1969.

Cummings, Bruce. *The Origins of the Korean War*. Princeton: Princeton University Press, 1990.

Freedman, Lawrence. *Kennedy's Wars: Berlin, Cuba, Laos, and Vietnam*. New York: Oxford University Press, 2000.

Garthoff, Raymond. "Berlin 1961: The Record Corrected." *Foreign Policy* 84 (Fall): 142–156, 1991.

Gleijeses, Piero. *The Dominican Crisis: The 1965 Constitutionalist Revolt and the American Intervention*. Baltimore: The Johns Hopkins University Press, 1978.

———. *Shattered Hope: The Guatemalan Revolution and the United States, 1944–1954*. Princeton: Princeton University Press, 1991.

Graham, Hugh Davis. *The Civil Rights Era: Origins and Development of National Policy 1960–1972*. New York: Oxford University Press, 1990.

———. *The Uncertain Triumph: Federal Education Policy in the Kennedy and Johnson Years*. Chapel Hill: University of North Carolina Press, 1984.

Greenstein, Fred I. *The Hidden-Hand Presidency: Eisenhower as Leader*. New York: Basic Books, 1982.

Haar, Charles M. *Between the Idea and the Reality: A Study in the Origin, Fate, and Legacy of the Model Cities Program*. Boston: Little, Brown, 1975.

Halpern, Robert. *Rebuilding the Inner City: A History of Neighborhood Initiatives to Address Poverty in the United States*. New York: Columbia University Press, 1994.

Haywood, Steven. "Broken Cities: Liberalism's Urban Legacy." *Policy Review* 88 (March–April) at <http://www.policyreview.org/mar98/cities.html>

Hoffman, Elizabeth Cobbs. *All You Need is Love: Peace Corps and the Spirit of the 1960s*. Cambridge, MA: Harvard University Press, 1998.

Howe, Harold, III. "LBJ as the Education President." Charlottesville, VA: Miller Center of Public Affairs, 1998.

Hunt, Michael H. *Lyndon Johnson's War: America's Cold War Crusade in Vietnam, 1945–1965: A Critical Issue*. New York: Hill and Wang, 1996.

Husock, Howard. "The Inherent Flaws of HUD." Cato Policy Analysis No. 292, December, 1997. <http://www.cato.org/pubs/pas/pa-292.html>

Immerman, Richard. *The CIA in Guatemala: The Foreign Policy of Intervention.* Austin: University of Texas Press, 1982.

———. *John Foster Dulles and the Diplomacy of the Cold War.* Princeton: Princeton University Press, 1990.

Jeffery, Julie Roy. *Education for Children of the Poor: A Study of the Origins and Implementation of the Elementary and Secondary Education Act of 1965.* Columbus: Ohio State University Press, 1978.

Kennedy, Robert. *Thirteen Days: A Memoir of the Cuban Missile Crisis.* New York: W.W. Norton, 1999.

Kornbluh, Peter. *The Bay of Pigs Declassified.* New York: The New Press. 1998.

Kunz, Diane, ed. *The Diplomacy of the Crucial Decade.* New York: Columbia University Press, 1994.

Launius, Roger D., and Howard M. McCurdy. *Spaceflight and the Myth of Presidential Leadership.* Urbana: University of Illinois Press, 1997.

Lemann, Nicholas. "The Unfinished War." *The Atlantic* (December 1988).

Lewis, Tom. *Divided Highways: Building the Interstate Highways, Transforming American Life.* New York: Viking, 1997.

Lowe, Peter. *The Korean War.* New York: St. Martin's Press, 2000.

Lynch, Grayson L. *Decision for Disaster: Betrayal at the Bay of Pigs.* Washington, DC: Brassey's, 2000.

Marmor, Theodore. *The Politics of Medicare,* 2nd ed. New York: A de Gruyter, 2000.

Martz, John D., ed. *United States Policy in Latin America: A Quarter Century of Crisis and Challenge, 1961–1986.* Lincoln: University of Nebraska Press, 1988.

National Security Agency. NSA and the Cuban Missile Crisis, <http://www.nsa.gov/docs/cuba/index.html>

National Security Archive. The Real Thirteen Days: The Hidden History of the Cuban Missile Crisis, <http://www.gwu.edu/~nsarchiv/sna/cuba_mis_cri/>

Office of the Chief of Military History. "The Army and the New Look," *American Military History.* Washington, DC: Center of Military History.

Olson, James S., and Randy Roberts. *Where the Domino Fell: America and Vietnam 1945–1990.* New York: St. Martin's Press, 1991.

Parmet, Herbert S. *Eisenhower and the American Crusades.* New Brunswick, NJ: Transaction Publishers, 1999.

Patterson, James T. *Grand Expectations: The United States, 1945–1975.* New York: Oxford University Press, 1996.

Patterson, Thomas G., ed. *Kennedy's Quest For Victory: American Foreign Policy 1961–1963.* New York: Oxford University Press, 1989.

Rabe, Stephen G. *Eisenhower in Latin America: The Foreign Policy of Anticommunism.* Chapel Hill: University of North Carolina Press, 1988.

Reeves, Richard. *President Kennedy: Profile of Power.* New York: Simon & Schuster, 1993.

Rickover, Hyman G. *Education and Freedom*. New York: E.P. Dutton, 1959.

Rogers, William D. *The Twilight Struggle: The Alliance for Progress and the Politics of Development in Latin America*. New York: Random House. 1967.

Scheman, L. Ronald, ed. *The Alliance for Progress: A Retrospective*. New York: Praeger, 1988.

Schlesinger, Arthur M., Jr. *A Thousand Days: John Kennedy in the White House*. Boston: Houghton Mifflin, 1965.

Schlesinger, Stephen and Stephen Kinzer. *Bitter Fruit: The Untold Story of the American Coup in Guatemala*. Garden City, NY: Doubleday, 1982.

Seely, Bruce E. *Building the American Highway System: Engineers as Policy Makers*. Philadelphia: Temple University Press, 1987.

Steigerwald, David. *The Sixties and the End of Modern America*. New York: St. Martin's Press, 1995.

Walker, J. Samuel. *A Short History of Nuclear Regulation, 1946–1999*. Nuclear Regulatory Commission, <http://www.nrc.gov/SECY/smj/shorthis.htm!AEC>

Walton, Richard J. *Cold War and Counterrevolution: The Foreign Policy of John F. Kennedy*. New York: Viking Press, 1972.

Wiersma, Kurt, and Ben Larson. Fourteen Days in October: The Cuban Missile Crisis, <http://library.thinkquest.org/11046/?tqship=1>

Wyden, Peter. *Bay of Pigs: The Untold Story*. New York: Simon and Schuster, 1979.

Zubok, Valdimir. "Khrushchev and the Berlin Crisis (1958–62)." Cold War International History Project. Working Paper No. 6. Princeton: Woodrow Wilson International Center for Scholars.

INDEX

About the Authors

JOHN A. KING, JR. teaches Social Studies at Ransom Everglades School, Coconut Grove, Florida.

JOHN R. VILE is Chair of Political Science Department at Middle Tennessee University. He is author of *Companion to the U.S. Constitution and Its Amendments* (Greenwood, second edition, 1997), *Encyclopedia of Constitutional Amendments, Proposed Amendments, and Amending Issues* (1996), and numerous other books on the United States Constitution.